SCHOOL CONSULTATION

SCHOOL
CONSULTATION

Readings About Preventive Techniques
For Pupil Personnel Workers

Edited by

JOEL MEYERS, Ph.D.
ROY MARTIN, Ph.D.
IRWIN HYMAN, Ed.D.
Temple University
Philadelphia, Pennsylvania

CHARLES C THOMAS · PUBLISHER
Springfield · Illinois · U.S.A.

Published and Distributed Throughout the World by
CHARLES C THOMAS • PUBLISHER
Bannerstone House
301-327 East Lawrence Avenue, Springfield, Illinois, U.S.A.

© *1977, by* CHARLES C THOMAS • PUBLISHER
ISBN 0-398-03485-0
Library of Congress Catalog Card Number: 75-20078

W-2
Printed in the United States of America

Library of Congress Cataloging in Publication Data
Main entry under title:

School consultation.

    Bibliography: p.
    Includes index.
    1. Personnel service in education—Addresses, essays,
lectures. I. Meyers, Joel. II. Martin, Roy.
III. Hyman, Irwin.

LB1027.5.S27   371.4   75-20078
ISBN 0-398-03485-0

CONTRIBUTORS

John Altrocchi, Ph.D.
University of Nevada
Reno, Nevada

Irving N. Berlin, M.D.
University of Washington
Seattle, Washington

Ralph F. Blanco, Ph.D.
Temple University
Philadelphia, Pennsylvania

David W. Brison, Ed.D.
Ontario Institute for Studies
in Education
Ontario, Canada

Anthony Broskowski, Ph.D.
Harvard University
Cambridge, Massachusetts

G. Phillip Cartwright, Ph.D.
The Pennsylvania State University
University Park, Pennsylvania

Carol A. Cartwright, Ph.D.
The Pennsylvania State University
University Park, Pennsylvania

Calvin D. Catterall, Ph.D.
Staff Development Consultants
Columbus, Ohio

Ace Cossairt, Ph.D.
Juniper Gardens Children's Project
Kansas City, Kansas

Vernon T. Devine, Ph.D.
University of Minnesota
Minneapolis, Minnesota

Carl Eisdorfer, Ph.D., M.D.
University of Washington
Seattle, Washington

Steven R. Forness, Ed.D.
UCLA Neuropsychiatric Institute
Los Angeles, California

Marvin J. Fine, Ph.D.
University of Kansas
Lawrence, Kansas

June Gallessich, Ph.D.
University of Texas
Austin, Texas

Allan Gerston, Ph.D.
New York University
New York, New York

Russell M. Grieger II, Ph.D.
University of Virginia
Charlottesville, Virginia

R. Vance Hall, Ph.D.
University of Kansas
Kansas City, Kansas

Leonard Handler, Ph.D.
University of Tennessee
Knoxville, Tennessee

Barbara Handler, Ph.D.
Knoxville, Tennessee

B. L. Hopkins, Ph.D.
University of Kansas
Kansas City, Kansas

v

James Kauffman, Ed.D.
University of Virginia
Charlottesville, Virginia

Daniel Langmeyer, Ph.D.
University of Cincinnati
Cincinnati, Ohio

Gilbert Levin, M.D.
Albert Einstein College of Medicine
Yeshiva University
Bronx, New York

Philip A. Mann, Ph.D.
Scott County Community Mental
  Health Center
Scott County, Iowa

J. Regis McNamara, Ph.D.
University of Georgia
Athens, Georgia

Loyce McGehearty, Ph.D.
University of Corpus Christi
Corpus Christi, Texas

Marshall W. Minor, Ph.D.
School District of Philadelphia
Philadelphia, Pennsylvania

K. Daniel O'Leary, Ph.D.
State University of New York
Stony Brook, New York

Beulah Parker, M.D.
University of California Medical
  School
San Francisco, California

Rita W. Poulos, Ph.D.
Port Jefferson, New York

Philip J. Runkel, Ph.D.
University of Oregon
Eugene, Oregon

Richard A. Schmuck, Ph.D.
University of Oregon
Eugene, Oregon

J. Neville Sikes, Ph.D.
Southwest Texas State University
San Marcos, Texas

Matthew Snapp, Ph.D.
Austin Independent School District
Austin, Texas

Charles D. Spielberger, Ph.D.
University of South Florida
Tampa, Florida

David D. Stein, Ph.D.
Psychological Services Institute
Sacramento, California

Milton M. Tyler, Ph.D.
College of the Pacific
Stockton, California

Ann R. Vicente, Ed.D.
Prince George Public Schools
Prince George, British Columbia,
  Canada

Sidney A. Winicki, Ph.D.
Jefferson County Public Schools
Lakewood, Colorado

James E. Ysseldyke, Ph.D.
The Pennsylvania State University
University Park, Pennsylvania

PREFACE

T HIS BOOK OF readings presents a variety of school consultation techniques which are available to pupil personnel workers. In recent years these techniques have become increasingly important due to the changing roles of teachers and pupil personnel workers.

American education currently reflects a rapidly changing society. During the past two decades this educational system has experienced some of the most dramatic changes in its history. The public continues to demand that educators accept some of the roles of traditional institutions, e.g. the family. The expanding mission of the schools has resulted in tremendous pressure for teachers to change their roles from classroom lecturers to learning facilitators. Teachers are evolving into traffic managers as they direct the flow of information and activity to create a meaningful learning experience. The growing proliferation of educational technology and hardware also promises to free the teacher to devote more attention to interpersonal relations with students. In addition, he cannot hope to master the vast contents of information which become increasingly available following improvements in educational technology. As a result, the teacher must augment his expertise as a facilitator in the process of education.

One way in which the teacher can improve his interpersonal skills as an educational facilitator is through psychoeducational consultation. Therefore, a crucial aspect of modern teaching lies in the teacher's opportunities to receive consultation and in his ability to effectively utilize the skills of consultants.

The second factor contributing to the growing need for consultation in the schools is the changing role of pupil personnel workers, i.e. counselors, psychiatrists, psychologists, social workers, etc. The quickly changing educational scene has had such an impact that the traditional roles of pupil personnel workers are becoming outmoded and inadequate. There is a serious shortage of manpower in the helping professions, and this problem has profound effects on the schools. There are clearly not enough pupil personnel workers available to reach all of the children who need help if the role models which stress direct service to individual children continue to dominate. Since the teacher has ongoing contact with children throughout each school day, one important role is for pupil personnel workers to influence the behavior of teachers. School consultation techniques constitute the primary way in which this role can be developed.

Although consultation is a function which has long been practiced in many helping professions, consultation techniques have recently received increased attention and development. For example, relevant journals in counseling, psychiatry, psychology, and social work have begun to devote considerable space to a discussion of consultation as a role model. This book of readings represents the first attempt to systematically describe the major approaches to psychoeducational consultation in the schools, and this is done in the context of a consistent conceptual frame of reference.

One purpose of this book is to stimulate practicing pupil personnel workers so that they may become more aware that school consultation can be an effective way to indirectly change the behavior of students through schools and teachers. It is hoped that as consultation procedures become better documented and more familiar, pupil personnel specialists will increasingly attempt to implement these techniques. A secondary aim of this book is to acquaint administrators, teachers, and others interested in schools with the consultation role model. As the model receives greater acceptance, it may become easier for practitioners to implement it, and there may be a resulting change in the role of some pupil personnel workers.

We are grateful to the authors and publishers who have given permission for their work to be reprinted. In particular we would like to take this opportunilty to thank the many students whose ideas and critical comments have helped to shape our thinking regarding consultation. Many students also helped in the extensive literature search which was done for this book, and their help is also appreciated.

J.M.
R.M.
I.H.

CONTENTS

Section I
INTRODUCTION

Section II
PSYCHOEDUCATIONAL DIAGNOSIS

Section V

ORGANIZATION DEVELOPMENT CONSULTATION

SCHOOL CONSULTATION

INTRODUCTION

T HE BEGINNING OF A technology for changing teacher behavior through consultation has recently emerged, and it is the purpose of this book of readings to present some of these early ideas about consultation. This book should make clear that, at present, the consultation literature is not a unified body of systematic attacks on a well-defined problem. On the contrary, it is a widely diverse body of anecdotes, admonitions, and demonstrations. In order to bring structure to the readings that follow, a general definition of consultation is presented.

Consultation as used in the context of this book is a term applied to the interaction between a psychologically trained professional (consultant) and a caretaker (consultee). The term client is generally used to refer to the persons under the consultee's care. Consultation always involves at least a three-person chain of service. The consultant interacts with the consultee who interacts with a client for whom he has responsibility. Since this book focuses on schools, the consultee is generally a teacher and clients are students. The goal of the relationship between the consultant and teacher is to maximize the teacher's functioning. In addition to helping the teacher, effective consultation should result in positive changes in the students under the teacher's care.

Some writers limit the term consultation to the situation where only adjacent members of the chain interact. That is, the consultant interacts directly with the consultee, i.e. teacher, but not the client, i.e. student. This restriction may be impractical for school consultation, and it is not considered in the definition of consultation used in this book. Following individual diagnosis or treatment of a client (i.e. student) by counselor or psychologist, a consultation conference will often be held with the child's teacher who is a consultee. This relationship between consultant and teacher will often be a consultation relationship even though the consultant has been and may remain intimately involved with the client.

Consultation is often initiated for remedial purposes. In addition to remediating the specific problem, however, an equally important consultation goal is a generalized improvement in functioning between the consultee and other clients currently and in the future. It is this emphasis on the preventive-educative aspects of behavior change that sets consultation apart from other remedial activities. Without this generalization, each crisis would be dealt with on an individual basis, and, therefore, there would be no advantage to the consultative model.

Another feature of consultation is that communication is not primarily unidirectional as would be the case with giving advice. Instead, the consultant and consultee *interact* in a series of actions and reactions focussed on the consultee's problem. Frequently the consultant and consultee are professionally trained in different disciplines where both have knowledge regarding different aspects of the referral problem. This is clearly the case when a counselor, psychiatrist, or psychologist consults with an educator. Consultation is, thus, best thought of as mutual problem solving.

One goal of consultation, as used in this book, is the improved psychological functioning of both the consultee and the client. Improved mental health is often a consultation goal. This is distinguished from the consultation in industry which is directed toward increased output. In education, the output is not so easily measured. Optimal psychological functioning on the part of the client may mean optimal academic production, or it may not. The goal of consultation as used in this book cannot be restricted to increased output in terms of numbers reflecting achievement. On the other hand, assessment of the effects of consultation is important, and the development of meaningful criterion measures is one significant area for research in school consultation.

One important feature of the process of consultation is that the consultee has the freedom to accept or reject what the consultant says. In this sense, it is essential that the consultant avoid taking on the role of supervisor. In other words, the consultant exercises no power over the consultee. This is clear in the sense that the consultant has no administrative power over the consultee, but it must also be clear in the quality of the consultant's interaction with the consultee. The way in which the consultant brings about change in the consultee is through influence rather than coercive power.

The consultant's influence may stem, in part, from the extent of the consultee's perception of the consultant as an expert with useful knowledge. Another source of influence is the consultant's interpersonal skills found in the qualitative aspects of the relationship, e.g. openness, friendliness, closeness, warmth etc. The processes used to influence the consultee and to change the consultee's behavior constitute a major focus of the readings selected for this book. The reader should try to recognize those aspects of the process of consultation which are used in each of the articles presented.

The Historical Development of School Consultation

Since psychology's inception as a distinct field of study it has been concerned with the process of learning. Early in its history psychologists focused on the development of theory and technique which others applied in the context of education. G. Stanley Hall's formulations regarding child study and educational psychology in the 1880s and Thorndike's use of statistical methods and learning theory, at the turn of the century, are outstanding examples.

Although theory in educational psychology is still important, psychologically trained personnel have now become directly involved with practical school problems in increasing numbers. The development of this role for psychologists can be traced to at least four movements in psychology: the testing movement, the vocational guidance movement, the mental hygiene movement, and the child guidance movement.

The testing movement in the United States was launched by the publication of the Goddard adaptation in 1911, and the Terman revision in 1916, of the Binet-Simon intelligence scale. The movement was strengthened with the appearance of the Otis group inteligence tests during World War I. Later, during the twenties and thirties, the increased interest in personality testing, e.g. Rorschach, Thematic Apperception Test, influenced the testing role of psychologists in the schools. Finally, special education has been an important force in developing the testing role of school psychologists, since a psychological examination is mandated to place children in special classes. This role has recently gained added importance as a result of legal problems in special class placement. This will result in a greater emphasis on careful and comprehensive psycho-diagnostic work.

The vocational guidance movement began as an attempt to match students with jobs in the decade between 1900 and 1910 with Frank Parsons in Boston and Jessie Davis in Detroit (Miller, 1961). This movement was important to the development of psychological services in the schools because it was the beginning of the process of assessing student aptitudes, needs, and interests, in order to match these traits with special curricula.

The mental health movement also had an impact on school psychological services. The National Committee for Mental Hygiene, founded by Clifford Beers in 1909, sought to arouse public interest in problems of mental health with particular attention to the prevention of mental illness. Mental illness was seen as a response to stress. It was hypothesized that psychological help offered at the time of stress could be a major preventive factor. The mental hygiene movement helped to create public interest in the prevention of mental illness through counseling in the schools.

The child guidance movement also influenced psychological services in the schools. The first clinical services offered in the schools were primarily medical services. However, Witmer at the University of Pennsylvania in the 1890s and William Healy in Chicago around 1910 began to apply psychological techniques in their clinics. Healy's techniques were soon desemminated to others and by 1914 approximately 100 child guidance clinics had been established.

Several professional groups developed which defined one or more of the functions outlined by these movements as their special area of service to schools. School psychologists performed the psychometric and child study functions, guidance counselors performed the vocational guidance and preventive mental health functions, and social workers, special educators, and a variety of other educationally trained personnel also became involved in these operations.

All of these movements tended to focus on the problem child and sought to treat his problems in a service delivery system modeled after that of medicine. That is, the "sick" child comes to a special, centralized place for the treatment of intellectual or personality malfunction. Spurred by the ascendance of clinical psychology after World War II and the concomitant dominance of Freudian based analytic techniques, the "clinical" trend in school psychological services probably reached its peak during the 1950s and early 1960s.

While the influence of the clinical trends in psychological services reached its peak, several other trends in psychology and education emerged which led to critical questions. First, psychologists began to note that children's behavior is a result of an interaction between their personal characteristics, i.e. cognitive abilities, personality traits etc., and the characteristics of the situation. The unit of study began to shift from an emphasis on the organism's characteristics to the organism-environment interaction. This point was stressed in Robert Sears' (1951) presidential address to the American Psychological Association. He stated that the study of personality theory and social psychology must focus on the dyad (two individuals interacting) rather than the individual.

At least three important influences stimulated educators to pay attention to this line of reasoning. First, Prescott (1957) encouraged teachers to use anecodatal records. By noting a child's behavior throughout the school day attention was focused on the important interactions between the child and his environment, i.e. teachers, peers, and classroom materials. Second, the development of scales to examine the interaction between teachers and their classes (Flanders, 1970) and the use of these scales in teacher training (Hyman, in press) has increased the awareness of some teachers that their style of interaction can have profound effects on students' behaviors. Finally, behavior modification approaches have been increasingly applied and demonstrated empirically in the schools (O'Leary and O'Leary, 1972). The behaviorists' message has been that relatively minor changes in the clasroom environment or teacher behavior, e.g. attention to appropriate student behaviors, can result in significant changes in student behavior. It has been argued that these changes can occur regardless of predispositions, past learnings, or personality of the child.

Another important basis for criticisms of the clinical approach to school psychological services stems from the notion that there may never be enough psychologically trained personnel to individually treat all the children who need help in the schools. One approach to this dilemma has been to use remedial techniques that can be effectively implemented in groups (Hyman, in press). Another approach to this number problem is to focus on the dyadic interaction between the teacher and child. With this approach one member of the dyad (the teacher) is constant in all the teacher-student interactions in a given classroom. Thus, if the behavior of the teacher can be changed a larger number of dyadic interactions can be changed.

The theoretical notions regarding the study of dyadic interaction and the deficient manpower allocation has contributed to questions about the clinical delivery system. However, the day to day experiences of school psychologists, counselors and related personnel regarding this model has probably contributed to these questions. For example, Caplan (1970) has described shortcomings of the clinical system that many practitioners will understand. In his attempts to aid developing school systems in Israel, he noticed that the children referred by a given teacher tended to have the same type of referral problem. Thus, for example, one teacher would usually refer acting out, aggressive boys, while another teacher might refer slow learners. Such differences would often occur even when teachers made referrals from the same group of youngsters. It became clear that schools often defined problem behavior in terms of the teacher and his concerns rather than in terms of the child's behavior. This kind of practical realization in conjunction with the above theoretical observations, makes it clear that efficient delivery of school psychological services demands a focus on consultation techniques which can help to change teacher behavior.

While there has been increased theoretical focus on school consultation in recent years, the practice of consultation in the schools has been gradually emerging for some time. In fact, many practitioners have always implemented some form of a consultation model where the focus was on changing the behavior of the child's caretakers, e.g. the teacher or parent. Similarly, before the development of a consultation model much was written about the importance of a free flow of information between psychologist and caretaker. However, recent developments in the consultation literature have refined this open-dialogue concept and may have given it added impetus in practice.

A Consultative Model

The purpose of this book is to present a selection of the current literature in consultation. This should help practitioners to broaden their perspective regarding the potential ways in which they can provide psychological services in the schools, and it should also help researchers to become more aware of the important issues in the field. One important way in which this can be accomplished is by trying to conceptualize each article in terms of the process variables which can be used to change teacher behavior.

The consultation process techniques derive from the literature in psychotherapy (e.g. Rogers, 1951) as well as consultation (e.g. Caplan, 1970), and the focus of these techniques is toward changing teacher behavior. The following are examples of some of these process techniques which have been described elsewhere (Meyers, Freidman, and Gaughan, 1975). (1) *Verbal reinforcement* is designed to increase the frequency of teacher statements related to her feelings, attitudes, and cognitions about teaching. Some examples include "uh-huh," "yeah," or reflecting the teacher's feelings. (2) *Clarification* is when the consultant uses his own words rather than the teacher's words to restate what the teacher has said. For example, the consultant might say, "You seem to be saying. . . ." (3) *Empathy* is a technique where the consultant communicates his understanding of the teacher's feelings. For example, the consultant might say, "I understand how you feel frustrated. . . ." (4) *Direct confrontation* about the teacher's attitudes, feelings, or cognitions can be used after rapport is established. For example, the consultant might say, "Although Johnny does talk out a lot, it seems that you feel unusually angry at him." (5) *Indirect confrontation* would be less threatening in that the consultant could confront the dynamics which may underlie the teacher's negative behavior by describing similar dynamics underlying the behavior of someone else like a child in the classroom. (6) *Probing for feelings* is a technique where the consultant asks the teacher to talk about feelings which are not being expressed. (7) Finally, *providing choice* is a technique in which the consultant will make several alternative suggestions as well as encourage the teacher to think of suggestions. The teachers must decide which suggestion to implement.

Although the above is not an exhaustive list, it is intended to give an idea of the process techniques which can be useful in consultation. When reading this book, one should observe what process techniques are used under what conditions. It is underscored that these process techniques may be important for any content technique, and, therefore, they may be significant for any of the approaches to consultation described in each of the following chapters. For example, verbal reinforcement is likely to be used to change teacher behavior in the behavior modification approach to consultation. On the other hand, it is likely that other important process variables may also be used with this approach even though these other techniques might not be directly stated. Thus, a behavioral consultant might use empathy or direct confrontation as a technique to convince the teacher to implement a behavior modification approach with the students.

The process variables should be distinguished from the content of consultation, and a second way in which to gain perspective regarding school consultation is to read the chapters in order to differentiate between the various content techniques. This book is structured in such a way as to facilitate this latter goal and this structure is derived from two recent attempts to describe the variety of viable school consultation approaches (Hyman, in press; Meyers 1973). Specifically, the consultation model presented in this book conceptualizes four content approaches to consultation which should be available to pupil personnel workers, and these four approaches constitute the four sections of this book. Section II contains chapters that represent the psychoeducational diagnostic approach to consultation; Section III presents the behavior modification approach; Section IV presents mental health consultation; and Section V contains articles representing organization development consultation. By understanding the content and process of school consultation, the reader should be able to form a conceptual scheme of the consultation approaches which are available to school personnel.

The Future

One trend in school consultation is a decrease in the individual case study functions of school pupil personnel workers. While individual casework is one of the important functions which should receive the careful and thorough attention of practitioners, the other approaches to consultation, i.e. behavior modification, mental health consultation and organization development, are also important and will become more prevalent for the reasons listed previously, i.e. manpower shortage, focus on organism-environment interaction, etc.

Perhaps the greatest single weakness which is found in the literature is an inadequate description of procedures for changing the consultee's behavior. This problem is found in each approach to consultation. While many articles discuss techniques which teachers can be encouraged to implement, there is virtually no detailed discussion of the techniques and process variables which help the consultant influence the teacher so that he is willing to implement suggested changes. Future work in practice, training, and research regarding consultation will have to attend to this problem and specific consultation procedures will have to be delineated more clearly.

Finally, the current state of the consultation literature indicates generally inadequate research for all approaches to consultation. If school consultation is to become a viable area for practitioners, and if the related skills are expected to have an opportunity to develop and improve, then research and evaluation is essential. It is encumbent upon practitioners, trainers, and researchers in the field of consultation to contribute to an increase in the sophistication and quality of consultation research in the future.

REFERENCES

Caplan, G.: *The Theory and Practice of Mental Health Consultation.* New York, Basic, 1970.

Flanders, N. A.: *Analyzing Teaching Behavior.* Reading, A-W, 1970.

Hyman, I.: The psychologist as a teacher trainer for head start. In Lapides, J. (Ed.): *Proceedings of Head Start Mental Health Conference, HEW Region III.* College Park, Maryland, University of Maryland—Head Start Regional Resource and Training Center, 1974 (in press).

Meyers, J.: A consultation model for school psychological services. *Journal of School Psychology, 11*:5-15, 1973.

Meyers, J.; Freidman, M. P., and Gaughan, Jr., E. J.: The effects of consultee-centered consultation on teacher behavior. *Psychology in the Schools, 12*:288-295, 1975.

Miller, F. W.: *Guidance: Principles and Services.* Columbus, Merril, 1961.

O'Leary, K. D., and O'Leary, S. G.: *Classroom Management: The Successful Use of Behavior Modification.* New York, Pergamon, 1972.

Prescott, D. A.: *The Child in the Educative Process.* New York, McGraw, 1957.

Rogers, C. R.: *Client-centered Therapy.* Boston, Houghton, 1951.

Sears, R.: A theoretical framework for personality and social behavior. *Am Psychol, 6*:476-483, 1951.

PSYCHOEDUCATIONAL DIAGNOSIS

ALFRED BINET WAS probably the first psychoeducational diagnostician to work as a consultant to schools. Binet was requested to develop a method by which children could be placed in appropriate educational programs. The eventual development of the Stanford-Binet and other well known individual intelligence tests, followed by the advent of personality testing resulted in what is now considered the traditional "medical model" for consultation. This model is based on the assumption that the problem lies within the child which necessitates an individual diagnosis of the problem child. Diagnosis could be followed by treatment procedures, e.g. therapy or special class placement, designed to focus on the problem within the child.

This approach to consultation has most often utilized school psychologists, psychiatrists, and social workers as the consultants. Recently, this model has developed into a team approach involving other specialists, such as learning disabilities specialists, speech pathologists, and audiologists. Generally, the problem child is initially referred by a teacher or principal. A form is often completed and forwarded to the consultant or a designate of the child study team. The most thorough evaluation will include conferences with the teacher and other knowledgeable school personnel, observation of the child in class, examination of all educational and medical records, interview with the parents to obtain all pertinent background information, evaluation of the child by specialists and a conference of specialists and the teacher to arrive at a diagnosis. This is then followed by recommendations communicated to the teacher, parents, and the child if he is able to understand. In the ideal situation the psychoeducational diagnostician acts as a consultant in terms of follow-ups. This provides the consultee with the opportunity to discuss success and failure of various recommendations and the consultant can thus help to make changes where needed.

One recommendation which can result from the psycho-diagnostic approach is to place a child in special education. Since a psychological evaluation is legally necessary for a school district to make such a placement, this approach to psychological services currently mandates the role of many pupil personnel workers. While this approach helps to insure that psychological services are provided in school, recently it has been criticized because of its failure to effect sufficient change in relation to the time and cost involved. Failure has often been linked to inadequate diag-nostic procedures and a lack of appropriate follow-up by the consultant. However, this approach offers a workable framework which often leads to positive changes for students when it is implemented in a thorough and competent manner. This section presents papers which provide an in-depth analysis of the major issues concerning psychoeducational diagnosis as a consultation approach.

The first chapter, by Forness, focuses on the precision of good diagnostic procedures and the historical lack of emphasis on recommendations resulting from the diagnosis. Forness indicates that more "testing of limits" and more use of naturalistic observa-tion might improve diagnosis, and he urges the consultant to eliminate jargon while offering teachers very specific recom-mendations.

The second chapter, by Brison, discusses the value of be-havioral data in psychoeducational assessment. Brison stresses the need to develop and use direct observation as an effective tool in diagnosis. The author presents a case study to support this point. Similarly, the third chapter, by Minor, stresses an ecological approach to gathering diagnostic information. In contrast with Brison, Minor does not use extensive direct observa-tion; on the other hand, he shows how a thorough understanding of the child's milieu is important.

Unfortunately, too often the psychoeducational diagnosis is followed by a written report with no direct teacher consultation. It is difficult to communicate effectively the diagnostic findings and recommendations with only a written report. The fourth chapter makes an effort to improve the quality of reports as Handler, Gersten, and Handler present some excellent examples of communicative and noncommunicative statements from psychological reports. They stress the importance of face to face communication and interpretation of test findings to teachers, and they present eleven specific recommendations for improved communication between psychologists and teachers.

The psychoeducational model deals basically with diagnosis and treatment. The consultant rarely provides the treatment since much of his time is occupied by diagnostic activities. In educational settings the teacher is most often the person providing the treatment and the recommendations are often spelled out in written form on a psychological or psychiatric report.

As noted above, the development of meaningful recommendations has been a problem in this approach to consultation. Consequently, in the fifth chapter, Catterall presents a theoretical orientation to developing recommendations. The author provides a guide for understanding the process of determining recommendations, and it is followed by Blanco's focus on the content of good recommendations. Blanco's chapter gives samples of the kinds of specific recommendations offered by participants in a national survey which he conducted. The seventh chapter, by Cartwright, Cartwright and Ysseldyke, deals with the issue of psychologists' recommendations in another manner. They present a model in which the teacher's diagnostic and remediation skills are improved through consultation from the psychologist.

The final chapter by Tyler and Fine, is concerned with the validity of the psychodiagnostic model. This is one of the few research papers to appear in the literature and it supports the intensive use of the psychodiagnostic consultation model.

Chapter 1

EDUCATIONAL PRESCRIPTION FOR THE SCHOOL PSYCHOLOGIST

Steven R. Forness

From the *Journal of School Psychology*, 8:96-98, 1970.

The malady of the school psychologist is described as a "paralysis of the analysis" in which traditional analysis of school learning or behavior problems does not seem to lead to meaningful educational recommendations. A model for assessment is prescribed wherein individual testing might prove more productive and which ultimately presents the school psychologist as a specialist in education and an observer *in situ*.

The school psychologist is not a well man. His malady, while not particularly acute, is nonetheless a chronic one, endemic to his profession. The patient often presents such symptoms as distension of the referral (Baker, 1965), rupture of the arteries of communication (Lucas and Jones, 1968), atrophied recommendations (Rucker, 1967), and accumulation of jargon deposits in the report (Rudnick and Berkowitz, 1968). The syndrome might best be designated as a "paralysis of the analysis" and a discussion of its pathology forms the basis for this paper.

The reported disenchantment with school psychological services has certainly not focused on the diagnostic ability of the school psychologist. On the contrary, teachers have often been

The author wishes to express his appreciation to Mrs. Juanita Ferjo, Educational Assessment Teacher, UCLA Neuropsychiatric Institute School, who has ably demonstrated the educational relevance of assessment. Related educational research is supported in part by U.S. Office of Education grant OEG-0-8-0030.9 and NICHD Grant HD 04612.

17

awed by the impressive and exacting analysis of school learning and behavior problems which form the bulk of psychological reports. The school psychologist, however, appears unable to move from the analysis of a child's problem to the next logical step: recommendations for remediation. Teachers have been shown to be the most concerned with the school psychologist's recommendations (Mussman, 1964); yet paralysis sets in precisely in this area. Recommendations tend to be vague or unrealistic and often leave the teacher with nothing but new terminology for an old problem (Rudnick and Berkowitz, 1968).

That such should be the case is not surprising. School psychologists have traditionally been trained in the mold of clinical psychologists, with emphasis on individual testing. In practice, the clinical psychologist serves as a resource person, constructing with his test results a framework from which the psychiatrist weaves his initial impressions of the patient's cognitive and affective functioning. The clinical psychologist is thus imbued, perhaps quite correctly, with the sanctity of test results. By dint of common training, the school psychologist tends to inherit the same respect for the product of testing. But often he is not trained to deal with the process of testing (the approach of a child to a test item, for example) and does not have an adequate basis upon which to formulate a meaningful recommendation for the teacher.

Volle (1957) suggested that individual intelligence testing might be considerably more productive if one were to "test the limits" of the child's responses. Should the child not respond, or respond incorrectly, to a test item, alternate methods of presenting the item might elicit the correct response. In other words, one might "teach" the child how to respond. Although the item is scored as incorrect, the educational techniques used in helping the child arrive at a correct response tend to be more important than the total score. Testing the limits of group achievement tests with individual children has likewise been productive in making recommendations to teachers (Ferjo and Forness, 1969).

Psychological assessment in a school context should, of course, include much more than the tests themselves. Weiner (1967) indicated that assessment goes beyond a determination of ability levels. She suggested observation of the "rate" of learning, the time required for a child to achieve a specific level. Bryant (1966) feels that assessment reports should include a description of educational methods and materials which were tried and some estimate of their effectiveness.

With the increasing acceptance of behavior modification techniques in the classroom (Hewett, 1968), the school psychologist should also consider an assessment of behavioral components as part of his diagnostic work-up. Lovitt (1967), for example, presented a schema for evaluation which includes observation of the stimulus materials best suited for an individual subject's learning, the mode and rate of his responses, the contingencies under which his responses are elicited, and the consequences or reinforcements under which he responds. Using such a system, a school psychologist could probably make substantive recommendations. Suggestions could be made along such dimensions as whether the subject responds at a higher rate if questions are written rather than oral, whether he learns more efficiently under fixed-interval schedules of reinforcement rather than fixed-ratio schedules, and to which types of reinforcement he best responds.

Recommendations must be formulated, however, within the context of classroom realities. It is here that, pathologically, the vital functions of the school psychologist appear most impaired. The trend towards certifying as school psychologists persons who have had no teaching experience or even course-work in curriculum or remedial methods is quite in evidence (California Administrative Code, 1969). Diagnostic evaluation should produce information which the teacher can transmit into an educational program. It is difficult to envision meaningful recommendations emanating from school psychologists in the absence of substantial experimental exposure to classroom management, educational terminology, curriculum materials, and other procedural aspects of both regular and special education classrooms.

More to the point, perhaps, it is difficult to imagine substantive recommendations on an individual child without reference to his classroom environment. One must consider the realities of the referral: the capabilities and personality of the teacher, his expectations for the child, the amount of individual attention he can give towards remediation, the materials available, and the many other factors which preordain success or failure for that child in that classroom.

It is no longer sufficient for a school psychologist to report test scores and elaborate on test behavior. Such medication might have served him in the past but perhaps only as a sedative. The supposed equilibrium between psychology and education which characterizes the school psychologist's training needs to be upset. The prescription is an increased dosage of education both in training and in practice.

Test results themselves probably serve no greater purpose than providing the legal criteria required to admit a child to a special class. Actual diagnosis and evaluation of a child are not products of testing; they are a process of teaching and continuous observation. And as McCarthy (1968) pointed out, the teacher is best qualified to carry out that function.

The school psychologist is the objective observer of the learning process. He is first an educator who is knowledgeable in that field, its techniques, and its language; but he has a fresh vantage point. He views the child in perspective similar to the teacher's but largely unencumbered by preconceptions which build as a function of continuous and often subjective observation. Trained in observation and experimental analysis, he can stand aside from many of the exigencies which prevent the teacher from reaching objectivity. The school psychologist, in effect, increases both the reliability and the validity of the teacher's observations.

The school psychologist, then, must be thoroughly familiar with the teacher's perspective and must be willing periodically to forsake the office for the classroom. Observation of the child in the referral situation would appear to be a necessary step in data collection. Particularly in the area of behavior problems, the psychologist must visit the classroom to observe antecedent and subsequent events which appear to maintain maladaptive behavior in each individual case. In learning problems as well, he must concern himself with the teacher contingencies under which a child's response rate appears to vary (e.g. Does a child misspell words at the chalkboard or in oral recitation at a higher rate than he does in a workbook exercise?) Observations in the specific educational setting might help the school psychologist make recommendations understandable to that specific teacher.

As the school psychologist refines his techniques, classroom observation through an educational perspective might substantially replace traditional adherence to psychological testing. The prognosis for useful analysis under such conditions appears quite good.

REFERENCES

Baker, H.: Psychological services: From the school staff's point of view. *Journal of School Psychology, 4*:36-42, 1965.

Bryant, N.: Clinical inadequacies with learning disorders—The missing clinical educator. In J. Hellmuth (Ed.): *Learning Disorders.* Vol. II. Seattle, Special Child Publications, 1966.

California Administrative Code. Title 5, Education, Sacramento, 1969.

Cason, E.: Some suggestions on the interaction between the school psychologist and the classroom teacher. *J Consul Clin Psychol, 9*:132-137, 1945.

Ferjo, J., and Folness, S.: Research in progress, 1969.

Hewett, F.: *The Emotionally Disturbed Child in the Classroom.* Boston, Allyn, 1968.

Lovitt, T.: Assessment of children with learning disabilities. *Except Child, 34*:233-240, 1967.

Lucas, M., and Jones, R.: Attitudes of teachers of mentally retarded children toward psychological reports and services. *Ohio State University Mental Retardation Traning: Technical Report Series 68-2,* 1968.

McCarthy, J.: Psychoeducational diagnosis: A derivative of classroom behavior. *Proceedings of Special Study Institute on the Visually Impaired Child with Multiple Handicaps.* San Francisco, California State Department of Education, 1968.

Mussman, M.: Teacher's evaluations of psychological reports. *Journal of School Psychology, 1*:35-37, 1964.

Rucker, C.: Report writing in school psychology: A critical investigation. *Journal of School Psychology, 5*:101-108, 1967.

Rudnick, M., Berkowitz, H.: Preparation of school psychologists: For what? *Psychology in the Schools, 1*:53-59, 1968.

Volle, F.: A proposal for "testing the limits" with mental defectives for purposes of subtest analysis of the WISC verbal scale. *J Clin Psychol, 13*:64-67, 1957.

Weiner, B.: Assessment: Beyond psychometry. *Except Child, 33*:367-372, 1967.

Chapter 2

THE SCHOOL PSYCHOLOGIST'S USE OF DIRECT OBSERVATION

David W. Brison

THE DIRECT OBSERVATION of children's behavior is one important function of the school psychologist. This technique supports the school psychologist in his role as a data-oriented problem solver (Gray, 1963). This function will be examined, not only in the context of the duties of the psychologist but also in relation to the school setting in which he works. It is the author's contention that systematic direct observation is largely neglected in education. The possible causes for this neglect will be outlined and an illustration of how the school psychologist has a unique opportunity to help correct this deficit will be presented.

Neglect of Direct Observation

One of the primary concerns of the school psychologist is deviant behavior patterns in children. The data involved in the interpretation of this behavior are normally subsumed under the heading of personality characteristics. Systematic direct observation is only one of the sources of data on personality. Bronfenbrener (1960) has categorized the sources of data on personality of children in a way that is conceptually helpful for the present discussion. He lists four sources of data:

1. Observation of behavior in selected situations.
2. Reports of behavior by the child or others.

From the *Journal of School Psychology*, 5:109-115, 1967.

3. Reports of attitude by the child or others.
4. Projective responses.

Research in both developmental and educational psychology has consisted mainly of the systematic collection of data. Several authors (Ausubel, 1958; Mussen, 1963) have said that research in these areas has not been directed by theory and has, therefore, not progressed beyond the level of preliminary observation and data collection. It is interesting to note that these data are mostly from sources 2, 3, and 4. Direct observation of children's behavior has been largely neglected (Wright, 1960) by researchers. (It is somewhat difficult to substantiate this from Wright's summary because he excludes studies where direct observation was used—as a dependent variable in a contrived situation.) On the other hand, educators have, despite their mistrust of researchers, often looked to researchers for instruments to evaluate behavior. Many tests now enjoying wide use in both education and counselling were initially developed for research purposes. Consequently, methods of systematic direct observation have not enjoyed wide usage in the schools.

There are various reasons why researchers have utilized sources other than direct observation. One reason is that it has often been difficult for them to get permission to observe in life situations. Secondly, observation is usually more time consuming. There are of course other reasons, but research in child psychology has had to rely largely on inferences about past behavior (learning, personality) drawn from a very limited but usually reliable sample of behavior in a test situation. As Bronfenbrener (1960) points out, this neglect is not because of a lack of either the reliability or validity of direct observation.

Of course, the above information does not really exclude the possibility that school psychologists actually spend time observing children in the classroom as a part of their work. It is the author's contention, based admittedly on only his observation as a school psychologist and his discussion with other school psychologists, that this observation is usually of a global subjective nature and does not consist of reliable, measureable recording of the specific type of behavior under consideration. Most school psychologists are uncomfortable in classrooms in the role of an observer and get out as soon as they can.

Reasons for Neglect of Direct Observation

There seems to exist in many areas of education a general reluctance to invade the classroom. This reluctance is perhaps particularly encouraged by the elementary teacher because the only time he has been observed was when someone was evaluating his teaching ability. The author thinks that many teachers are wary of this type of observation mainly because they feel that judgments on their teaching ability are based on inadequate data. In addition, many teachers have simply not been observed to any great extent since their practice teaching days, and over a period of years come to question the validity of their own practices and actually are afraid to let others see them work.

However, once teachers overcome their initial resistance, most of them welcome observation, particularly if it does not result in global evaluations of their own ability or premature analysis of children's behavior.

If the psychologist is systematically recording some aspects of children's behavior, the teacher is apt to conclude that he is involved in some kind of a research project. Many educators seem to have a built in distrust of research, and the psychologist is apt to initially suffer by association. The validity of the assumption that educators distrust research can be debated at length but it is not within the scope of this paper. However, the educator certainly has legitimate reasons for distrust of research. Several primary reasons are premature extrapolation of basic psychological research (the extrapolation can be premature either because the necessary developmental research has been neglected or because the investigator does not take into account the difference between laboratory conditions and "real life"); unwarranted application of purely empirical results which have no generalization because they do not elucidate causal factors that operate in all situations. Bereiter and Engelmann (1966) have presented a fascinating critique of Hunt's premature use of sensory deprivation studies as an explanation for the learning deficits of culturally disadvantaged children.

For the above reasons, many school psychologists divorce themselves from direct observation of a systematic nature, especially if it involves note taking. Unfortunately, this is true even if they are not involved in research but are using direct observation as part of a clinical examination of an individual child.

The last reasons for school psychologist's neglect of direct observation are that they do not agree on what to observe, how to observe, or the purposes for which direct observation can be used. It is the answers to these questions which will be the concern of the rest of this paper.

The School Psychologist's Relationship to Systematic Collection of Data

School psychologists should develop the skills of a data-oriented problem solver (Gray, 1963); that is, they should convey by their actions that educational plans and decisions should be made on this basis of data that is available or could be collected. As indicated, the psychologist can make a real contribution in this area because there is an urgent need for this attitude in the schools.

The systematic collection of data can assist the psychologist in several aspects of his role. First, in helping teachers understand children it is necessary to refer to a common base of observations that have the same meaning for both teachers and counselors. Too often nebulous terms, such as rejection, aggression, regression, lack of security, result in poor communication because they have different meanings to different people. Data collection can also be used as a method of measuring change in individual children's behavior. Finally, data can be used to formulate hypotheses about what maintains deviant behavior. The teacher and psychologist can both participate in this process of hypothesis formulation and subsequent testing of these hypotheses.

Interpretation of Data

Once personality data have been collected, they can be interpreted in various ways. At one extreme of a hypothesized interpretation continuum are the behavioral therapists (Bijou and Baer, 1961; Ullman and Krasner, 1965) who maintain that one should not make inferences about the organism from observed behavior. They claim that interpretation of behavior as goal directed, or as an expression of underlying dynamic conflicts is neither parsimonious nor advantageous.

A middle position is that observed behavior can be utilized to make inferences about the child which enable the observer to predict with some accuracy how the child will react in another situation. The theory guiding these inferences varies widely but some typical inferences are about self-concept, direction of certain goal seeking behavior, and ego strength.

At the other extreme of this interpretation continuum are those who interpret behavior as the symbolic representation of dynamic conflict. The conflicts are usually explained by either traditional psychoanalytic or neo-psychoanalytic theory.

It is not possible in this context to contrast further these different positions. Fortunately, it is not important in terms of our discussion of direct observation of children's behavior. For once the data have been reliably collected, they can be interpreted any way the observer chooses. What is important is that the original data be available for other interpretations. Unfortunately, this has often not been the case in diagnosis in counseling and psychotherapy. Quite often interpretation has been a value judgment and the basis of this judgment is known only to the observer or those holding a close theoretical viewpoint. Both the reliability and validity of these judgments are questionable.

Strategies of Observation

The focus of our observation is the child in interaction with his environment. It is obvious that this is a continual, complex flow of interaction and any attempt to record it has to be selective. Even when observing a single child for only one minute, it is impossible to record all his behavior and all aspects of the environment that could be acting on the child. Those operating within a general Skinnerian framework have attempted to fragment this continuous interaction by examining functional relationships between children's responses (operants) and the consequences of those responses. Others have used general personality traits, aggressiveness, dependency, and withdrawal, to guide their observation. The assumption underlying this approach is that the presence of these traits predisposes a child to certain types of interaction with his environment.

A clear, concise but clearly inadequate answer to the question of what to observe is, "Observe only useful information." An understanding of what information is of potential value is not going to drop out of the sky and unfortunately theory cannot at present time give any definite direction but only some promising leads.

It should be obvious that direct observation of children's behavior cannot proceed without some guiding selective principles. If observation is guided by a single theoretical system then potentially useful information might very well be lost. On the other hand, if the selective principles are too broad then not enough information is collected about any one aspect of the child's interaction with his environment.

As an example, consider the problems involved in developing an instrument for the observation of aggressive behavior. First, the reader should note that concentration on aggressiveness narrows the range of the child's interaction that is being observed. Further, a theoretical explanation of aggression, such as the frustration-aggression hypothesis, would restrict even more the range of our observations. Suppose, however, that the school psychologist is not interested in testing theory or being guided in his observations by a single theoretical system.

The next problem then is to define what is meant by aggression. Bandura and Walters (1963) after surveying the literature, find two general categories of aggression definitions: (a) "the class of pain-producing or damage-producing responses that could injure or damage if aimed at a vulnerable object" and (b) definitions of aggression that involve the *intent* of a person to injure. The first definition is rather easy to operationally define but potentially valuable information about aggression is excluded. Most aggression which we regard as deviant or bothersome involves intent on the part of a child to injure another. Intent is, however, difficult to infer because the observer often has to know something about prior events in the classroom.

In the stage of constructing an instrument for recording of

aggression by direct observation, it is necessary to define operationally, as clearly as possible, what is meant by an aggressive
act. The only way the success of this operation can be tested
is to see if different judges come to the same conclusion after
observing the same behavior. In order to obtain this interjudge
agreement, it is necessary to limit the inferences that have to be
made while the observer is recording. Again it should be emphasized that the observation, once recorded, can be interpreted
in any manner the observer wishes. Also, the development of
an instrument of this type is going to involve preliminary observations and many revisions before reaching the point where different
observers will agree.

Observation and the School Psychologist

In actual practice, the use of observational techniques is not
as difficult as it might seem. First, there are available instruments
which have demonstrated reliability (interjudge agreement) so
the construction stage can often be circumvented. An interesting
instrument for observation in the classroom has been developed
by Spaulding at Duke University for the Ford Foundation Education Improvement Project. It subdivides the child's response in
the classroom into thirteen categories. Spaulding originally devised the instrument for teacher training purposes but is currently using it to measure classes of operant behavior in young
culturally disadvantaged children. Secondly, in classroom situations the problem of what to observe is not so difficult. Most of
us would agree that we value such things as attention to task,
and rewarding social relationships and devalue hyperactivity
which deviates from the mean, withdrawal, and highly dependent
behavior.

Psychologists are apt to get referrals from parents, teachers,
and principals that fit into precisely these categories. The psychologist should then try to get some kind of an objective measure
of the type of behavior in question. This measure should include
aspects of the situation in which the behavior occurs. Then
hypotheses should be formulated about why the behavior is
maintained; they should be checked and appropriate plans devised

based on appropriate methods of producing change. The final stage would be the application of the observation instrument to see if change is produced.

To illustrate the purpose of this paper, the following case is outlined. Last week a teacher described a child in her class who was particularly disturbing to her. He raised his hand repeatedly in response to questions, criticized answers other children gave, had the tendency to try to dominate class discussion with little lectures he prepared, and constantly demanded her attention by bringing in items from the newspaper even though they were not relevant. His general high level of activity was also a constant irritant.

The psychologist should first go into the classroom and observe the child. The observational technique of the specimen description (Wright, 1960) might be used at this stage. Here the psychologist describes in narrative form the behavior of the child for a specified period of time, for instance five minutes. Several specimen descriptions of different types of classroom activities could be collected. This description includes aspects of the situation, such as teacher or peer responses. The counselor has several general constructs to guide his observation, namely: attention-getting, aggression, and general hyperactivity. After analyzing the behavior sampled in the specimen description, the psychologist might construct a check list and then again observe the child noting the *incidence* of behaviors in the categories mentioned. It might be necessary to sample the whole class so that a normative contrast could be made. Also the psychologist would have a check list for the teacher's behavior with general categories including approval, disapproval, attention, and attempts to ignore.

The next step would be to formulate hypotheses about why the problem exists and how it is maintained. For instance, the psychologist might postulate that the child's behavior is a defensive reaction against real or imagined rejection. Alternatively, he might feel analysis in terms of what is reinforcing the behavior is a correct approach. In any case, the hypotheses should lead to plans of action. There might be attempts to provide a secure counseling relationship or conversely to change environmental contingencies. The most important last step would be measurement of change in behavior, using the same instruments after treatment has been instituted.

The approach briefly outlined will certainly raise questions in many school psychologist's minds. It may be true that most do value certain kinds of behavior, but the categories mentioned do not exhaust all behaviors we value and for some they do not even assume very high priority. What about creativity, spontaneity, self-actualization, and openness to feelings? In fact, these are terms usually associated with a mental health point of view. Also, how does one choose the values to which we assign high priority? Is it enough to accept others' (teachers', parents') definitions of problems? The answer to these questions is twofold: this approach is envisioned as only part of the school psychologist's job although admittedly a major function. Secondly, behavior in all categories listed interferes with effective school learning and psychologists ought to be primarily concerned with promoting effective learning. Lastly, collection of data and efforts to measure change are not specific to certain values, this approach can be utilized with other values such as creativity and self-expression.

This paper has dealt with direct observation as a means of data collection. The author feels direct observation should assume highest priority as a means of data collection in the schools. This does not mean that collection of personality data in the other categories listed by Bronfenbrener (1960) is omitted. Demonstration of the effective use of such data could be a real contribution of the school psychologist.

There is the implication, in this discussion of the use of a technique, that the school psychologist should function in part as a behavioral trouble shooter. This is the author's assumption. However, the major point is that the success of this venture should be measured.

REFERENCES

Ausubel, D. P.: *Theory and Problems of Child Development.* New York, Grune, 1958.

Bandura, A., and Walters, R. H.: *Social Learning and Personality Development.* New York, HR&W, 1963.

Bereiter, C., and Engelmann, S.: *Teaching Disadvantaged Children in the Preschool*. New York, P-H, 1966.

Bijou, S. W., and Baer, D. W.: *Child Development: A Systematic and Empirical Study*. Vol. I., New York, Appleton, 1961.

Bronfenbrener, V., and Ricciuti, H. N.: The appraisal of personality characteristics in children. In P. H. Mussen (Ed.): *Handbook of Research Methods in Child Development*. New York, Wiley, 1960.

Gray, S.: *The Psychologist in the Schools*. New York, HR&W, 1963.

Mussen, P. H.; Conger, J. J., and Kagan, J.: *Child Development and Personality*. New York, Har-Row, 1963.

Ullman, L. P., and Krasner, L. (Eds.): *Case Studies in Behavior Modification*. New York, HR&W, 1965.

Wright, H. F.: Observational child study. In P. H. Mussen (Ed.): *Handbook of Research Methods in Child Development*. New York, Wiley, 1960.

Chapter 3

SYSTEMS ANALYSIS AND SCHOOL PSYCHOLOGY

Marshall W. Minor

Traditionally the activties of professionals supplying mental health services to schools have been guided by a medical model which stressed intrapsychic dysfunction. This model is contrasted with an ecological orientation utilizing a systems approach for preventing or alleviating problems. The case history method is used to demonstrate how school psychologists actually perform within this model and to illustrate some of the general characteristics of the ecological approach; it also demonstrates how teacher consultation, family therapy, and study role playing are organized into a meaningful and unified strategy directed at helping a child in trouble.

T RADITIONALLY, SCHOOL PSYCHOLOGISTS have utilized a clinical, or medical, model to define their roles and determine their professional activities. This model has dictated that children whose academic or social behavior deviates from the cultural mores of the classroom or larger school system possess some defect which has resulted in their failure to function successfully. Following this model, the school psychologist's function has been one of determining the nature of the hypothesized defect and devising necessary remedial or treatment strategies which are intended to remove or alleviate it.

Recently, however, the traditional medical model of behavioral dysfunction is being challenged. Mental health professionals

From the *Journal of School Psychology*, 10:227-232, 1972.

argue with increasing frequency that it is circular and semantically confusing to take behaviors (academic failures, strange verbalizations or mannerisms, etc.) which have been adjudged atypical by some societal code or standard as evidence for the existence of some underlying mental dysfunction. Unlike the case of paresis, where the rationale for inferring underlying disturbance rests upon anatomical and physiological referrents, the inference of mental illness is usually based solely on the presence of those same or similar behaviors which the hypothetical mental illness was supposed to explain in the first place (Szasz, 1961).

Rhodes (1969), for example, has argued that it is meaningless to discuss problems of behavior in isolation from the systems or contexts in which those problems arise, since it is these very contexts (e.g. classroom) which define the behavior as disturbing in the first place.

de Meuron and Auerswald (1969) have taken a similar view and recommend that professional activity not be directed toward diagnosing and treating individual psychopathology, but, rather, it should concentrate upon understanding and changing the relationships which exist between the troubled child and the ecological systems in which he is embedded.

While not denying that the traditional model has benefited numerous children and has provided a rich source of information concerning the intrapsychic life, the purpose of the preceding comments was to suggest that school psychology needs to develop a new conceptualization of human behavior if it is to respond adequately to, and help with, the current problems confronting the schools, particularly with reference to the development of preventive programs. Recent developments in psychoanalytic ego psychology, general systems theory, social psychiatry, family therapy, and communication theory are beginning to merge into a still loosely organized model of human functioning and disability which would seem to hold promise for providing school psychology with an alternative to the medical model. This developing model might be called an ecological systems approach.

Some of the basic characteristics of this newer orientation will be contrasted to those of the traditional medical model. In order to demonstrate how such an orientation could be utilized by a school psychologist, some of the details of an actual school referral will be discussed.

The child in question was Gloria, a fourth grader. Gloria had brought to class what the teacher considered to be pornographic pictures. This incident led the teacher to request a meeting with the child's parents. The mother arrived with her current paramour, who lived with the family. Rather than listening with regret to the description of her daughter's misconduct, as the teacher had planned, the couple began to attack the teacher and the school for their intolerance and degrading manner toward the child. The teacher left the meeting shaken and somewhat frightened by the encounter with this couple. It was at this point that she asked the team to help her. The team consisted of a school psychologist and a community worker who were part of an ecologically oriented, school mental health program serving Title I elementary schools in the inner-city area.

Characteristics of the Ecological Model

Unit of Diagnosis

In contradistinction to the medical model, where the object of study and treatment is the individual patient, the ecologically oriented psychologist's point of reference is the entire psychosocial or ecological field within which the referring problem arose.

The interest in analyzing the system instead of the individual stems from the assumption that human behavior is not so much a function of instinct, constitution, or intrapsychic dynamics as of the conditions of the interpersonal context within which the behavior takes place.

From this standpoint, terms such as personality, attitudes, and symptoms are thought of as ". . . describing the individual's typical interactions which occur in response to a particular interpersonal context, rather than as intrapsychic entities" (Jackson, 1967).

The ecological view maintains that a behavioral problem represents not a symptom of intrapsychic disease, but a disequilibrium in the interaction processes occurring between the individual and the environment (Zwerling, 1968). The psychologist who ascribes to this view will necessarily find himself as interested in the person who is disturbed, e.g. referring teacher, parent, as in the disturber, e.g. child. The appropriateness of this orientation in Gloria's case can be seen in that the magnitude of the teacher's concern stemmed more from contact with the parents than from Gloria's behavior.

With the foregoing principles in mind, the team's first goal was to determine what important psychosocial entities appeared to be involved in Gloria's present difficulties.

The teacher's involvement was, of course, obvious at the time of referral. In addition, the fact that the referral and the teacher's interest in possibly removing Gloria from the school seemed prompted by the meeting with Gloria's parents helped to identify another important system and to lead the team to set up a family meeting.

Behavior is Socially Significant

While traditionally oriented mental health specialists recognize the influence of past environmental inputs, e.g. mother-child relationship, traumatic events, etc., as causative factors in behavioral dysfunction, they tend to ignore the present social significance of these disturbed behaviors.

The traditionalist may interview parents and teachers in order to obtain a historical record of what *caused* the present problem, but he tends to assume that past causes are largely independent of the current environment.

The ecological or systems view, however, maintains that behavior is constantly being shaped by, and in turn shapes, the present environment. It follows from this assumption that behavior can be made intelligible, or understood, in terms of its present social significance.

This hypothesis, if study and evidence prove its validity, provides the practicing psychologist with a tremendous advantage over his more traditionally oriented colleagues. If behavior is considered to be the result of intrapsychic processes, the professional who has assumed responsibility for making things better is limited to trying to alter processes and structures which he cannot see or manipulate directly, e.g. fixations, minimal brain damage, etc., and which were caused by some temporarily distant past event. If, on the other hand, as the ecological model maintains, behavior is best understood as represented outcomes of psychosocial or interpersonal processes which are current and observable, then the psychologist has at least a chance of influencing these processes positively.

When the community consultant met with Gloria's family, his objective was not to focus solely on the child, but to learn about the entire family and its relationships with one another and the outside world. While some family history was obtained, the information was assumed to represent more of a statement concerning how the family was trying to handle the interviewer and how it presently functioned rather than an accurate account of the family's history.

The family session strongly suggested that one of Gloria's roles in the family was to get rid of the mother's various paramours when the mother could no longer tolerate their presence in the home. Gloria would achieve this feat by causing so much trouble for the family, e.g. getting in trouble at school, stealing, etc., that the home would become chaotic, and the man would leave in desperation. Although the home would then return to relative quiescence, the system remained unchanged.

Treatment Consists of Rule Changing

The ecological approach maintains that a person's behavior is frequently more intelligible and adaptive than it might otherwise appear to be when considered within the framework of the significant social groups of which that person is a member. Outside agents, such as a teacher or therapist, who focus only on the individual, may not see that what appears to be odd or disorganized behavior is actually an appropriate response to a social system, e.g. family, of which the agent is not a member. It follows from this hypothesis that treatment or behavior change would most appropriately consist of altering the rules which govern these important behavior-determining systems.

The team determined that Gloria's family would have to be included in its intervention strategies, because much of her difficulty seemed to be related to the role her family had assigned her.

Although the family had agreed to have another family session, the day after the first session Gloria created an incident which threatened to cause her expulsion from school and bring an end to the team's involvement with her family. Gloria had led a band of children from a neighboring school in an attack on some of her classmates.

At this point, the team was faced with a set of interlocking subsystems, all of which were attempting to reduce their states of tension by labeling Gloria as the sole cause of their discomfort. The family, teacher, classmates, and Gloria herself all seemed set on having her transferred out of school.

The team was able to have the teacher, albeit reluctantly, see that expelling Gloria at this time would only be playing into the family's hands. By expelling Gloria, the school would be accepting the myth that Gloria was the sole source of the family's problems. Expulsion would have also once again allowed the family to use Gloria to rid itself of outside discomfort. Instead of a paramour, Gloria's misconduct would this time have served to rid the family of the team's interventions.

Had the team been working with only the family and not the teacher, Gloria would probably have been expelled after her attack on her classmates. This would have prevented the team from offering any more help and, moreover, would have further reinforced the family's pattern of using Gloria's misconduct to solve its problems. Similarly, the team probably would have met with failure had it limited its interventions to the classroom or to individual sessions with Gloria. This child was fulfilling an essential role in her family and it would be foolhardy to expect that she could change in isolation from her family.

It also seems important to note that had the team felt no urge to understand Gloria's behavior in terms of the relationships she had with the family system, or had met with the family only to gain information for a more adequate psychiatric diagnosis, her attack on her classmates would have seemed totally aberrant and commensurate with a view that she possessed some sort of intrapsychic defect. By its willingness to try and understand the rules and interactions which characterized Gloria's family, the team was able to understand this incident as socially meaningful behavior designed to end the team's therapeutic involvement with the family.

Because it felt that Gloria would manage to have herself expelled before subsequent family sessions could be held, the team decided to enlist the support of another powerful system in Gloria's life space, namely her classmates, to offset this possibility.

The team had the class role play the gang fight which Gloria had led. Initially hostile, Gloria finally broke down and said she wanted to be friends when several of the children assured her they wanted her to join them.

The impact of her improved relations at school showed up during the second family session, which the mother began by saying that Gloria had gotten worse because she was not coming home for lunch. This discussion proved very useful, for it allowed the team to explore with the mother her objections to her daughter's staying for lunch, since most of the other children in school did so.

Although it was too early to confront the mother, it seemed apparent that the mother had collusively supported her daughter's poor relationships and failures at school so that she would remain loyal to the family system and continue to play the role of the bad child who chased away the mother's male companions. The fact that Gloria had stayed for lunch for the first time suggested that some intervention had begun to be made into this pattern. The close of school concluded the team's involvement with Gloria at this point.

A follow-up of Gloria's school performance six months later showed that her new teacher felt her to be an average student for her class, and that she had two close friends. The fact that Gloria's absenteeism, however, was high suggested that much work remained to be done with Gloria's family and with the attitudes and strategies utilized by the school in dealing with the children.

Conclusion

The foregoing presentation was not intended to suggest that the team's interventions had completely alleviated Gloria's situation, nor was its aim to obviate the importance of individual dignity and experience. It was hoped that the discussion did reveal some of the advantages accruing to the mental health practitioner who maintains an interactional view of the human problems which he confronts.

Perhaps the biggest advantage accruing to the therapist who enlarges his perspective to include the child's social environment is the element of hope. When diagnosis or assessment is limited to specifying individual psychopathological conditions, the therapist is limited in the power he can bring to bear for alleviating problems. When he includes those significant social systems which surround the child in his treatment plan, the therapist greatly enhances his chance of success and similarly avoids scapegoating a child with oftentimes self-fulfilling labels.

A psychologist who says that a child cannot learn because he has some intrapsychic defect is considerably more limited in terms of his intervention alternatives than is the one who assesses the child's difficulties in terms of the social environment which is intimately involved with those difficulties.

REFERENCES

deMeuron, M., and Auerswald, E. H.: Cognition and social adaptation. *Am J Orthopsychiatry, 39*(1):57-67, 1969.

Jackson, D. D.: The individual and the larger contexts. *Family Process, 6*(2):139-147, 1967.

Rhodes, W.: The disturbing child: A problem of ecological management. In P. S. Graubard (Ed.): *Children Against Schools.* Chicago, Follett Educational Corporation, 1969.

Szasz, T. S.: *The Myth of Mental Illness: Foundations of a Theory of Personal Conduct.* New York, Hoeber-Harper, 1961.

Zwerling, L.: Conceptual alternatives in the definition of community psychiatry. Paper presented at conference on Community Psychiatry and the Responsive Environment, Temple University, Philadelphia, March, 1968.

Chapter 4

SUGGESTIONS FOR IMPROVED PSYCHOLOGIST-TEACHER COMMUNICATION

LEONARD HANDLER, ALLAN GERSTON, AND
BARBARA HANDLER

WHEN TEACHER AND psychologist pool their observations and knowledge of a child, the result is that both obtain a clearer picture of the child's strengths and weaknesses, difficulties, and abilities. Everyone benefits under such a program; the teacher gains added insight in complex personality functioning, and in planning an individual student's program; the psychologist gets a clearer picture of how the child reacts, and can use such material in making a more extensive diagnosis. The child benefits from the increased understanding of both the psychologist and the teacher.

An important factor in teacher-psychologist relationships is mutual respect. It is important for the teacher not to view the psychologist as a threatening figure. On the other hand, the psychologist should not be rigid and closed minded; he must not dismiss the teacher's ideas and interpretations on the basis of, "What does he know, he's just a teacher." Diplomatic relations can do much to ease a tense situation where the common problem, the child, becomes obscured by petty personality conflicts.

Perhaps one of the most important areas of conflict and confusion is the area of psychologists' reports. One source of confusion is that test data and observations tap different levels of behavior, test data often tapping unconscious processes, and observable behavior usually reflecting the child's adjustment to

From *Psychology in the School,* 2:77-81, 1965.

these unconscious processes. Data from one source may seem to contradict data from other sources, and it is, therefore, important for the psychologist to designate which level of observation and inference he is speaking about at any given moment. Since the main purpose of the psychologist's evaluation is to shed new light on the understanding of the individual being tested, he should realize that a psychological report should not be a demonstration of his erudition, or a medium by which he demonstrates his professional competence. Instead, the report should be used to describe the psychologist's findings and should give his impressions of the child as clearly and as concisely as possible. It would be helpful if the results were translated into possible problems in educational planning, and particular problems in academic functioning. Technical language is to be avoided, and if necessary, psychologists should prepare several different reports to communicate their findings to various professional and nonprofessional groups (Bellak, 1959). It would be helpful if the teacher were provided with a relatively uncomplicated presentation of specific personality dynamics, with special reference to the way in which the child can be expected to behave, the reasons for his behavior, and suggested methods for effectively dealing with and helping the child.

For example, the fact that a child may be fixated at the oral stage of psychosexual development will have less meaning to a teacher than a statement that the child is extremely dependent, and needs a good deal of reassurance, support, and security. While both phrases essentially say the same thing, the latter not only informs the teacher of the child's difficulty, but in addition, it also guides him in his relationships with, and planning for the child. In an effort to clarify the above point, the following excerpts from two reports are presented; one is replete with technical terms, and the other is more simply and clearly written.

An Uncommunicative Report

John is a boy with an IQ of 123, which places him in the superior range. He approaches all tasks in a highly abstract manner, although at times he tends to become stimulus bound.

He manifests a great deal of perseveration in completing the tasks presented, almost to the point where an obsessional quality is suspected. His ability to function on an abstract level may indicate a potentially greater IQ than the one reported.

Despite John's relatively flexible intellectual functioning, he tends to display a rigid personality structure. He places much emphasis on his ability to "beat out" his siblings, and consequently, his peers. It is suspected that such overachieving may have resulted from the birth of his sister, which was traumatic for John, as evidenced by his power strivings. His fixation may be seen in terms of an anal character make-up, typically rigid, with obsessional overtones. His excessive cleanliness is probably a reaction-formation toward earlier impulses to dirty himself.

It is recommended that John's teacher and guidance counselor present him with a flexible model to follow. It is necessary that he identify with a male who will not be threatening in his power struggle with authority.

A Communicative Report, of Use to Teachers

John has an IQ of 123, which indicates that he has superior intellectual ability. This IQ does not mirror the boy's true ability, however. John is quite able to grasp many complex relationships required for higher level thinking. However, because he is not usually satisfied with anything but a perfect performance, he tends to miss more obvious and simpler answers in his search for perfection. It would seem that less of an emphasis should be placed on perfection, while more of an emphasis should be placed on fundamental concepts. It is thus expected that John should do considerably better than the average student in his class. The teacher, however, should remain alert to the possibility that he may not fare as well as might be expected on what he considers to be "baby stuff."

John appears to have had a great deal of trouble in getting along with his sister. He was quite jealous of her when she was born, and still remains so. This is reflected in his relationships with other children; he tries to be a domineering figure, and yet he is quite anxious in the company of his peers. He is thus apt to strike out at the other children because of a fancied insult. It may be best if the teacher remain somewhat tolerant of this apparently uncalled for aggressiveness. In a firm way she might label his actions and point out their implications. The teacher should also represent a kind but a stern figure to John. He should set up limits for John's behavior, something which is not done at home. It would be helpful to remain aware of the fact that because such limits are new to John they will meet initial resistance. However, the teacher would do best to persevere in his attempts to maintain rational limits. Above all, the teacher should never play favorites where John is concerned. We may thus attempt to overcome the rampant favoritism he encounters at home.

It is recommended that the teacher and guidance counselor hold a few brief counseling sessions with John. These sessions might be used to help John cope with or come to accept the everyday frustrations one inevitably meets in social situations. This might be done by realistically explaining to John what is expected of him in social situations. The teacher and counselor may even want to act out a situation with John, or give him some examples and guidelines to follow. The teacher may also help John to see that things are not all black or all white, but that there are shades of grey in between. Finally, both the teacher and the guidance counselor should represent realistic authority figures to John; they should set up limitations on John's behavior, and explain the reasons for these limitations.

The first report is laden with psychological cliches, which obscure rather than clarify the way this boy is likely to function. It would be of relatively little help to the teacher, who has every right to expect that the report will help him in his efforts to better understand the child. The second report, in contrast, portrays the boy as a real person, with real problems. It describes the way he functions, but it goes beyond the descriptive level in that it also tells what may be expected of the boy in the future. It also outlines a plan which the *teacher* may realistically employ in dealing wtih the child.

Very often psychologists neglect to make recommendations

for the teacher to follow because they feel he lacks adequate training to help the child. However, the tremendous importance of the teacher in a child's life has often been grossly underestimated, especially by psychologists who feel they know so much more and can do so much more for the child. The obvious fact that a teacher spends a great part of the day, five days a week, in meaningful contact with the child, is often overlooked. Thus, while in theory communication between the teacher and the psychologist should abound, in actual practice the situation is quite the reverse.

Part of the problem of the limited and often one-sided communication between teacher and psychologist is a result of reliance on the written report, as opposed to the oral report. This last approach involves working closely with the teacher and employing both case consultation methods, and case presentation procedures. Thus, face to face relationships are initiated. This often results in the establishment of many time-saving and integrating procedures for the benefit of the child. In these meetings it is important for the teacher to feel free enough to accept the ideas of the psychologist, if applicable; the psychologist, however, should have confidence in the ability and the judgment of the teacher so that he may be a meaningful contributor rather than a silent observer. The inclusion of the teacher in case consultation sessions, along with the psychiatrist, psychologist, and social worker, would do much in helping him to understand the child as well as the personality dynamics he sees displayed in the classroom every day. The teacher's oral presentation of the child's reactions to everyday situations can be of value in understanding a child, and may be of value in making recommendations for treatment or placement.

On the other hand, teachers may benefit from more intensive training in the area of personality dynamics, mental hygiene, and psychological evaluative procedures, especially if they are to function as "team" members. Not to help the teacher develop his psychological knowledge and ability constitutes a loss to the many children who will never receive psychological or psychiatric treatment, but who nevertheless are in need of such help. Training is needed to make the teacher more aware of the possible areas of conflict and difficulty in childhood, and also to reduce the abuse and misuse of psychological tests in the classroom.

Appropriate training may include courses and discussion groups in mental hygiene like the one described by Rankin (1955). The teachers in the group met for sixteen sessions of 2½ hours each. In addition to films and recordings, each session included a lecture by a psychiatrist, and a discussion led by a psychologist. Some of the topics covered included, "The Prevalence of Mental Conflicts," "Pre-adolescents and Their Problems," "Aggression and Hostility," and "Withdrawing Behavior." The teachers, it was reported, emerged from this course with a better understanding of their pupils, as well as a better understanding of themselves.

Just as serious as the teacher's lack of knowledge of psychological problems is the psychologist's lack of knowledge about what goes on in the classroom. The psychologist has studied the processes of learning from books, and perhaps in the laboratory, but he has had little contact with actual classroom activity and classroom procedure, other than rather vague memories of his own student days. Such lack of experience severely limits the quality and specificity of the recommendations he can make. While the requirement of teaching experience for all those planning to become school psychologists sounds like a good idea, perhaps the same ends may be accomplished by something similar to a course in student teaching.

Sources of Conflict

Some sources of conflict and irritation which prevent integration and cooperation have been summarized by Cason (1945). One of the major problems, and one that tends to be overlooked because of its obviousness, is the failure of the psychologist to report back to the school. The teacher becomes resentful, and rightly so, at being left in the dark. Another sore spot is the fact that the psychologist often does not give credit to the teacher for any aid in the handling of a case. Additional antagonism comes from the fact that psychologists often make only general recommendations, which are of little help in starting a rehabilitation program. The psychologist may also make recommendations which are impossible to carry out because of actual physical limitations e.g. inadequate facilities or lack of time. This tends to make the teacher feel inadequate, through no fault of his own. The psychologist may also make recommendations to the teacher in an area where the teacher does not concede the psychologist's competence, an area the teacher regards as his own speciality. Finally, a report which heaps criticism on the teacher, whether it is justified or not, does not lead to constructive and harmonious relationships.

Suggestions for Improved Communications and Cooperation

1. The psychologist should relieve the teacher's uneasy feelings by sympathetically reviewing the problem with him.
2. The psychologist and teacher should both help to define the various aspects of the problem or problems.
3. The steps to be taken should be planned together, be it observation, interviewing, testing, etc.
4. The information available should be pooled; the total amount of information will thus be increased, and additional insights may be gained.
5. The psychologist should prepare a specific plan for the teacher, taking into account his capabilities as well as his limitations.
6. The psychologist might well supplement the written report to the teacher with an oral report. This would help to insure that the teacher does not place exaggerated value in the written psychological report. To do so might result in the teacher shunning his responsibility, and placing the entire matter into what he feels are the omnipotent hands of the psychologist. He may feel that the problem will now be magically solved; this attitude will lead only to frustration and disappointment on the part of the teacher.
7. The psychologist should explore with the teacher the ways in which the personnel, the resources of the school and community may be advantageously used.
8. The teacher should be relieved of the responsibility for behavior of the child over which he has no control. He

might be reminded that the home should share such responsibility.

9. It is the responsibility of the psychologist to make certain that the teacher does not expect immediate results. Such unrealistic expectations would only prove frustrating and disheartening for the teacher.

10. The teacher should be encouraged to adopt a variety of methods in dealing with his students; flexible procedures should be stressed.

11. It is the psychologist's responsibility to remain available for help in future consultations, when they are requested.

It seems fitting to close this paper with a quotation from Cason (1945) who aptly summarizes many of the problems discussed in this paper.

> School psychologists cannot operate in an ivory tower. Whenever the welfare of a child is at stake, several individuals share the responsibility. The school psychologist's value depends not only on the keenness of his diagnosis, the adequacy of his predictions about future behavior and his own therapeutic work, but also on his ability to stimulate in the school personnel an understanding of the child and a willingness to bring their best efforts to bear upon his needs.

REFERENCES

Bellak, L.: Psychological test reporting: a problem in communication with psychologists and psychiatrists. *J Nerv Ment Dis, 129*:76-91, 1959.

Cason, E.: Some suggestions on the interaction between the school psychologist and the classroom teacher. *J Consult Clin Psychol, 9*:132-137, 1945.

Rankin, P.: Fostering teacher growth. In P. A. Witty (Ed.): *Yearbook of the National Society for the Study of Education, 54*:Part II, 1955.

Chapter 5

TAXONOMY OF PRESCRIPTIVE INTERVENTIONS

CALVIN D. CATTERALL

A taxonomy of the interventions available to all school personnel as they attempt to intervene for and on behalf of students is organized around four major approaches:

a. Things that can be done around the student—environmental interventions

b. Things that can be done to the student—installed interventions

c. Things that can be accomplished by the student—assigned interventions

d. Things that can be done with the student—transactional interventions

Although aimed at the school psychologists, this paper suggests the use of a variety of interventionists and implies a more active follow-through role than has typically been taken by psychologists in the schools.

To be of greatest use in the educational setting, a taxonomy of interventions should classify all of the major approaches that are available to school personnel for effecting behavioral change as they attempt to intervene on behalf of students. The format catalogs the large variety of things that an interventionist can introduce between the events of a student's life in order to produce a desired change. Such a model implies that the psychologist/interventionist will emphasize follow-up and follow-through activities more than has traditionally been the case with

From the *Journal of School Psychology*, 8:5-12, 1970.

school psychologists. In this report, limitations of space have made it necessary to minimize documentation of the effectiveness of the interventions. A well-organized taxonomy should facilitate much needed research on when specific interventions can be used most effectively; it should also encourage better communication between professionals in this area.

A method of identifying the major forces around which specific interventions can be organized and which can be utilized by a number of different people has proven to be helpful. Although most of the interventions are not new or unique, this system has been developed in the belief that many professionals become "role bound" in their attempts to help students. Each group feels that they can and cannot do certain things to be effective. Instead of the limited number of approaches that many training programs bring to the task of helping children, we need a broad variety of interventions which lead, insofar as is possible, to goals that can be defined and evaluated in terms of specific behaviors.

Although many of these interventions are applicable in almost all settings where people come between the events in an individual's life in such a way as to induce change, this analysis focuses on those interventions which are applicable in the school setting. Although at times careful assessment will indicate the need for change in the basic communicational pattern of the child's home, this normally is not under the control of and, therefore, not the direct responsibility of the school. Although home/school communication and cooperation are valuable, the educational interventionist should place his primary emphasis on insuring that the school represents the best possible learning situations. Whereas the school has a responsibility to interpret to the community the need for appropriate referral services and should effectively communicate with them, it should not take on direct counseling of all of the parents with whom it comes in contact.

The activities to be described will be "prescriptive;" they lead to a positive plan of action for a student which: is based upon an assessment/analysis but which moves on to a specific, preferably short-termed plan of action; implies a systematic, programmed application of known principles of helping people; and leads to the realization of specific behavioral objectives with appropriate feedback and opportunity to evaluate effectiveness.

The plan should be an "intervention" in that it describes the actions of an interventionist as he comes between the events in a student's life in such a way as to bring about a desired result. Such plans assume that the vast majority of the students can be helped with an appropriate amount of effort: if they are based on a correct assessment/analysis, if the intervention is started early enough, and if all appropriate resources are utilized. They should be practical within an educational setting and primarily aimed at those exigencies operating in the school over which it can and does have control. They should also make use of and involve a variety of people, such as the teacher/interventionist, the principal/interventionist, the parent/interventionist, etc.

Interventions can be organized in several ways. One technique would be to classify them as to where the focus of the approach takes place (whether you are attempting change in the total environment or trying to focus on the individual in a more personal way). Another approach divides interventions along a continuum of the directness of approach (whether or not they work with the individual in a direct or indirect way). One advantage that the school has over many other treatment agencies is that it can work both directly and indirectly with the student. Thus by working on improving the curriculum we can help students who are already in trouble, and, hopefully at the same time, prevent problems in future students. Those indirect techniques which avoid the problems inherent in "identifying the patient" provide us with some of our most powerful, albeit only minimally used, ways of helping people.

Another analysis suggests that there are four major ways one can use to intervene in the process of helping students. (1) Something can be done *around* the student, by working indirectly with him on the total setting in which he exists, environmental interventions. (2) Something can be done *to* the student, by focusing directly on the factors which affect him but in a way which de-accentuates the interpersonal relationships, installed interventions. (3) Something can be done *by* the student, by using a personal relationship with the student to bring about specific behavioral changes indirectly, assigned interventions. (4) Finally, something can be done *with* the student, by working directly with the student in a personal way which capitalizes on the interpersonal relationship, transactional interventions.

		INDIRECT	DIRECT
		Directness of Approach	
ENVIRON-MENTAL	Focus of Approach	ENVIRONMENTAL	INSTALLED
PERSONAL		ASSIGNED	TRANSACTIONAL

Figure 5-1.

The Intervention Format

Environmental Interventions: All of the techniques described under this heading indirectly attempt to help the student by making adequate provisions for him in the total curriculum/ environmental setting. The school, as it is currently constituted, causes or severely aggravates the great majority of all of the problems for which the school psychologist is called upon for help. Energy spent to make the total environmental/curricular setting more individualized, more relevant, and more totally positive is well spent. If we can meet an individual's needs and help him to find success day after day in the school situation, he will be less likely to have difficulty and need to be referred.

(a) *Program Management* describes interventions which have to do with the organizational and programmed aspects of a child's curriculum: where it should begin, how it should be introduced, how fast it should proceed, etc. Subcategories include the following:

1. Developmental adjustments—adjustments which reflect the student's level of skill in the academic and social areas.
2. Learning uniqueness—intraindividual adjustments made to meet the needs of the child's learning pattern.
3. Interest—adaptations appropriate to the child's experiences and interest level.
4. Goal oriented—helping a student relate what he is doing in school today to what he wants to build toward tomorrow.
5. Pacing—adjustments which take into consideration the appropriate speed at which the material should be presented to the child.
6. Feedback—facilitation of learning through appropriate knowledge of results.

(b) *Placement* is the heading used to describe the various types of groups or classes into which a child can be placed. Adjustments within the school:

1. Preselecting an environment—placing students in certain groups or with specific teachers where they will be most likely to make progress.
2. Adjustments within the class—using special seating or grouping to meet various health, social, or academic needs.
3. Adjustments within the organized curriculum—including such techniques as team teaching, the ungraded school, staggered reading, etc.
4. Resource centers—individualizing through classroom or schoolwide resource centers.
5. Retention or replacement—although over-used in the past with minimal success, still a specific intervention.
6. Double acceleration—advancing the student more than one grade in a year.
7. Supplementary education—placing students in special education, corrective speech, discussion groups for the gifted, etc.

Adjustments between schools, interventions that lie outside the child's regular attendance area:

1. Dual eligibility—the student has part of his needs met in one school (preferably his home school) and part in another.
2. Lend lease—transferring a student to another school in order to give him a "fresh start" or to meet some other specialized need.
3. Special education programs—total specialized programs designed to meet major physical or learning needs.

(c) *Structuring* refers to alterations in the stability or order in the child's environment.

Clarification of the rules:

1. New students—helping the new student understand and adapt to the rules.
2. Consistency—attempting to enforce the rules as consistently as possible.
3. Walking through the rules—most helpful for children who learn best motorically.

Additional structure:

1. Establishing more meaningful rules—including consistent follow-through.
2. Scheduling—making and carefully following a schedule.

Less structure:

1. Free time—giving a child freedom to do what he wants or time to think and explore on his own.
2. More activity—interspersing movement activities among those which require sitting still.
3. Changing assignment—breaking the monotony of routine with "change of pace" activities.

Installed Interventions: In these interventions, some technique, person, stimulus, etc. is added to or taken away from the child's environment or life space. Instead of emphasizing a personal relationship with the child, the installed intervention attempts to manipulate specific aspects of the student's social and/or physical environment directly.

(a) *Catalyst*, which in its technical meaning refers to a substance or supply that when added to a specific situation causes or accelerates a specific change, refers, in this taxonomy, to adding another person's knowledge or skill to the child's life in order to facilitate growth. The emphasis is on the things or supplies the interventionist brings to the situation rather than on the interpersonal relationship. One of the most promising techniques to be developed in recent years is the increase in the use of a large number of people in trying to help others. Catalysts include the following:

1. Other students.
2. Members of the professional staff.
3. Other adults in the school.
4. Parents.
5. Volunteer adults from the community.
6. Paid teacher-aides.
7. Special catalytic groupings within the school—brought together to help with specific problems.

(b) *Stimulation* describes the process of adding needed stimuli to the child's environment.

1. Sensory stimulation—finding an experience or treatment which stimulates growth in a deficit area.
2. Modeling—providing the student with an appropriate model toward which he can grow.
3. Experiential stimulation.
4. Language development.
5. Concept development.
6. Academic-intellectual stimulation.
7. Stimulation through competition.
8. Self-enhancement.
9. Medical stimulation.

(c) *Moratorium* refers to a variety of procedures used to induce someone to discontinue specific activities for diagnostic, prognostic, or demonstrational purposes.

1. Vacuum—a regimen which exists to the degree that the interventionist is able to remove, for a period of time, all

of the elements of a student's life which have been causing dissention.

2. Diagnostic moratorium—again planned inactivity in order to help the interventionist make an adequate "diagnosis."
3. Experimental moratorium—to give something up for an "experiment" or to "try something out."
4. Medical moratorium—reducing the medical stimulation to see what effect this has on the child's behavior.

(d) *Destimulation* includes those interventions that reduce distractive stimuli.

1. Time out—trying to help the child by reducing the amount of distractive stimuli.
2. Carrels or offices.
3. Limited day.
4. Systematic exemption—the child enters into a contract wherein he agrees that he will leave the classroom when he cannot maintain previously agreed-upon standards of behavior.
5. Self-signal—the child signals when he recognizes that he needs to retreat to some prearranged place to regain his composure.
6. Limiting personal contact—reducing the number of people trying to provide service for the child.
7. Medical destimulation.

(e) *Positive Reinforcement* involves the systematic use of positive reinforcement to change behavior. These techniques show a tremendous amount of promise in helping us alleviate a wide variety of behavior and learning problems. They will usually be more powerful if utilized in conjunction with some of the program management techniques described under environmental intervention.

1. M&M's® and other primary reinforcers.
2. Signals—using buzzers, lights, etc. to indicate appropriate responses.
3. Prizes, rewards.

4. Token cultures—the child earns marks or tokens which can later be traded.
5. Attention.
6. Special privileges—including free time from other required activities or permission to do preferred academic work where curriculum reinforces other curriculum.
7. Verbal reinforcement.
8. Payroll—using money as a reinforcer.

(f) *Punishment,* although it tends to be ineffective because of its overuse in our culture, would probably be more effective if its uses were better understood. Withdrawal of something pleasant:

1. Withdrawal of rewards.
2. Reducing social support—helping peers withdraw social approval and attention from its association with negative behavior.
3. Restriction—limiting certain kinds of freedom.

Introduction of unpleasant stimuli:

1. Negative or aversive stimuli.
2. Corporal punishment.
3. Suspension, exemption, expulsion.
4. Exhaustion—exhausting the undesirable response by enforced repetition.

Negative reinforcement—the removal of unpleasant stimuli thereby causing a positive reaction.

Assigned Interventions: This includes those indirect techniques which are aimed at changing specified personal/social behavior. A specific activity or role is assigned to a student which will artificially affect his adjustment within a social setting with enough force to eventually bring about a more permanent change.

(a) *Behavior Exercise*—wherein certain behaviors or activities are prescribed to a student.

1. Physical/developmental exercises.
2. Social-contact exercises.
3. Cognitive/intellectual exercises.

(b) *Role Shift* attempts to increase the individual's role flexibility and sensitivity to others through the assignment of specific roles.

1. Assigned roles—getting the student to adopt specific roles.
2. Role emergence—using role playing techniques to help the student evolve into behavior that he could not previously support.
3. "Experimental" roles—assigning short-term roles to "see what happens."
4. Games and simulation theory—helping the student increase his behavioral repertoire by becoming aware of the "rules of the game."

(c) *Attitude Shift* describes the use of fairly precise methods of helping the student change his outer behavior with the goal of also changing his more basic attitude.

Transactional Interventions: These include a variety of techniques in which the interventionist works with the student in a direct, personal way. As used in this framework, a transaction refers to an event in which all of the participants, both the interventionist(s) and the student(s), gain meaning from their active participation in the relationship.

(a) *Sensitization Techniques* describe a series of procedures in which the interventionist attempts to help students either increase or decrease their sensitivity to specific stimuli.

1. Immunization—introducing minimal doses of hurt or frustration into a student in a controlled setting to build up his tolerance.
2. Injection—providing massive amounts of love, care, concern, respect, praise, etc.
3. Desensitization—reducing anxiety by using relaxation techniques with successive approximations toward an object or situation which was once associated with fear.
4. Role rehearsal—increasing sensitivity to certain situations by rehearsing (acting out) and discussing a role.
5. Crutches—helping a child adopt "face saving" crutches which will help him through specific situations.

(b) *Records-production Dialogues* organized personal on-going transactions around something the student produces.

Record data, structuring the interaction around notes or expressive art forms:

1. Notes-reports.
2. Calendars-diaries.
3. Autobiographies.
4. Tapes.
5. Expressive art.
6. Bibliotherapy.

Contact-schedule method—on-going transaction at regularly scheduled times around something the student produces:

1. Art work.
2. A story.
3. Construction.
4. Games.
5. Serial testing.

(c) *Group Dialogue* includes all those interventions which change behaviors through group interactions and/or discussions.

1. Human relations—stimulating discussions which try to develop a better understanding of interpersonal relationships.
2. Study skill groups—organizing sessions around either information-giving or a problem-oriented basis.
3. Simulation—using games to help the individual learn to attend to a variety of important stimuli, use specific rules to make decisions, and/or begin to see the consequences of his decisions.
4. Decision making—helping groups gain understanding and skill in making decisions.
5. "Service" groups—trying to get a group selected on the basis of some specific problem to invest themselves in service activities.
6. Student effectiveness training—improving interpersonal communication through such techniques as "active listening," receiving and reacting to the feelings of others, etc.

7. Basic encounter groups—helping groups of people primarily through the improvement of communication skills.
8. Family therapy—all of the members of a family who can profit from such an experience are helped to work on communication problems.
9. Role playing and psychodrama—bringing groups together for the purpose of reciprocal role taking.
10. Group therapy—using the group process to help the individual develop insight.

(d) *Personal Dialogue* includes direct, personal, one-to-one encounters while trying to help students.

1. Reality therapy—Glasser's approach based on the personal needs for love and worth, involvement, and commitment.
2. Direct information giving confrontation—confronting the student with the consequences of his actions.
3. Nondirective counseling—reflection of feelings and holding up a "mirror" to the student.
4. Existential counseling—deemphasizing "gimmicks" and emphasizing the value of becoming "transparently real."
5. Supportive—accepting the student and giving him encouragement.
6. Touch therapy — establishing warm personal contact through the sense of touch.
7. Insight therapy—helping students improve their current level of functioning by gaining insight into their past.
8. Play therapy—encouraging catharsis and insight development through playing games.
9. Decision making—helping students develop skill in solving problems and making their own decisions.
10. Behavioral counseling — techniques where the student identifies a specific objective and then is helped to attain it.

Discussion

Determining what intervention to use depends on what resources are available and currently tends to assume more of the proportions of an art than a science. Once a taxonomy of interventions has been worked out and generally accepted, we will be in a much better position to do large scale research to identify those techniques which are most useful for helping particular types of students and, even more important, we will be able to communicate our results to each other more meaningfully.

The specific interventions to be used will be determined by an assessment/analysis. Although in some instances this will involve psychological testing, the primary tool of the assessment/ analysis is careful observation, and thus is available to interventionists not skilled in direct testing. Adoption of the interventionist role by others in the educational setting should reduce the number of children who are currently not being helped because they are waiting for the services of a psychologist. In making an assessment/analysis it is important to focus on both the learner and the learning situation and to identify the specific behavior to be changed.

Interventions will normally be used in "stereo," in conjunction with each other, rather than singly. The two concepts of "adding to" and "taking away" of life forces must both be kept in mind. The goal is to bring enough interventions into play in the proper balance with enough force to effect the desired change in behavior. There should be a continual reevaluation to determine whether or not there is movement toward the desired goal; if there is no progress, a change should be made in the intervention strategy.

Pressures within the profession of school psychology push us into what would appear to be two different directions on two different continua at the same time. We are urged toward greater professionalism and higher levels of training; at the same time, we are finding that people with little or no training can be used to help other people. We are urged to develop a more efficient and precise technology; at the same time we are finding that the interpersonal encounter, relevance, and improved communication are being emphasized.

It is felt that this taxonomy of interventions has a potential contribution in that it helps us to:

(a) Become more professional. It describes a widely varying, important consultative role for school psychologists, wherein we can bring to the school situation the best that psychology has to offer and points the direction for us to become master interventionists.

(b) Involve more paraprofessionals. It describes a framework which involves more people (both professionals and paraprofessionals) to help young people.

(c) Develop more efficient technology. It should help us sharpen our thinking about how to help students, force us to improve our technology, and encourage us to make a more systematic evaluation of the interventions we are using.

(d) Help make education more personally relevant. It continues to direct our attention to the need for all educators to learn to use themselves, to improve their communication skills, and to take an active part in making the whole process more relevant and meaningful.

It is hoped that this intervention format provides a broad framework within which many of these seemingly opposing activities can be brought into focus.

Summary

A taxonomy has been described of the multiplicity of interventions available to the schools in their attempts to help students.

(a) The approach should present a map to the school psychologist as he uses himself and others more systematically and effectively when intervening on behalf of the learner.

(b) Rather than focusing primarily on diagnosis, its emphasis is on involving a large number of people in an effective follow-through.

(c) It encourages the interventionist to look at both the learner and the social setting in which he may be having difficulty.

(d) It points the way for psychologists to become consultants in helping a great many people utilize a variety of techniques in the process of intervening on behalf of children.

The path toward the systematic analysis of human behavior and of our attempts to change it is replete with pitfalls. Corrections, clarifications, additions, substitutions, discussions, etc. would be most welcome.

```
┌─────────────────────────────────────┐
│                                     │
│          Chapter 6                  │
│                                     │
```

A FOCUS ON REMEDIATION IN SCHOOL PSYCHOLOGY

RALPH F. BLANCO

```
│                                     │
└─────────────────────────────────────┘
```

School psychologists sometimes suffer from a remediable peculiarity: they possess considerable skill in diagnosis, but too often have a paucity of treatment plans for exceptional children. It was not known what recommendations were being offered by school psychologists to the teachers and parents of handicapped children. Through a grant, the investigator completed a Division Sixteen-wide research survey and received 3,700 psycho-educational recommendations to aid such children. The concepts were classified, edited, and compiled into a manual for trainees and experienced professionals. The survey's rationale, methodology, and results are briefly discussed.

O NE OF THE major deficiencies in school psychology today is the lack of comprehensive psycho-educational recommendations to aid exceptional children and those academically handicapped in school. Although school psychologists and related professionals are often remarkably expert in diagnosis, they frequently have difficulty in formulating treatment plans. All too often recommendations are stereotyped, nonindividualized, intangible, and irrelevant.

From the *Journal of School Psycholgoy,* 9:261-269, 1971.

Preparation of this article was supported in part by a grant (OEG-0-70-0010-607) from the Bureau of Education for the Handicapped, U.S. Office of Education, H.E.W. Grateful acknowledgment is given to Joseph G. Rosenfeld, Project Consultant, for invaluable assistance in the execution of this research project and to the 146 psychologists who competently contributed their ideas.

Many excellent books (Blackham, 1967; Kessler, 1966) and journals have discussed the diagnostic and etiological considerations of exceptional children. Yet none has specified the broad array of remedial procedures which concern all major exceptionalities. Most relevant texts (Jones, 1970; Palmer, 1970; Shaw, 1966; Ullmann and Krasner, 1969) and journals devote chapters or articles to psychotherapy and behavior-shaping techniques or to special education placement. Occasional references give excellent recommendations for particular diagnostic categories (Valett, 1968) or special problems (Marine, 1968-69). However, one does not find an accessible reference describing a truly full range of treatment plans for the selection of discerning school psychologists and treatment-oriented specialists.

In being unable to resolve some of the learning and social problems of school children, the school psychologist too often falls short of the legitimate expectations of teachers and parents, to say nothing of the immobilized progress of the children in question. It becomes more and more clear that the specialty must address itself to a broad spectrum of treatment plans or else become extinct. The relative absence of remedial plans for childhood exceptionalities will no longer be tolerated by educators or parents.

In addition, an open profession must reveal all the options for treatment to its young professionals in training. Although such a desk reference does not exist currently in psychology, special education, guidance, or psychiatry, by contrast medicine has the *Merck Manual of Diagnosis and Therapy* (Lyght, 1966) and other treatment guidelines (Conn, 1965; *De re Medica*, 1951; Gustafson and Coursin, 1964). A comparable manual of treatment plans would be very useful to school psychologists. Such plans are, in effect, the missing link in school psychology and as such deserve our research attention.

Abbreviated Rationale

No longer in its infancy, school psychology must face up to the reasonable expectations held for it or else it may become replaced by less well-trained but more result-oriented groups in education or industry (McNeil, 1965). In and around school psychology and special education the cry is, "Diagnosis is dead." True, it is dead, dead for those psychologists who never made it come alive or for those not capable of bringing a comprehensive diagnosis to a successful conclusion (i.e. helping a child to change for the better). Perhaps diagnosis is dead for teachers and parents who expected ideas for change but did not receive them. The author believes that sometimes this unsettling state of affairs has occurred because well-intentioned school psychologists simply did not know how to effect change and thus failed to fulfill their major responsibility.

A small unpublished study at the investigator's university of the reactions of special education teachers to the reports and consultations of school psychologists reveal that 40.7 percent of their 184 criticisms dealt with the lack of specific clinical and educational recommendations to help teachers with referred children. The following quotations are representative of the teachers' disappointments.

> Their reports are too sketchy for specific programs of remediation and do not tell what to do to change the situation.
> I get only an 'official label' for the child, no real help. Reports and discussions with the psychologist only describe the child and his problems; what about ideas to help the child?
> My school psychologist is overworked and would like to spend time in developing remedial programs.

Often the teachers' complaints are quite justified. Over the years, a list of questionable recommendations made by a few, certified, experienced school psychologists in the field has been compiled. The following are not defective because they are out of context, since often there was no real context.

> This boy has a weak ego. He has not had adequate opportunity for growing pains.
> Give him opportunity for mistakes.
> Provide the child every opportunity for success.
> The teacher should use various methods of instruction to aid academic growth.
> Give the child emotional support.

What then about the dozens of other ideas which may help the child, his teacher, and his parents? Where can behavior modification techniques help, for example, with a child's impulsivity, attention span, or motivation to learn? What insight should the child gain through teacher counseling? What might his parents change in their attitudes and behavior about child rearing? What needs are most neglected and can be met through specific environmental manipulation and social change? What specific kinds of reading help could be started, through what modality, and for what incentive.

The whole point of psycho-educational assessment is remediation (Palmer, 1970). An exquisite grasp of diagnosis, dynamics, and etiology gives one an excellent understanding of the development, intensity, and direction of the exceptionality, but it does not provide a plan of action. School psychologists must help answer the legitimate question, "Now what is to be done?" But the lack of organized knowledge is so profound that a former U.S. Associate Commissioner of Education, James J. Gallagher (1969) remarked, "Among the needs of special education are a greatly increased supply of *remedial experts* who can provide both cognitive and affective treatment programs."

Such deficiencies are probably based upon (a) lack of adequate training, (b) lack of resource material, and (c) uncertainty about the effectiveness of treatments, all problems which concern our profession. In addition, many of the educational and clinical approaches suggested in the literature have not been subjected to rigorous experimental controls to test their validity. It is hoped that they will be and that the profession will learn of their precise application. While it is well to consider only quantitatively documented remediations, the immediate exigencies of the individual case and the existence of large groups of exceptional children do not allow the practitioner the luxury of waiting for all research to be completed before taking action. Furthermore, it is often from the curiosity about creative practices that much research is derived.

This particular research study does not purport to be a definitive effort to verify experimentally each and every recommendation received from contributors, although many such ideas are clearly based upon well-validated, data-oriented research in behavior modification references (Ullmann and Krasner, 1965). Other researchers have developed several valuable research designs to tap the effectiveness of a single recommendation or. remedial approach on one child, compared to classroom peers (Chansky, 1970).

The major goals of this research were the identification and compilation of psycho-educational recommendations about exceptional children. The basic question was as follows: what are the treatment approaches which school psychologists offer for handicapped children? Could such recommendations be compiled and rated according to a predetermined classification system by experienced practitioners? Lastly, an inquiry was made to determine statistically the differential effects of the contributors' training and experience upon the choice and utilization of their recommendations.

Procedure

It was decided to gather the data by conducting survey research on all 1350 members of Division 16, School Psychology, of the American Psychological Association.* These psychologists had a professed interest in the speciality of school psychology and many of them had worked in a treatment capacity at an advanced, experienced level. In addition, the investigator was experienced with large-scale survey research (Blanco, Franklin, Braybrook, and Reuveni, 1968).

In 1969, all members of Division 16 were sent the following items as part of the survey research: (a) a cover letter explaining the research and its goals; (b) a letter of sponsorship from Dr. Edward L. French, President of Division 16, representing the majority vote of the Executive Board, 1968 through 1969; (c) instructions; (d) a Survey Sheet upon which to note the recommendations; (e) a Personal Data Sheet for contributors to enter their academic qualifications and professional experiences; (f) a

---

* For a detailed discussion of the basic rationale, survey forms, symptom list, etc., see Blanco (1971).

Symptom List (a portion of which was obtained with permission of the Group for the Advancement of Psychiatry, 1966) from which to select problems requiring treatments; and (g) the then unpublished "Fifty recommendations to aid exceptional children" (Blanco, 1970).

To help guarantee adequate response and to elicit fifteen to forty relevant concepts from each psychologist, they were sent the Fifty Recommendations noted above, sent another 100 recommendations upon receipt of their own, listed in the final report as contributors, and notified when the report was to be published. The remedial suggestions were classified and coded by the contributors themselves through ratings for presumed effectiveness, appropriateness in age ranges, and the suggested recipient of the treatment plans, a teacher or parent.

A questionable approach was the ordinal estimate about the "effectiveness" of each recommendation, as such ratings obviously depended upon the unique case, data, the circumstances of the school and home, the capability of the psychologist who prescribed it, etc. Such a rating did provide for interesting statistical comparisons between groups of recommendations and groups of contributors.

It appeared early in the creation of this study that no matter what identifying terms or definitions were used in the Symptom List, obfuscation in meaning and implication was rather certain to follow. It did not seem reasonable to wait for the professional specialty of school psychology to decide upon terms acceptable to each potential respondee. Some potential contributors actively seek major or minor imperfections in any survey as an excuse to reject it instantly. And because some psychologists never respond to any survey and others are simply too busy, the survey researcher can never reach the full range of potential respondees or obtain a perfect random sample. Some members rejected the survey because the material had no reference for speech handicapped or gifted children, for example. It was hoped that the Symptom List would encompass perhaps 95' percent or more of all school-related exceptionalities and learning difficulties in children. It was postulated that even those psychologists with an extreme "psychodynamic" or "behavior modification" orientation could respond comfortably and offer treatments for particular deviations.

Results

A total of 146 psychologists (10.8% of Division 16) responded to the survey and contributed 3,700 psycho-educational recommendations. In general, the concepts ranged from the commonplace to the ingenious. In a most strenuous experience, the investigator and his project consultant edited each idea at least three times according to specific criteria dealing with duplications, "Aunt Fanny" generalizations (Tallent, 1963), readability, etc. A total of 1,376 recommendations survived the editing process. The eclectic orientation of the two editors in no way prohibited the inclusion of any recommendation from a "pure" reinforcement or "pure" psychodynamic orientation.

The 146 contributors were a well-qualified group of psychologists. Almost one half of them had doctorates; the remainder had at least one masters degree. They were trained in many of our major universities and represented urban, suburban, and rural institutional and educational settings in their present work. Most of them majored in school psychology through departments of psychology or education. Some 57 percent had noncollege teaching experience. Actually, 145 of the contributors were or had been full-time or part-time school psychologists. The male psychologists averaged eleven years and the females about thirteen years of experience.

Their ideas generally reflected three psychological orientations: reinforcement theory, psychodynamic theory, and need theory. Approximately one third to one half of the treatment plans seemed based upon a reinforcement approach.

By virtue of the qualifications of the contributors (advanced degrees, specializations within certain graduate programs, years of experience in the areas tapped by the survey, and the theoretical basis of the bulk of the recommendations), it is believed that adequate content validity and a variation of construction validity exist within this compilation. The recommendations clearly appear to be logical deductions from the three main theoretical orientations noted above. It is fully recognized that the term "construct validity" is ordinarily used in reference to test construction, but it was deemed appropriate for use here in an analogous way to relate theory and derived practice. Should a psychologist accept a theoretical orientation as generally valid for treatment, it seems reasonable that he also accept treatment plans logically deduced from such a frame of reference.

Very few clear trends were apparent after statistical analysis of the efficacy ratings due primarily to small Ns in certain cells. There were no overall significant differences between ratings of males and females or between less-experienced and more-experienced psychologists. Doctor of education and masters personnel gave significantly higher (.05 level) efficacy ratings to their recommendations compared to the doctor of philosophy group. The typical rating of all contributors, however, was slightly higher than "moderate" confidence. Psycho-educational prescriptions were offered more frequently to teachers than to parents and were deemed by contributors to be most appropriate at the Elementary Age and All-Age Levels.

The results are generalizable only to the 146 contributors who comprised the sample. Thus, the conclusions are not necessarily appropriate to any larger group of psychologists.

Discussion

Obviously the selection of a specific treatment plan requires comprehensive psycho-educational assessment and discretionary clinical judgment. There are no more guarantees from the investigator that the recommendations will be either effective or carefully implemented in any given clinical application than there are guarantees that diagnostic texts will produce astute diagnosticians. The professional who uses these ideas and techniques bears the burden of responsibility in initiating, maintaining, and evaluating the treatment program derived from such concepts. The problem is not with the organized reference, but with the people who use it, their training, and their judgments.

In terms of this manual of recommendations, the main danger is the potential misapplication of knowledge by incompetent people. But then, the same danger exists in all professional fields. Those who perceive this approach as automated and dehumanizing are asked to consider the impossibility of applying the fifty-three treatments suggested for "school phobia." It simply cannot be done in automatic, "cookbook" fashion. Such a book requires no judgment, whereas this reference demands it.

To suggest to a physician that he should not have to depend upon one of his desk references is not only absurd, it is also unrealistic, perhaps unsafe. It is equally absurb for psychologists to hold such unrealistic expectations for themselves.

Examples

A few examples of the edited recommendations are noted below. Space limitations do not permit a thorough explanation of the key.

First Brackets: (Subjective assessment of contributor)

3 = High effectiveness depending upon circumstances.
2 = Moderate effectiveness depending upon circumstances.
1 = Low effectiveness but may have value.
Second Brackets:
Age range appropriate
Third Brackets:
Recipient: *T*eacher or *P*arent

Mildly Retarded: Allow as much time as possible so the child can express himself verbally since he is apt to respond negatively if urged to speak too quickly or perfectly. Do not permit him to use body language entirely, grunts, or finger pointing as substitutes for verbal expression.

(3) (8-12) (T)

Mildly Retarded: It is good educational policy for some or perhaps all retarded children to attend school in the summer part time since they need to work closer to their maximum potentials than most others. This plan may violate a tradition, but an exception can be made to provide socialization and education for retarded children. Some may welcome such an experience while older ones may have to be weaned away from the television set.

(3) (All) (T)

Mildly Retarded: Behavior modification techniques will be very helpful in establishing a more acceptable level of performance. Daily work assignments should be tied to a specific amount of work performed, at a specific level of accuracy, with specific and tangible rewards or tokens. The teacher can encourage motivation by offering rewards of value to the child: food, candy, tokens, free-time, a special seat, money, play time, etc.

(2) (5-15) (T)

Mildly Retarded: If a parent shows a marked reluctance to admit her child to a retarded class, request the parent or another child in the same room make a social call on the new mother to discuss the educational program; perhaps both may visit the class and observe the children together.

(3) (6-17) (P)

Aggressive Behavior—Externally Directed: The teacher may try a time-out procedure so that an aggressive child will have fewer opportunities to react against peers. He may be placed out in the hall or in a time-out room.

(3) (All) (T)

Aggressive Behavior—Externally Directed: In extreme cases, shorten the length of the school day; consider attendance on alternate days or possibly only in the morning or part of the morning. Always discuss such plans with parents. Advise therapy.

(3) (6-18) (T)

Verbally Aggressive, Ridicules Others: If the child ridicules and abuses others, one may suspect that there is a considerable sense of inferiority. The teacher should develop ego-supportive activities for him, such as special privileges, special errands, the choice of desired activities, release play-time, etc. that will enhance the reader-child relationship as well as make school a more pleasant place. The teacher must also make it very clear that repeated incidences may deprive the child of these privileges if he is unwilling to control himself in the future.

(2) (All) (T)

Lying to Authority and Parents: Suggest that the parents unwittingly may be contributing to such behavior by inflicting too high standards on the premise that the parents may be perfectionistic. Advise them to be more tolerant, to look for favorable qualities, and not to overreact to those forms of behavior which may be displeasing. It is possible that parents may value the child only for what he does academically. This narrow viewpoint should be aired with the parents and discredited.

(2) (All) (P)

Excessive Fantasy, Daydreaming: The teacher should interrupt the fantasy by calling the child's name, asking him to recite or contribute often, by standing near him, by touching him or perhaps asking his opinion or getting him to help another.

(3) (5-2) (T)

Isolating Behavior: A child who will not talk to his teacher or peers will frequently speak through hand puppets.

(3) (2-7) (T)

Underachievement—Passive Aggressive: If the student is deficient in writing or has a problem about doing written assignments or tests, give him oral examinations.

(2) (7-18) (T)

Underachievement—Passive Aggressive: Differentiated assignments are needed for an under-achiever since he cannot maintain the pace of the class regardless of high ability.

(1) (All) (T)

Low Anxiety Tolerance: Give the anxious child points for each correct answer and not demerits for each incorrect answer. When a reasonable number of points accumulate, give the child a small reward: gum, candy, a chance to sit near a buddy, a chance to do nothing, etc. If the "normal" children want to try such a system, go ahead for them to but make their rewards a bit more difficult to obtain since they can tolerate more effort.

(2) (All) (T)

Blind and Partially-sighted: Touch typing is often recommended to children of average ability from the fourth grade up as this can become an invaluable tool for children with progressive eye disorders.

(3) (All) (T)

Blind and Partially-sighted: Give extensive training to the blind children in the social skill of polite refusal of help since many kind but infantalizing offers will be extended to them.

The more unnecessary help they accept, the more dependent they may become and reduce their chances for mature adjustment.

(2) (All) (P)

Deaf and Hard-of-hearing: For the children who refuse to wear their hearing aids or glasses by conveniently "forgetting" them at home or in the school desk, attempt to reinforce the wearing by (a) heavy reward at first, (b) a chart system for consecutive "wearers" who may earn a weekly prize, (c) withdrawal of privileges for "forgetting."

(3) (All) (T)

REFERENCES

Blackham, G. J.: *The Deviant Child in the Classroom.* Belmont, Wadsworth, 1967.

Blanco, R. F.: Fifty recommendations to aid exceptional children .*Psychology in the Schools,* 7(1):29-37, 1970.

Blanco, R. F.: A Study of Treatment Plans for School Psychologists for Exceptional Children. Project No. 482192, Grant No. OEG-0-70-0010 (607), Bureau of Education for the Handicapped, Office of Education, H.E.W.: Temple University, January 1971.

Blanco, R. F.: Prescriptions for children with learning and adjustment problems. Springfield, Thomas, 1972.

Blanco, R. F.; Franklin, D. L.; Braybrook, W. M., and Reuveni, U.: Career Motivation of Army Personnel—Junior Officer's Duties Questionnaire. Technical Report 1-212, Contract No. DAHC-15-67-C-0279. The Franklin Institute Research Laboratories, 1968.

Chansky, N. M.: Research designs for school psychologists. Paper presented at the Professional School Psychology Institute of the American Psychological Association Convention, Miami Beach, September 1970.

Conn, H. F. (Ed.): *Current Therapy: Approved Methods of Treatment for the Practising Physician.* Rev. 17. Philadelphia, Saunders, 1965.

De re medica. Rev. 14. Indianapolis, Eli Lilly & Co., 1951.

Gallagher, J. J.: Psychology and special education—The future: Where the action is. *Psychology in the Schools,* 7:219-226, 1969.

Group for the Advancement of Psychiatry: Psychopathological Disorders in Childhood: Theoretical Considerations and a Proposed Classification. New York, Group for the Advancement of Psychiatry, 6, Report No. 62, June 1966.

Gustafson, S. R., and Coursin, D. B.: *The Pediatric Patient.* Philadelphia, Lippincott, 1964.

Jones, R. L. (Ed.): *New Directions in Special Education.* Boston, Allyn, 1970.

Kessler, J.: *Psychopathology of Childhood.* Englewood Cliffs, P-H, 1966.

Lyght, C. E. (Ed.): *Merck Manual of Diagnosis and Therapy,* 11th Ed. Rahway, Merck, Sharp, & Dohme Research Laboratories, 1966.

Marine, E.: School refusal—Who should intervene? (diagnostic and treatment categories). *Journal of School Psychology,* 7:63-70, 1968-69.

McNeil, E. B.: Is counseling a rat fink operation? *Psychology in the Schools,* 2(1):24-31, 1969.

Palmer, J. O.: *The Psychological Assessment of Children.* New York, Wiley, 1970.

Shaw, S. B.: *The Psychiatric Disorders of Childhood.* New York, Appleton, 1966.

Tallent, N.: *Clinical Psychological Consultation.* Englewood Cliffs, P-H, 1963.

Ullmann, L. P., and Krasner, L. (Eds.): *Case Studies in Behavior Modification.* New York, HR&W, 1965.

Ullmann, L. P., and Krasner, L.: *A Psychological Approach to Abnormal Behavior.* Englewood Cliffs, P-H, 1969.

Valett, R. E.: *The Remediation of Learning Disabilities.* Palo Alto, Fearon, 1968.

Chapter 7

TWO DECISION MODELS: IDENTIFICATION AND DIAGNOSTIC TEACHING OF HANDICAPPED CHILDREN IN THE REGULAR CLASSROOM

G. Phillip Cartwright, Carol A. Cartwright, and James E. Ysseldyke

As evidence that concerns the relative ineffectiveness of traditional special-education services has mounted (Bennett, 1963; Cassidy and Stanton, 1959; Dunn, 1968; Ellenbogen, 1957; Johnson, 1962; Reynolds and Balow, 1972; Sparks and Blackman, 1965; Thurstone, 1960), the school psychologist has come under repeated attack for his role (usually dictated) as "gatekeeper of special education" (Garrison and Hammill, 1971). Dunn (1968) has advocated strongly abolishment of special classes, special schools and their resultant pigeonholing and categorization and argues that, "Never in our history has there been a greater urgency to take stock and to search out new roles for a large number of today's special educators . . ."

Role identification is not a new problem for school psychologists, and a variety of roles have been proposed within the last decade (Baker, 1965; Bijou, 1970; Buktenica, 1970; Cardon and Efraemson, 1970; Catterall, 1970; Ebert, Dain and Phillips, 1970; Fine and Epstein, 1969; Jackson, 1970; Phillips, 1967; Ruckhaber, 1970; Singer, Whiton and Fried, 1970). The search for identity has involved a movement away from the traditional psychometric model and a greater emphasis on serving handicapped children

From *Psychology in the Schools*, 10:4-11, 1973.

in regular classroom settings. Few would argue with Newland's (1970) statement that the overriding commitment of school psychologists is facilitation of learning by school children. As Newland (1970) has stated, "the major responsibility of the school psychologist is (and has long been) *to work with teachers in the interests of children. . . .*"

Discussions of changes and trends in special education (Cartwright, Cartwright, and Robine, 1972; Lilly, 1970, 1971; Reynolds and Davis, 1971; Ysseldyke and Sabatino, 1972) repeatedly emphasize heavier involvement of the regular classroom teacher in the identification and management of handicapped children. School psychologists long have advocated inservice training designed to facilitate teacher's abilities to identify and manage handicapped children. With increased emphasis upon an inservice function, however, school psychologists cannot afford to operate in the absence of the stated objectives that they are attempting to meet and a model or models within which to meet those objectives.

A dual approach is needed in the school psychologist's attempt to meet the needs of handicapped children in regular classes. He first must attempt to prepare regular classroom teachers to identify and provide appropriate educational strategies for handicapped children within the regular classroom setting. Teachers must be trained to provide individualized instruction designed to ameliorate or alleviate existing and incipient learning problems early in a child's career. Second, teachers, especially early childhood educators, must be sensitized to the value of early detection of problems and trained to provide instruction directed to the prevention of serious learning problems in children.

This paper proposes two models, an identification model and a diagnostic teaching model, that may be uesd effectively by the school psychologist in his efforts to assist teachers in the identification and educational management of handicapped children. The models are designed to help teachers make intelligent decisions about children in their classrooms and specify both those things that a teacher must know and how he is to behave. The competencies required of teachers in both the processes of identification and diagnostic teaching are presented in flow-chart format, since the systematic sequencing of behaviors and alternative courses of action are as critical as the competencies themselves.

The specific objectives of the identification and diagnostic teaching models should assist the school psychologist in the delineation of new roles when he works with regular classroom teachers. An ongoing school psychologist-regular classroom teacher interaction and a continuous evaluation and modification of the models are implicit in the discussion that follows.

Decision Model for the Identification of Handicapped Children

The following six objectives are proposed as the set of competencies that are required for adequate identification of handicapped children.

   A. Know the characteristics of handicapped children and be aware of signs that indicate potential learning problems;

   B. Be able to screen all children in regular classroom programs for deviations and determine the extent of the interindividual differences;

   C. For those children with deviations, be able to select and use appropriate commercial and teacher-constructed appraisal and diagnostic procedures in order to obtain more precise information as to the nature of the deviation;

   D. Be able to synthesize information by preparing individual profiles of each child's strengths and weaknesses on educationally relevant variables;

   E. Be able to evaluate the adequacy of the information available in order to make appropriate decisions about referral to other specialists;

   F. Be able to prepare adequate documentation for the case when the decision to refer is affirmative.

It is expected that individuals who exhibit the competencies listed above will evaluate systematically children's learning potential and formulate appropriate educational plans according to the Decision Model for the Identification of Handicapped Children (Identification Model) outlined in the following section.

The six objectives are associated directly with the six steps in the Identification Model (see Fig. 7-1). The first two steps in the Identification Model require that the teacher evaluate all the children in the classroom in order to identify those children who exhibit deviations from "normally expected" behavior. Objectives A and B are related directly to these first two steps.

Evaluation of children is a continuous process that is an integral part of the total educational effort. The model proposes that teachers be trained to organize the behavioral data that children constantly generate in the classroom and effectively use these data to make identification decisions. Information that concerns both normal behavior and possible abnormal behavior in each of the domains (cognitive, affective, and psychomotor) is the prerequisite for the task of screening children in terms of deviations. By the nature of his training the school psychologist should be able to: (a) provide teachers with training that concerns learning characteristics sufficiently deviant to cause concern; (b) stress the importance of dealing with observable behaviors of individual children; and (c) describe the educational relevance of certain observed behaviors. Since the model is especially appropriate for teachers who work with preschool and primary children who may not yet manifest clear-cut signs of atypical behavior, emphasis will have to be placed on the more subtle clues to incipient problems while an awareness of what certain behaviors may suggest as well as what they may not suggest is developed.

The school psychologist, in his training attempts to satisfy Objective B, may well focus on: (a) the relative nature of normality in terms of sociocultural factors and societal and educational expectations; (b) inter- and intraindividual differences; (c) interpretation of the results of group tests; and (d) the continuous and circular nature of the screening process.

During the first phase of the Identification Model, the teacher surveys the entire group of children for performance on certain relevant variables in order to select those who exhibit deviations sufficient to warrant more intensive diagnosis. With the completion of the screening at any one time, the teacher will have

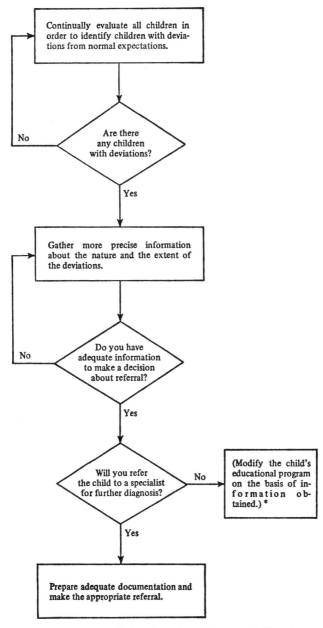

Figure 7-1. Decision Model for the Identification of Handicapped Children. * This step is the subject of the second decision model.

formulated "suspicions" or hypotheses about some of the children in the group and will proceed to the third step in the Identification Model for these children.

In the third step (Objective C), the teacher and the school psychologist gather precise information as to the nature and extent of intraindividual differences.

Inservice training related to Objective C should include methods of data collection and interpretation that emphasize individual appraisal for each child in terms of deviation noted during screening. The nature of the data collected will depend on the nature of the deviation for which the child was screened out of the total group.

Tentative completion of the third stage in the Identification Model, together with achievement of Objectives D and E, enables the teacher to evaluate the comprehensiveness of the obtained data and, therefore, to make the decisions required in steps four and five. Inservice training associated with Objective D should include construction and interpretation of profiles that depict educationally relevant data. Training relevant to Objective E should consist of: (a) criteria to determine the comprehensiveness of the obtained data; (b) information about the specialists who can be expected to provide various types of intensive diagnostic services for children; and (c) descriptions of the classroom teacher's role in relation to the roles of various specialists.

When a negative decision is reached at step four, it is necessary to return to step three and continue to collect the information required to complete the child's profile chart before one proceeds through the fifth step. However, when an affirmative decision is made at step four, the teacher should proceed to the next decision block and decide whether referral is in order. When he formulates an answer to the question of referral posed at step five, the teacher asks himself: have I exhausted all sources of information available to me in my role as a classroom teacher? Can I make educational plans for this child on the basis of information currently available? Do I need more information before I make educational plans for this child?

When the decision at step five is for referral, the teacher will proceed to step six and prepare documentation prior to the referral. Prior to this, the school psychologist should assist the teacher in specialist selection, referral documentation, referral procedures, and referral follow-up.

When the decision for referral is negative, the teacher accepts responsibility for modification of the child's educational program within the regular classroom setting. The role of the school psychologist in assisting with these modifications is the topic of the model for Diagnostic Teaching.

Decision Model for Diagnostic Teaching

School psychologists play a major role in assisting teachers to provide individualized instructional programs for children by offering consultation and inservice experiences in the various steps of the Diagnostic Teaching Model. The following eight objectives are proposed as the set of competencies that are required to carry out the Diagnostic Teaching Model.

A. Identify characteristics of individual children that indicate the need for special teaching or management procedures.
B. Specify relevant educational objectives for individual children.
C. Select techniques for effective classroom management.
D. Choose and use specialized teaching strategies to reach specific objectives for children with varying behavioral and learning characteristics.
E. Choose and use special materials in association with specific strategies.
F. Identify and use appropriate evaluation procedures.
G. Draw upon existing sources of information as to specialized strategies and materials.
H. Consult with available resource persons for assistance.

These objectives are correlated directly with Figure 7-2, Decision Model for Diagnostic Teaching (Diagnostic Teaching Model).

The first step of the Diagnostic Teaching Model is a recapitulation of the content of the Identification Model.

Administration and interpretation of traditional diagnostic tests and procedures often will not yield adequate information

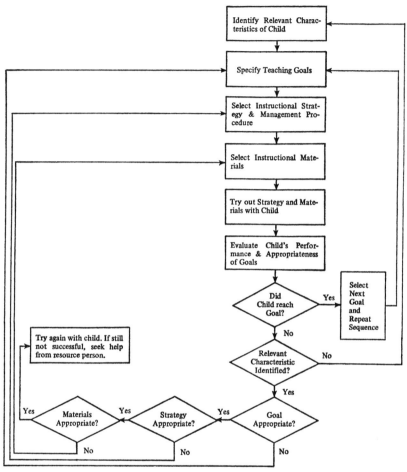

Figure 7-2.   Decision Model for Diagnostic Teaching.

about a learner. The school psychologist should assist teachers
in development of observation skills to include (a) setting up
the environment as a "test" for certain observable behavioral outcomes; (b) determining which observable behaviors will be
recorded; (c) designing records for observational data; and (d)
interpreting observational data in light of possible errors or
limitations in the data collection procedures.

After specific needs and relevant characteristics for an individual learner have been determined, the teacher should be ready to move the child forward by specifying appropriate objectives for the child. A majority of the information related to the second step in the model (Objective B) should be designed to formulate and sequence behavioral objectives. In order to formulate appropriate objectives, teachers should be able to perform task analyses of several broad subject areas. This competency will allow the teacher to delimit and sequence specific behavioral objectives within various subject areas. The teacher should be able to state objectives in terms of observable behaviors to be displayed by the learner, the conditions under which the behavior is to be exhibited, and the criteria for an acceptable performance.

Extensive consultation between the teacher and the school psychologist is essential for successful implementation of the third level (and Objective C) of the Diagnostic Teaching Model. This step involves awareness on the part of the teacher as to the range of instructional procedures available to manage the educational problems of children.

Inservice training related to Objective C should include topics, such as setting limits, developing routines, behavior modification, providing learning and behavioral models, physical arrangements (furniture, materials, storage, dividers, etc.) of the classroom, and techniques of talking with children to promote mental health.

Objectives C, D, and E, and the third, fourth, and fifth steps in the process should be accomplished by focusing the teacher's attention on general and specific instructional procedures (strategies and associated special materials) that can be employed to assist the child in the regular classroom to accomplish the educational objectives that have been described for him by the teacher. A sampling of specialized strategies and materials (Objectives D and E) should focus on the underlying principles involved in making a match between the unique characteristics and needs of the learner and the unique properties of the strategy and materials.

The fifth step in the model (Objective E) requires the teacher to select appropriate instructional materials and, with a preferred instructional methodology, try out the prescription with a child for whom a diagnosis has been made.

The teacher who satisfactorily accomplishes Objectives A through E will be prepared to write a remedial prescription for individual children who evidence a wide range of educational problems. The teachers will be able to collect pertinent data, recognize when to seek the advice of consultants and other resource people, to generate pertinent educational objectives that are appropriate to various situations, to evaluate which educational methodology seems appropriate for individual children, and to consider the instructional devices that can be used to facilitate the accomplishment of the educational goals for individual children.

The teacher competency associated with Objective F (the sixth step in the model), to identify and use appropriate evaluation procedures, is especially pertinent in view of the experimental nature of a diagnostic teaching situation. Since there is no formula one can apply in order to select the teaching strategy for a learner, any match between learner needs characteristics, and strategy material is tentative and must be validated empirically. The use of evaluation procedures that yield *immediate* information about learning performance should be emphasized. Criterion-referenced rather than norm-referenced evaluation is suggested. Interpretation of evaluative data and implications for changing strategy and materials and/or objectives derived from the evaluative data also should be included in inservice experiences directed toward attainment of Objective F.

Teachers should be able to decide upon the appropriateness of various evaluative techniques; make decisions about adjustments that need to be made in goals, methods, and/or materials; consider what additional resources and/or consultants may be helpful to decide on an effective and efficient management program; and review the steps that can be taken to organize school personnel and parents of the children.

A major part of the inservice training about Objectives G and H should be knowledge of the retrieval systems associated with regional resource and special education materials centers.

The teacher needs to be aware of descriptors required for information retrieval and the type of information he can expect from the resource centers. A great variety of special educational strategies and materials currently are being described and published; it is incumbent upon the teacher and the school psychologist to be aware of available information. A teacher cannot be expected to develop specialized strategies and materials for each individual child in his class. However, he should be expected to be aware of available resources related to instructional strategies and materials.

When diagnostic teaching is successful, an affirmative response to the question of goal achievement will be forthcoming. The same sequence of behaviors then is followed again for the next learner objective. When the child did not reach the goal, the model indicates the type of systematic analysis needed to determine which step in the diagnostic teaching sequence was in error. If an error is found to be associated with one of the steps in the process, the teacher simply cycles back and reenters the system at the error point, corrects the original error, and continues again through the main sequence of diagnostic teaching behaviors.

REFERENCES

Baker, H. L.: Psychological services: from the school staff's point of view. *Journal of School Psychology,* 3:36-42, 1965.

Bennett, A.: *A Comparative Study of the Progress of Subnormal Pupils in the Grades and in Special Classes.* New York, Columbia U Pr, 1963.

Bijou, S. W.: What psychologoy has to offer education—now. *Journal of Applied Behavior Analysis,* 3:65-71, 1970.

Buktenica ,N. A.: A multidisciplinary training team in the public schools. *Journal of School Psychology,* 8:220-225, 1970.

Cardon, B. W., and Efraemson, M. W.: Consulting school psychology in the urban setting: Philadelphia process follow through. *Journal of School Psychology,* 8:231-236, 1970.

Cartwright, C. A.; Cartwright, G. P., and Robine, G. G.: CAI course in the early identification of handicapped children. *Except Child,* 38:453-460, 1972.

Cassidy, V., and Stanton, J.: *An Investigation of Factors Involved in the Educational Placement of Mentally Retarded Children: A Study of*

Differences Between Children in Special and Regular Classes in Ohio. Columbus, Ohio St U Pr, 1959.

Catterall, C. D.: Increasing innovation and behavioral change through collaboration with a school staff. *Journal of School Psychology, 8*:215-219, 1970.

Dunn, L. M.: Special education for the mildly retarded—is much of it justifiable? *Except Child, 35*:5-22, 1968.

Ebert, D. W.; Dain, R. N., and Phillips, B. N.: An attempt at implementing the diagnostic-intervention class model. *Journal of School Psychology, 8*:191-196, 1970.

Ellenbogen, M. A.: A comparative study of some aspects of academic and social adjustment of two groups of mentally retarded children in special and regular grades. Unpublished doctoral dissertation, Northwestern University, 1957.

Fine, M. J., and Epstein, S. J.: The school psychologist's contribution to the community mental health center. *Journal of School Psychology, 7*:70-74, 1969.

Garrison, M., and Hammill, D.: Who are the retarded; *Except Child, 38*:13-20, 1971.

Jackson, J. H.: Psychoeducational therapy as the primary activity of school psychologists. *Journal of School Psychology, 8*:186-190, 1970.

Johnson, G. O.: Special education for the mentally handicapped—a paradox. *Except Child, 19*:62-69, 1962.

Lelly, M. S.: Special education: a teapot in a tempest. *Except Child, 36*:43-49, 1970.

Lilly, M. S.: A training based model for special education. *Except Child, 37*:745-759, 1971.

Newland, T. E.: The search for the new: frenzied, faddish, or fundamental? *Journal of School Psychology, 8*:242-244, 1970.

Phillips, B. N.: The teacher-psychological specialist model. *Journal of School Psychology, 6*:67-71, 1967.

Reynolds, M. C., and Balow, B.: Categories and variables in special education. *Except Child, 38*:357-366, 1972.

Reynolds, M. C., and Davis, M. D. (Eds.): *Exceptional Children in Regular Classrooms.* Minneapolis, University of Minnesota, Department of Audio-visual Extension, 1971.

Ruckhaber, C. J.: An elementary school mental health program: the Stark School model. *Journal of School Psychology, 8*:197-201, 1970.

Singer, D. L.; Whiton, M. B., and Fried, M.: An alternative to traditional mental health services and consultation in the schools: a social systems and group process approach. *Journal of School Psychology, 8*:172-179, 1970.

Sparks, H. L., and Blackman, L. S.: What is special about special education revisited? *Except Child,* 5:242-249, 1965.

Thurstone, T.: *An Evaluation of Education of Mentally Handicapped Children in Special Education Classes and in Regular Grades.* Chapel Hill, University of North Carolina, 1960.

Ysseldyke, J. E., and Sabatino, D. A.: An alternative to self-contained special education classes. *Illinois Education Review,* 1:59-65, 1972.

Chapter 8

THE EFFECTS OF LIMITED AND INTENSIVE SCHOOL PSYCHOLOGIST-TEACHER CONSULTATION

MILTON M. TYLER AND MARVIN J. FINE

Effects of two modes of school psychological consultation were examined against four main outcomes: (1) changes in teacher understanding of the child, (2) the direction of the changes in teacher understanding of the child, (3) teacher satisfaction with consultation, and (4) teacher follow-through on psychologist's recommendations. The two consultative modes were differeniated by the amount of time and by the length and elaboration of the psycholocial report. Eight school psychologists alternated in acting out the different consultaive modes, plus a control condition, with a total of 120 teachers who had referred children. Data were obtained through paper-and-pencil questionnaires completed pre- and post-consultation by teacher and psychologist. The results strongly supported the intensive over the limited consultation, and any consultation over no consultation.

E FFECTIVE SCHOOL PSYCHOLOGICAL consultation has been viewed by many as being closely associated with the teacher's response to the service. Actual changes in teacher attitudes, understanding, or behavior may be the objectives of the consultation. But even if the objectives are more narrowly defined in terms of changes in pupil behavior, the teacher is often the change agent and also the individual most integral to enhancing or defeating

From the *Journal of School Psychology*, 12:8-16, 1974.

implementation of a program initiated by others. Despite the importance of the teacher, the factors within a psychologist-teacher consultation that increase teacher receptivity have remained primarily speculation and opinion.

A study by Kaplan and Sprunger (1967) did attempt to investigate the consultation variable of time spent with the teacher. Its results failed to discriminate between the conditions of more and less time spent, but did support that either of their consultative conditions led to positive changes in the teacher over the condition of no consultation. Unfortunately the Kaplan and Sprunger study was limited in several important respects, including differentiation of the two treatment conditions.

This study is in part a replication of aspects of the Kaplan and Sprunger study, but it has also broadened the scope of inquiry. On a relatively pragmatic level four research questions were posed.

1. Does psychological consultation lead to a change in teacher understanding of the child?
2. If change occurs, does the teacher's understanding of the child become more or less like the psychologist's?
3. To what extent are teachers satisfied with psychological consultation?
4. Does the teacher actually follow through with the psychologist's recommendations?

These four questions actually deal with the outcomes of consultation and as such are dependent variables. The independent variables in this study were two consultation modes that were differentiated primarily in two ways: the amount of time spent with the teacher and the length and elaboration of the report. Eight hypotheses, expressed in null form, were postulated and these will be presented under analysis of data.

Method

Participants: Eight Kansas school psychologists agreed to participate in the study as field workers. Each psychologist was to use the next fifteen referrals meeting the criteria of the child's not being a special class candidate. This procedure led to the involvement of 120 different teachers and 120 different children. Each teacher and child was involved only once.

Treatments: The term "consultation" has been given varied meanings in the psychological literature and there is no consensus as to common definition. The position assumed in this study was that any professional encounter between psychologist and teacher that required the psychologist to apply his technical skills toward the resolution of some problem could be termed a consultative experience. The actual procedures followed in this study were variations on the referral-child study-report paridigm and were approximations of Caplan's case-centered consultation (Caplan, 1970).

The two consultative treatments employed were labeled the intensive and limited modes. The intensive consultation consisted of a (a) fifteen- to twenty-four-minute preassessment psychologist-teacher contract, (b) a thirty- to forty-minute interpretive, postassessment contact, and (c) a psychologist's report of at least three double-spaced typewritten pages detailing the psychologist's findings and itemizing specific recommendations. This report was submitted at the time of the final contact. The limited consultation consisted of (a) a five- to ten-minute preassessment conference, (b) a ten- to fifteen-minute interpretive, postassessment conference, and (c) a 1 to 1½ page summary report which included a nonelaborated listing of recommendations.

Aside from the specifications of the two consultative modes, each school psychologist was free to use whatever diagnostic, interview, or observation procedures he wished. Since cases were randomly selected and the study focus was on teacher-psychologist interaction, the actual workups were not deliberately controlled.

A control group was also included and will be discussed in the next section.

Procedure: Each psychologist was instructed to alternate sequentially the assignment of referral cases to the two treatment conditions and to the control group, as the cases were received. This insured randomization of assignment. Each teacher was then sent a modified fifty-seven item form of the S.R.A. Youth Inventory (Remmers, 1951) to complete and return on the referred child. This instrument was used in the Kaplan and Sprunger study (1967) and was found appropriate for eliciting teacher perceptions of a child. The instructions to each teacher stated that the child was selected to be a part of a study. The teacher was then asked to complete the inventory from the viewpoint of the child.

Following the completion of the inventory the psychologist proceeded to act out the predetermined consultation with that teacher. It was estimated that each consultation would cover approximately a two-week period. At the termination of consultation the teacher was asked again to complete the modified S.R.A. Inventory and also an eight-item questionnaire that focused on such things as teacher satisfaction with the time spent by the psychologist, teacher estimate of the psychologist's helpfulness, and teacher beliefs as to the psychologist's interest. Each of the eight items was rated on a five-point scale.

The control teachers were sent the S.R.A. Inventory after they were initially identified and again after a two-week period, but they had no contact with the psychologist during the duration of the study. The teacher instructions for completing the inventory the second time were similar to the first occasion. While it might be anticipated that the control teachers would be frustrated by having to complete the inventory a second time without having received any service, there were no reported difficulties and a high percentage of the inventories were returned. An effort was made to offer the control teachers psychological services as soon as possible after the two-week lapse.

Following his workup of the referred child, the psychologist also completed the S.R.A. Inventory. In every case the inventory was completed from the point of view of the child and, therefore, represented an indice of teacher and psychologist understanding of that child.

One week after termination of consultation the psychologist visited the teacher to discuss the implementation of his recommendations. Then the psychologist completed a five-point rating scale on the extent of teacher implementation of the recommendation.

Eleven of the total of 120 teachers failed to complete their questionnaires adequately and those data were deleted from the study. For most of the analyses the sample was composed of thirty-six teachers in the limited consultation group, thirty-five teachers in the intensive consultation group, and thirty-eight teachers in the control group. On the last analysis requiring psychologist rating of the teachers, the total sample of forty teachers per consultation group was used, since this data had been obtained satisfactorily in total from the participating psychologists.

Analysis and Results

The concern of the first three hypotheses was simply whether the different treatments would relate to quantitative changes as measured by the S.R.A. Inventory. A change was noted if from pre- to postinventory an item was added or deleted.

One-way analysis of variance (Guilford, 1965) was used to test null hypotheses one through three which state that there will be no difference in change scores between limited, intensive, and control groups, pre- to posttest scores on the S.R.A. Inventory.

Hypotheses one through three were as follows:

1. There will be no significant difference in the quantity of change of teacher understanding of the child between groups of teachers receiving limited psychological consultation and no psychological consultation.
2. There will be no significant difference in the quantity of change of teacher understanding of the child between groups of teachers receiving intensive psychological consultation and no psychological consultation.
3. There will be no significant difference in the quantity of change of teacher understanding of the child between groups of teachers receiving limited and intensive psychological consultation.

The means and standard deviations of change scores for the intensive, limited, and control groups are presented in Table 8-I.

The F value of 17.99, significant at the .01 level, indicated

TABLE 8-I

PRE- TO POSTTREATMENT CHANGE SCORE DATA

Group	*Intensive* (N=35)	*Limited* (N=36)	*Control* (N=38)
X	19.77	15.63	10.54
SD	7.36	7.12	4.03

that differences existed among the three groups (see Table 8-II).

To test for differences between means, the Tukey test for gaps (Myers, 1966) was applied. As shown in Table 8-III differences between means for all groups were significant beyond the .01 level.

Since the mean differences were significant between the limited and control groups, the intensive and control groups, and the limited and intensive groups, hypotheses one, two, and three were all rejected at the .01 level of confidence.

TABLE 8-II

ANALYSIS OF VARIANCE OF SRA CHANGE SCORES FOR LIMITED, INTENSIVE, AND CONTROL GROUPS

Source of Variation	*Sums of Squares*	*Df*	*Mean Square*	*F*
Treatment	1,495.60	2	747.80	17.99**
Within Treatment (error)	4,241.03	102	41.58	
Total	5,736.63	104		

**$p < .01$

The next three hypotheses were concerned with the direction of change in the S.R.A. ratings. To obtain the relevant data, first the teacher pretreatment S.R.A. Inventory was compared with the psychologist's S.R.A Inventory and the number of agreements were noted. This procedure was repeated with the teacher posttreatment S.R.A. Inventory. The t test analysis then focused on examining the differences between pre- and posttreatment agreement scores for the experimental and control groups.

Hypotheses four, five, and six were as follows:

4. There will be no significant differences between the pre- and post-consultation teacher-psychologist agreement in

TABLE 8-III

TUKEY ANALYSIS OF DIFFERENCES BETWEEN MEANS FOR THE
LIMITED, INTENSIVE, AND CONTROL GROUPS

Group	Control	Limited
Limited	5.09**	
Intensive	9.23**	4.14**

**p < .01

understanding of the child of the teachers receiving limited consultation.

5. There will be no significant differences between pre- and postconsultation teacher-psychologist agreement in understanding of the child of the teachers receiving intensive consultation.

6. There will be no significant difference between the change of positive agreement with the psychologist's understanding of the child of teachers receiving the limited and intensive consultations.

The results of related t test (Guilford, 1965) analyses between teacher pre- and postconsultation S.R.A. agreement scores with psychologist S.R.A. scores for both the limited and the intensive groups are presented in Table 8-IV. The t value for the limited group was .89, indicating no significant difference in change scores from pre- to posttesting. This permitted the acceptance of hypothesis four. The intensive group, however, changed significantly from pre- to posttesting. The t value of 2.29 for the intensive group was beyond the .05 level of confidence, which required rejection of hypothesis five.

TABLE 8-IV

t TEST ANALYSIS OF TEACHER-PSYCHOLOGIST SRA AGREEMENT
SCORES, PRE- AND POSTCONSULTATION

	Agreement Scores				
	Preconsultation		Postconsultation		
Group	X	S.D.	X	S.D.	t
Limited (N=36)	28.83	7.52	31.09	8.83	.89
Intensive (N=35)	30.80	9.75	35.29	11.39	2.29*

*p < .05

TABLE 8-V

ANALYSIS OF AGREEMENT GAINS SCORES

Group	Limited (N=35)	Intensive (N=36)	t
X	2.26	4.49	1.96
SD	3.99	5.38	

The results of the unrelated t test analysis between agreement gains scores of the limited and intensive groups is shown in Table 8-V.

The obtained t value of 1.96 failed to reach significance at the level of confidence, leading to the acceptance of hypothesis six.

An additional concern of the study was to examine teacher attitude toward the school psychologist in relation to limited and intensive consultation. An eight-item instrument was accordingly designed to determine teachers' attitudes concerning the two modes of consultation.

The median test (Siegel, 1956) was used to test null hypothesis seven.

Hypothesis seven was as follows:

7. There will be no significant difference regarding satisfaction with psychological consultation among groups of teachers receiving limited and intensive consultation.

Each subject's total score for all eight questions was first derived and analyzed with the median test. The analysis yielded a chi square value of 17.34, which for one degree of freedom exceeded the critical value at the .01 level of confidence, and accordingly hypothesis seven was rejected. These results indicated that the teachers receiving intensive consultation were more satisfied with the psychologists' services than were teachers receiving limited consultation.

In addition, the Kilmogorov-Smirnov two-sample test (Siegel, 1956) was employed to examine differences between the limited and intensive groups on each of the eight questions of the instrument. These data are summarized in Table 8-VI.

Analysis of the teachers' responses on all questions except

TABLE 8-VI

KOLMOGOROV-SMIRNOV TWO-SAMPLE TEST OF DIFFERENCES
BETWEEN INTENSIVE AND LIMITED GROUP SCORES OF
TEACHER SATISFACTION WITH PSYCHOLOGISTS'
SERVICES BY QUESTION

Question	*K Value**
1. The school psychologist's interest in my problems	$K = 12**$
2. The school psychologist's interest in my point of view regarding the referred child	$K = 11**$
3. The helpfulness of the psychologist regarding my understanding of the child	$K = 10**$
4. The helpfulness of the psychologist's written report	$K = 5$
5. The amount of time spent in conference with the psychologist	$K = 19**$
6. The helpfulness of the psychologist's recommendations	$K = 9**$
7. The applicability of the psychologist's recommendations	$K = 11**$
8. The psychologist's overall helpfulness	$K = 11**$

* All of the significant K values were in favor of the intensive group.
** $p < .01$

question 4 yielded K values sufficiently high so that the differences found between the intensive and limited groups' scores on these questions were significant statistically at the .01 level of confidence. On question 4 there was no statistical significance between intensive and limited group scores.

Both the overall analysis and the analysis by question yielded highly significant differences between the limited and intensive groups' scores regarding their satisfaction with the school psychologists' services. These results indicate that teachers receiving intensive consultation were generally more satisfied with the school psychologists' services than were the teachers of the limited group.

The final concern of the study was to examine the extent of teacher follow-through on psychologists' recommendations in relation to the mode of consultation. Each of the eight school psychologists rated each of their participating teachers in the limited and intensive groups one week following the interpretive conference. The teachers were rated on a five-point scale ranging from no implementation of psychologists' recommendations through maximum implementation.

Hypothesis eight was as follows:

8. There will be no significant difference between the extent of follow-through on psychologists' recommendations be-

tween groups of teachers receiving limited and intensive consultation.

A summary of the school psychologists' ratings of the degree of teacher implementation of psychologists' recommendations for both the limited and the intensive groups is shown in Table 8-VII.

TABLE 8-VII

RATINGS OF TEACHER FOLLOW-THROUGH ON
PSYCHOLOGIST RECOMMENDATIONS

Scale Value	Limited	Intensive
5	11	12
4	10	15
3	9	7
2	6	6
1	4	0

The Mann Whitney U technique (Siegel, 1956) yielded a U value of eight, which failed to reach the level of significance required to reject hypothesis eight at the .05 level of confidence. Therefore, hypothesis eight was accepted.

The findings were generally in favor of the intensive over the limited contacts between psychologist and teacher. In relation to the intensive experience, teachers changed more in their understanding of the child and significantly in the direction of greater agreement with the school psychologist. Also, the teachers indicated greater satisfaction with the intensive experience.

As to the fourth question on teacher follow-through, it is interesting to note that while statistical significance was not obtained, the data quantitatively were supportive of the intensive mode of consultation. Also, each of the consultation modes seemed to have led to rather substantial teacher follow-through. The findings of no significant difference between the two consultation modes and the rather substantial follow-through by both groups need some qualification.

Since the psychologists were responsible for the ratings, the possibility of bias definitely exists. These psychologists were aware of which teachers were in the respective consultation groups and possibly were inclined to favor the intensive mode. A counter bias, however, would likely have been the psychologist's desire to see substantial teacher follow-through regardless of consultative mode. Even if the psychologists attempted to control their personal biases, the teachers may have had some reluctance to communicate a lack of good follow-through. A more objective means of assessing teacher behavior ought to be utilized in future studies to bypass the potential biasing of reports by involved psychologists and teachers.

Literature regarding the characteristics of a facilitative relationship contributed toward attempts to explain the several findings of this study. Certainly the psychologist's willingness to spend the amount of time with the teachers necessitated by the intensive mode of consultation was valued by them, as shown by their response to the teacher questionnaire on satisfaction with psychological services. A productive direction for future research may be to examine more closely the nature of a facilitative relationship between psychologist and teacher. Such factors as the psychologist's theoretical orientation to service and the extent to which the teacher perceives his possessing Rogers' (1959) facilitative characteristics could be studied and would bring some theoretical bases to an otherwise pragmatically studied area.

As stated earlier, this study was in part a replication of the Kaplan and Sprunger (1967) study. Its findings will be reviewed as they relate to the current study. Kaplan and Sprunger found that both the limited and intensive modes of consultation led to significant changes in teacher understanding of the child, but that there was no significant difference in change of understanding between the two treatment groups. The current study also found that both limited and intensive consultation led to significant changes in teacher understanding of the child; however, a significant difference was obtained between the treatment, with the intensive group revealing significantly greater changes over that of the limited group.

Another finding of the Kaplan and Sprunger study was that both modes of consultation led teachers to view the child significantly more as the psychologist viewed him. Significant difference in this change of agreement with the psychologist were not obtained between treatment groups. The current investigation obtained somewhat different findings. The intensive group did change significantly in the direction of the psychologist's understanding of the child, while the limited group did not change significantly in this direction.

This study supported the basic thesis of the Kaplan and Sprunger study that school psychological consultation does have an impact upon the teacher. But this study seemed to be showing greater discrimination in results as related to the two treatments. One criticism levied against the Kaplan and Sprunger study was its difficulty in really implementing two separate treatments. The reported findings were interpreted as giving support to this criticism, since greater control over differentiation of treatment was a characteristic of the current study.

REFERENCES

Caplan, G.: *Theory and Practice of Mental Health Consultation*. New York, Basic, 1970.

Guilford, J. P.: *Fundamental Statistics in Psychology and Education*. New York, McGraw, 1965.

Kaplan, M., and Sprunger, B.: Psychologcial evaluations and teacher perceptions of students. *Journal of School Psychology*, 5:287-291, 1967.

Myers, J. L.: *Fundamentals of Experimental Design*. Boston, Allyn, 1966.

Remmers, H. H.: *S.R.A. Youth Inventory*. Chicago, Science Research Associates, 1951.

Rogers, C. R.: Significant learning: In therapy and in education. *Educational Leadership*, 16:232-242, 1959.

Siegel, S.: *Nonparametric Statistics for the Behavioral Sciences*. New York, McGraw, 1956.

BEHAVIOR MODIFICATION

T HEORIES OF LEARNING have a long history in psychology and comprise one of the major cornerstones of the discipline. However, the application of learning theory to changing behavior in the hospital, clinic, and classroom is a recent development. Despite its youth, behavior modification is one of the major movements in applied psychology. Since the middle of the 1960s when behavior modification research began to appear in quantity, an enormous literature has accumulated and much of this literature focuses on classroom applications.

Despite its rapid growth, a review of the research regarding classroom application of behavior modification reveals that the technology is in its infancy. The controlling stimuli (reinforcing stimuli) that have been researched make this point clear. Investigators have focused almost entirely on simplistic kinds of reinforcers, such as verbal praise or inexpensive trinkets. However, psychologists have hypothesized for years that more subtle variables have important effects on behavior. Eye contact, posture, and qualitative aspects of speech (e.g. pitch and speed) are examples of such variables. In the classroom a variety of subtle teacher behaviors probably has an important effect on students. The teacher's choice of students to answer questions, and the clues which a teacher can give following incorrect answers exemplify such influential teacher behaviors.

Even though the development of behavior modification technology has just begun, it has repeatedly been demonstrated to be an effective tool, and large numbers of psychologists have attempted to apply this tool in schools, hospitals, and clinics.

However, many attempts have not been as successful as one would expect from reading the research literature. Although programs fail for many reasons, one important cause that has been discussed is the inadequately developed consultation approaches to behavior modification programs.

For the reasons that have been referred to in Section I, many psychologists function primarily as consultants, and almost all who apply operant technology in schools, hospitals, etc. function in this role. Thus, consultees (i.e. teachers, ward attendants, parents) deal directly with the client and carry out the specifics of the behavior management program. The problem is that consultees often do not behave in a manner that will produce change in the client, even after the consultant has conscientiously tried to encourage the consultee to behave in such a manner. Thus, behavior modifiers increasingly recognize that the process of changing the consultee's behavior is a difficult but essential step in changing the client's behavior.

Unfortunately, the great bulk of the behavior modification literature does not deal explicitly with the interaction between consultant and consultee. Most studies simply report a brief outline of the material covered while noting that aides, parents, peers, or teachers were instructed in the rationale and procedures of behavior modification. Difficulties in getting the consultee to follow directions, and methods for dealing with these difficulties are rarely described. The behavioral consultant knows that if the teacher behaves in a certain fashion there is a good chance the student(s) will behave in a prescribed fashion. If the first attempt at behavior modification is unsuccessful, adjustments are made and empirical evidence indicates that eventually an appropriate arrangement of reinforcement contingencies should result in the desired student behavior. Behavioral consultants need a technology of consultation which will help to maximize their ability to develop teachers' skills as behavior modifiers. In other words, behavioral consultants need to know effective consultation techniques for controlling teacher behavior.

Two general approaches have emerged from the few attempts to attack this problem. The first includes both a description of the kinds of resistance encountered while attempting to train behavior modifiers, and a description of how these problems are dealt with. The second includes systematic manipulations of the consultant-consultee interaction, and an investigation of the effects of these manipulations. Several papers of each type are presented in this section. The first four are position papers or descriptions of the consultation process as applied to behavior modification. The last two are empirical studies of this consultative process.

A major theme running through this book is that the content of consultation must be thought of as separate from the process of consultation. In this section the content is generally behavior principles that will aid the teacher in dealing with the behavior of his students. The processes by which the consultant motivates the consultee to use appropriate behavior principles varies. Techniques that have been discussed to date are (1) appeal to rationale arguments, (2) promise of reward, (3) actual reward, (4) mini-training sessions, and (5) various techniques for improving teacher-child communication. Particular attention should be given to the consultative processes used in each chapter in this section, and these processes should be compared to those used in psycho-educational diagnosis, mental health consultation, and organization development.

The introductory article by Kauffman and Vicente underscores the central issue of the section that knowledge of learning theory is not enough to successfully implement behavior modification programs in the schools. The light-hearted tone of the article helps to increase the impact of the message.

Next, two articles are presented which discuss possible responses to questions raised by parents, teachers, and principals about management systems using tangible rewards. In both chapters objections are dealt with on a rational plane. In other words, the authors present logically based arguments which the consultant can utilize to convince the reluctant teacher that tangible rewards should be used. In the first of these papers, O'Leary focuses on practical questions which are often raised about tanglibe reward systems (cost of materials, cost of consultant time, time demands on teachers, etc.), while in the second, O'Leary, Paulos, and Devine consider philosophical questions. These include, is rewarding children bribery? Will programs using tangible rewards teach greed? Should people be rewarded for behaviors that are required in daily living?

The fourth paper by Grieger discusses teacher attitudes that interfere with behavior modification programs. The reader will notice points of similarity between the teacher attitudes discussed by Grieger and O'Leary particularly with regard to what Grieger calls the "should-ought" syndrome. However, the kinds of processes Grieger outlines for overcoming teacher concerns are somewhat different than those discussed by O'Leary. Grieger's techniques include mini-modification programs, constructive communication of affect and direct rational appeal.

It is implicit in the discussion of the preceding three papers that "resistances" are considered to be the result of misinformation (O'Leary), real philosophical conflict (O'Leary, Paulos, and Devine), or inappropriate and confused attitudes (Grieger). In contrast to these positions the reader is referred to Tharp and Wetzel's (1969) discussion of resistances which takes the position that any attempted change in individuals or in institutions will result in resistance by those who are the focus of change. Their discussion of resistances encountered in carrying out a major consultation project is a useful addition to the material presented in this section.

The second section of this section is devoted to papers that empirically investigate the consultant-consultee relationship. As the reader will notice, research in this area is just beginning, but the selections included provide some answers and, more importantly, offer suggestions for further research.

Most behaviorally oriented writers who have talked about consultation have suggested that the consultant use the same techniques to control consultee behavior as are used to control client behavior i.e. praise or reward contingent on appropriate behavior. The first chapter in this section investigates the efficacy of this recommendation.

McNamara reports data on one teacher which suggest that mild punishment, reward, and feedback each had approximately equal effects on consultee behavior. However, the use of punishment and reward conditions on only one subject suggests a cautious interpretation of these data.

Cossairt, Hall, and Hopkins studied the effects of instruction, feedback and praise on teacher attending behavior. They found that praise in conjunction with instruction and feedback was more effective than instruction or instruction plus feedback. They conclude that praise is essential in maintaining appropriate consultee behavior. This finding with regard to praise parallels the findings of the general behavior modification literature. In addition, since praise is a motivational variable, there should be further investigations of the more subtle interpersonal and motivational processes which the consultation literature suggests are important.

Chapter 9

BRINGING IN THE SHEAVES: OBSERVATIONS ON HARVESTING BEHAVIORAL CHANGE IN THE FIELD

JAMES M. KAUFFMAN AND A. R. VICENTE

Problems encountered by behavior modification consultants working in public schools are described in the form of a parable. Two sowers (consultants) are used as examples of successful and unsuccessful attempts to provide assistance to teachers in the use of behavior modification techniques. It is suggested that extensive field experiences, the ability to speak the language of teachers, adaptation of techniques to special school situations, sagacity in the choice of first efforts in the schools, modification of teacher behavior, demonstration, adequate follow-up, and sensitivity are essential elements of successful consultation. Examples are given of the responses of school personnel and parents to successful and unsuccessful consultation.

Prologue

Behold, a sower went forth to sow; And when he sowed, some seeds fell by the wayside, and the fowl came and devoured them up; Some fell upon stony places, where they had not much earth: And when the sun came up, they were scorched; and because they had no root, they withered away. And some fell among thorns; and the thorns sprung up and choked them: But others fell into good ground, and brought forth fruit, some a hundredfold, some sixtyfold, and some thirtyfold (Matthew 13:3-8).

P OPULARIZATION OF OPERANT conditioning technology within the past decade has brought an aura of revivalism to the behavior

From the *Journal of School Psychology*, 10:263-268, 1972.

modification efforts of many special educators. The gospel according to Skinner (1953) and the revelation unto Premack (1959)
are now heralded by a growing number of priests and proph-
etesses. The act of the apostles have become ever more bold
(Forness and MacMillan, 1970). Miracles have been performed
by true believers (Zimmerman and Zimmerman, 1962; Stolz and
Wolf, 1969). Early writings have been canonized (Ullmann and
Krasner, 1965; Krasner and Ullmann, 1965). Translations and
commentaries in the vernacular have been made available to
the laity (Smith and Smith, 1965; Patterson and Guillion, 1968;
Deibert and Harmon, 1970; Zifferblatt, 1970), who are urged to
consequate* the behavior of their young to the betterment of
mankind.

Operant technologists embrace a common creed: *behavior
is a function of its consequences.* But the faithful have experienced schismatic differences in matters of practice (Lovitt, 1970).
Some have championed the datum of rate and the six-cycle
vehicle of its expression† with fundamentalist fervor (Bradfield,
1970), ignoring matters of verifiability and reliability which
others have made articles of faith (Baer, Wolf and Risley, 1968).
The imminent threat to the promulgation of the gospel, however,
appears not to be differences in expression of faith among
believers, but communication problems common to all who would
testify to the power of consequation. Hear, then, the parable
of two sowers.

THE PARABLE OF TWO SOWERS

And it came to pass that Midian, after many years of toiling
in the field of Pedagogy, did return unto the seat of learning for
further instruction. And there he did first hear words of wisdom
from a behaviorist. And Midian questioned the behaviorist,
saying, "Are these truly new words which thou speakest and new
acts which thou doest? Or are they that which wise leaders of

---

* Consequate: A neologism meaning to apply systematic consequences to
a behavior.

† Some persons suggest that behavior is most efficiently analyzed as movements per minute recorded on special logarithmic paper.

the young have always spoken and done; yea, even from the beginning of time?"

Midian's days with the behaviorist were spent systematically planting the seeds of behavior modification; and he learned well the necessity of good growing conditions, and of tilling the soil. And he did develop hybrid seed to fit his needs and the needs of his bretheren, and of the soil he was tilling. And he worked in the field with other sowers of exceeding cunning and skill until the day that he was ready to test his seed, even in the field of public school. And he was called Midian, the Facilitator.

And lo, Mishma was residing also at a seat of learning. Verily, he ventured not forth from the womb of the great university. There he sought the seeds of behavior modification in many books; and he found them and devoured them all; and he watched his knowledge of behavioral science grow, with the added fertilizer of pigeon boxes and rat experiments. And Mishma's seeds of wisdom which he ate did spring forth and grow and produce new seeds, which were rigorous research and laboratory methods. And his experiments were of exceeding might, and he was called Mishma, the Knower.

And behold, gathering unto them their seeds, the two sowers went forth. And Midian sowed his seed in the field of public school. Likewise, Mishma did come to the field of public school to sow his seed. And they did labour, both Midain and Mishma, in the same field together.

And Midian cared for his seeds as a good steward, taking care not to waste his seed nor to cast his seed thoughtlessly about the school. And as he toiled in the field with teachers he watched them and listened to their words and learned them. He sought diligently for the perfect soil to receive his first seed. And lo, the teachers saw within him the light of one who understood their problems, and the complexities of their charges. And the teachers marveled at his tales of small but significant successes, saying, "Do not our hearts burn within us? Is he not like one of us?" And Midian used his knowledge of behavior modification to reinforce the appropriate behavior of the teachers. For secretly he saw the soil being plowed and prepared for the seed by warm responses and rapport.

But Mishma wrapped his seeds in small volumes and made great haste to get them growing. And as he hastened into the field he quickly cast his seed upon the ground, crying with a loud voice, "Hear ye the word of the prophet; harken now unto my voice and turn from your wicked ways and be saved; read now the words of this book and call upon my name in your distress." Gathering his seeds in both arms, he ran unto as many elementary schools as possible each day. And behold, Mishma's seeds were left behind at his every pause.

And as Midian worked, he saw that the soil in his field was sufficiently prepared unto the time of planting; And it was good. He chose wisely the tilled fields in which his seeds could be fruitful and multiply. There he did plant his seed and did water and prune the young plants with gentle words and deeds, yea, even with demonstration. And behold, he was always at hand for consultation.

And as Midian watched his seeds growing in the field he rejoiced at his choice of good ground and his watchful sowing and tender care. For all about him he saw his seed bearing fruit and producing new seed unto a bountiful harvest of behavioral change.

But the seeds that Mishma had scattered were growing in an unseemly manner. And the fruit borne of his seed was without form and void. And Mishma ran from field to field, watering the young plants with his technical vocabulary. But alas, his seed did not spring up and bear good fruit. And lo, teachers did pile up notes, and phone messages, and distressing reports before him in great number; and Mishma cried for help unto Midian and said, "Wherefor art thou Midian? For my sowing is for naught, but thy seed is sprung up unto a bountiful harvest." And Midian came unto Mishma and they together did harken unto the crises of Mishma's teachers and to the seed which he had planted. And they did hear:

Seed devoured by wayside fowls. "That's bribery! I will not reward things that children are *supposed* to do. If I pay them for working they will not work unless they know what the reward will be. Children should learn for the joy of learning" (fear of corrupting children).

"I tried to praise the good things my children did, but nothing good ever occurred. And I ignored Tom's sleeping in class, but my principal wrote me a note about not letting students sleep in class" (disenchantment with formulas for behavior management).

"You are not letting the children be free and creative. When you treat them like this they have to conform to survive" (fear of manipulation).

"I just haven't the time. I cannot do that in my room. There's already too much to do. Besides I don't think that would work for me" (fear of failure).

Cries heard from stony places. "Delbert has never talked in the four months I've had him in class, so I promised him an M&M for every word he said loud enough for the class to hear, but he's still not talking. Then, today, I wanted everyone in the class to sit quietly and listen during the whole ETV program and it just didn't work" (lack of ability to shape behavior).

"For a while they stopped fighting and I was really glad; but now they are right back to where they started" (quick short-term changes without long-term effects).

"No matter what he does I just praise and praise him, but he's still failing everything" (inability to make reinforcement contingent upon appropriate behavior).

"I tried rewarding with raisins but five children didn't like them, so I *had* to quit" (lack of flexibility and inventiveness in selecting reinforcers).

"I promised a surprise on Friday for good behavior during the week, but by Wednesday afternoon they were just awful" (lack of behavior definition and immediacy of reinforcement).

"I can only praise in the morning, I just have too many interruptions after lunch. And for the past two days I had to quit because we were too busy taking six-weeks tests" (inability to generalize procedures).

Young plants choked by thorns. "Mrs. Mitchell said to me, 'In our house we demand certain behavior and no one deserves a reward just for doing his part. His father and I feel you must punish children. As soon as you threaten to spank him he'll shape up, that's how we do it at home. Can't you just send a note? I don't have time to visit after school. He'll shape up. We had the same problem with the older boys'" (parent resistance).

"Every time I give Bill a reward, three other children are bad and beg to get a reward for being good. I can't do it for all of them, and it's not fair for just a few" (peer problems).

"My principal won't even listen when I tell him how well things are going. And now that I've found a good reinforcer, the principal says I can only use the play ground at assigned times. He says other teachers are complaining because my children tell their children about being able to eat candy in class. Sometimes I feel like everybody is waiting for me to fail, and if I don't get some support I will" (administrative indifference).

"We made playing in the water a reinforcer, and Bobby has done good work to earn time in the water. He's actually learned to swim! The school nurse says a boy in his condition *can't* swim. But he can. Now, the other psychologist said it was a home problem and I shouldn't expect so much work from him" (conflicting and irrelevant consultation).

"I've spent six dollars on M&Ms this month. I can't afford it. No one will rechannel money to help pay for some small prizes" (personal costs).

"After all, it was started by the Russians. It just might be a communist plot"(!!!).

Then looked they upon the harvest that was Midian's and they beheld:

Seeds planted in good ground. "When I saw I could change the behavior of one child, I tried it on the whole class and it really worked" (thirty-fold seed).

"I find I no longer have to scream at the children. The days are *so* pleasant, and my students and I enjoy each other. It just makes teaching nicer" (sixty-fold seed).

"Now that I am more positive, I find I can work well with other teachers and my principal. Mrs. A. even asked me yesterday if I would help her set up a behavior modification program in her room" (one hundred-fold seed).

Many long hours toiled they together. And Mishma beheld within Midian a prophet of truth; yea even a holy man, who could show unto him the way to vast harvests. And Midian went unto Mishma and fell on his neck and kissed him (for he was a sensitive behaviorist), and raised up his right hand and inscribed upon a tablet of stone:

IT AIN'T JUST THE SEEDS YOU GOT, BABY, BUT HOW YOU TILL THE SOIL!

Epilogue

Say not ye, There are yet four months, and then cometh harvest? Behold, I say unto you, Lift up your eyes, and look on the fields; for they are white already to harvest (John 4:35).

REFERENCES

Baer, D. M.; Wolf, M. M., and Risley, T. R.: Some current dimensions of applied behavior analysis. *Journal of Applied Behavior Analysis, 1*:91-97, 1968.

Bradfield, R. N.: Precision teaching: A useful technology for special education teachers. *Educational Technology, 10*(8):22-26, 1970.

Deibert, A. N., and Harmon, A. J.: *New Tools for Changing Behavior.* Champaign, Research Press, 1970.

Forness, T., and MacMillan, D. L.: The origins of behavior modification with exceptional children. *Except Child, 37*:93-100, 1970.

Krasner, L., and Ullmann, L. P. (Eds.): *Research in Behavior Modification.* New York, HR&W, 1965.

Lovitt, T.: Behavior modification: The current scene. *Except Child, 37*:85-91, 1970.

Patterson, G. R., and Gullion, M. E.: *Living with Children: New Methods for Parents and Teachers.* Champaign, Research Press, 1968.

Premack, D.: Toward empirical behavior laws: I. Positive reinforcement. *Psychol Rev, 66*:219-233, 1959.

Skinner, B. F.: *Science and Human Behavior.* New York, MacMillan, 1953.

Smith, J. M., and Smith, D. E. P.: *Child Management: A Program for Parents.* Ann Arbor, Ann Arbor Publishers, 1965.

Stolz, S., and Wolf, M. M.: Visually discriminated behavior in a "blind" adolescent retardate. *Journal of Applied Behavior Analysis, 2*:65-77, 1969.

Ullmann, L. P., and Krasner, L. (Eds.): *Case Studies in Behavior Modification.* New York, HR&W, 1965.

Zifferblatt, S. M.: *You Can Help Your Child Improve Study and Homework Behaviors.* Champaign, Research Press, 1970.

Zimmerman, E. H., and Zimmerman, J.: The alteration of behavior in a special classroom situation. *J Exp Anal Behav, 5*:59-60, 1962.

Chapter 10
ESTABLISHING TOKEN PROGRAMS IN SCHOOLS: ISSUES AND PROBLEMS
K. DANIEL O'LEARY

ANY ATTEMPT TO establish a token reinforcement program in a public school will prompt a barrage of questions from principals and teachers. Some of these questions are little more than reflections of resistance to change, but others are well intentioned and often probe at the critical issues inherent in a token program. It is to the latter type of question that this paper will be directed.

The questions posed by principals frequently concern cost, necessary consulting time, teacher training, and probability of success. Let us discuss the cost of reinforcers first. Consider a class of fifteen disruptive children in an elementary school. If they all received back-up reinforcers worth 5¢ every day for one month (20 school days), then received 40¢ prizes every other day for one month, received 60¢ prizes every third day for one month, and finally received $1.00 prizes every fifth day for one month, the cost of back-up reinforcers would be less than $300.00 for a four-month program.* If the aim of the project director is to transfer control from back-up reinforcers, such as candy and toys to praise and other social reinforcers, one should make a

---

Paper presented at the Annual Meetings of The American Psychological Association, Washington, D.C., 1969.

* One might use less expensive back-up reinforcers *and* quickly increase the behavioral criterion required for various reinforcers in order to maximize the possibility of maintaining prosocial behavioral after the tangible back-up reinforcers are withdrawn.

114

transition to social reinforcers as soon as possible. From my own experience with children from first to fourth grade, such a transition could certainly be made within three to four months without loss of appropriate behavior.

In a junior or senior high school the transition to social reinforcers would probably take longer and the cost of back-up reinforcers would undoubtedly be greater. However, McKenzie et al. (1968) have significantly changed the academic behaviors of ten- to thirteen-year-old children in a learning disabilities class by using grades as tokens and allowances as back-up reinforcers. The parents managed the exchange of tokens for back-up reinforcers under supervision of the experimenters, and since the parents were accustomed to giving their children allowances, neither parents nor the school assumed added costs.

Although some school systems or organizations like the PTA, the Rotary, and Kiwanis have provided for the cost of back-up reinforcers for children, most published studies of token reinforcement programs have had government or university research funds cover such costs. The use of token programs has grown dramatically, but because of the dearth of outcome and follow-up research with token programs in classrooms, it seems best to continue to have the cost of back-up reinforcers covered by research funds where possible. In fact, it is my contention that any token program would be best conducted on a research or "pilot study" basis, even if it is not the intention of the psychologist to publish his results. Having an observer or teacher keep some records of the child's progress provides all people concerned with constant feedback and evaluation about the effectiveness of the program, one of the most beneficial effects of the whole behavior modification thrust.

Administrators and teachers will also wish to know about the necessary consultation time. It is of prime importance that a token program get off to a good start, and that any program receive at least one hour of consultation time per day during the first week of the program from someone knowledgeable in the application of learning principles to classroom management. The consultation time could then gradually taper off to two hours per week. Compared to the number of therapist hours spent in more traditional therapeutic centers where children are seen individually outside the classroom setting, such consulting time is probably an extremely effective use of professional services.

It has been demonstrated that teachers can use a token program and effect some change in children's behavior without participating in a course in learning principles or without having extensive consultation (Kuypers, Becker and O'Leary, 1968). However, care must be taken not to rely solely on the "heavy duty" back-up reinforcers since only partial change will result. Token and back-up reinforcement is but *one* method of producing change in the children's behavior, and it is critical that attention be paid to the types of cues, threats, and frequency and consistency [of] social reinforcement the teacher uses on a minute to minute basis. Particulary important is the effective shaping of the children's behavior in the time between the distribution of ratings or token reinforcers. In addition, adherence to the rules concerning exchange of back-up reinforcers is critical. Several years ago the author dealt with a teacher who became so frustrated with the child that she occasionally allowed them to take any back-up reinforcers, regardless of the amount of token reinforcement. As you might guess, the program had little effect on the children's behavior.

The amount of time a teacher has to spend in giving out the token and back-up reinforcers may be a teacher's greatest concern. Even where we used ratings which were placed in children's booklets every twenty or thirty minutes, the amount of time it took the teacher to place a rating in each of twenty children's booklets and give just a few words of feedback to each child was only three to four minutes. Furthermore, we have found that after a token program has been in effect, the teacher can use less aversive control and spend less time in simple classroom mangement. Thus, the initial time spent in giving ratings and exchanging back-up reinforcers may be well worth the effort. It also should be emphasized that simply having the teacher send home a statement about the child's good behavior or giving the child a plastic token which the parent knows is indicative of good behavior can be used to effectively change a child's classroom behavior with a minimum amount of effort and time.

Questions about the probability of success of such a program are much more difficult to answer. From a review of token programs now being completed by Ron Drabman and the author, it is estimated roughly that 70 to 80 percent of the children in a token program in a preschool or elementary school class for emotionally disturbed, retarded, or educationally disadvantaged children would show significant gains in appropriate social behavior and that these gains would be appreciably greater than those shown by control children in a regular special education class (O'Leary and Becker, 1967; O'Leary, Becker, Evans and Saudargas, 1969). With regard to academic improvement, and particularly to changes on standardized tests, conclusions are more difficult to make, but studies by Birnbrauer, Bijou, Wolf and Kidder (1965), Hewett, Taylor and Artuso (1969), Miller and Schenider (1969), Walker, Mattson and Buckley (1968), and Wolf, Giles and Hall (1968) suggest that academic behavior *per se* can indeed be significantly enhanced by a token program. However, it should be emphasized that a token program is no panacea for increasing the academic repertoire of children. A token reinforcement program is a means of effectively reinforcing behavior, but any token program is intrinsically bound to the adequacy of the presentation of academic materials. In a sense, a token program is an emergency device for prompting and maintaining academic and social behaivor but it tends to remain a prosthetic device if the presentation of academic material is boring and poorly programmed.

It has been quipped that behaviorally oriented psychologists are wart removers while analytically oriented psychologists are the heart surgeons of psychological problems. This remark may be particularly relevant to men who apply token programs but worry little about academic programs and the factors that will control the child's behavior after he has graduated from the token program. With regard to this issue of generalization, the question posed by an administrator or teacher is simply, what will happen when the token program is withdrawn? The answer to that question is straightforward. If special procedures are not devised specifically to maintain the children's appropriate behavior when the program is withdrawn, the children's appropriate behavior will decline. On the other hand, it appears that if some procedures are followed the appropriate behavior of the children can be maintained after the formal token program is withdrawn. Because the problem of maintaining gains in a token program is presently such a key issue, a number of suggestions for enhancing long-term effects of token programs will follow.

1. Provide a good academic program since in many cases you may simply be dealing with deficient academic repertoires, not "behavior disorders."

2. Give the child the expectation that he is capable and that his good behavior is the result of his own efforts. This suggestion has been amply followed in the Engelmann-Becker Follow-Through Program where immediately following a child's correct answer, the teacher very enthusiastically says, "Yes, that's a smart answer; you're a smart boy!" In this regard, it should also be emphasized that the teacher should convey an attitude that she feels or expects the token system to work and succeed.

3. Have the children aid in the selection of the behaviors to be reinforced, and, as the token program progresses, have the children involved in the specification of contingencies, a procedure effectively used by Lovitt and Curtiss (1969). For example, the child rather than the teacher could specify the amount of recess he should earn for a certain number of correct responses.

4. Teach the children to evaluate their own behavior.

5. Try in every way possible to teach the children that academic achievement will pay off. For example, pick something you know a child likes, e.g. clothes, and tell him how he will be able to buy many nice clothes if he studies hard and gets a good job.

6. Involve the parents. Most published studies on token programs in classrooms have not involved parents, probably

for reasons of experimental control. However, the author has not yet been involved in a token program where it was not thought that its long-term effectiveness could have been enchanced by parent involvement. The effective use of parents in school-related token programs has been well illustrated by McKenzie, Clark, Wolf, Kothera and Bensen (1968) and by Walker, Mattson and Buckley (1968).

7. Withdraw the token and the back-up reinforcers gradually, and utilize other reinforcers existing within the classroom setting such as privileges, recess, and peer competition, e.g. boys vs. girls and group contingencies.

8. Reinforce the children in a variety of situations and reduce the discrimination between reinforced and nonreinforced situations. Most of the evidence at this point strongly suggests that behavior is very situation specific and when it is clear to the children that their behavior pays off in one situation but not in another, they behave accordingly.

9. Prepare teachers in the regular class to praise and shape children's behavior as they are phased back into the regular classes, and bolster the children's academic behavior, if needed, with tutoring by undergraduates or parent volunteers.

10. Last, in order to maintain positive gains from a token program it may help to look at the school system as a token system writ large with a whole chain or sequence of responses and reinforcers from the children to the teacher, to the principal, to the school superintendent, and finally to the school board. When viewed in such a manner, the consultant or research investigator should attempt to facilitate the process of reinforcement not only for the children but for the teachers, the principal, and the school board. Praise to a teacher from a principal, frequent feedback and follow-up results given to the principal from the investigator, and some publicity about the program in local papers sent especially to school board members are but a few examples of the types of interactions which may

serve to maintain interest in both the long- and short-term effects of token programs.*

In conclusion, a word of encouragement and a word of caution is in order. First, there definitely are a number of studies which demonstrate that a token program can be successful in changing the behavior of children in a classroom. However, a token program is but one of a variety of techniques which can be used to help a teacher. Because of the problems of withdrawal of token and back-up reinforcers, other procedures should be tried first, such as making rules clear, using praise and shaping, ignoring some disruptive behavior, diminishing the use of threats and verbal reprimands, and focusing on a good academic program. Where such procedures fail and where there is a great deal of peer reinforcement for disruptive behavior (not just one or two disruptive children in a class), token program may well be a very useful procedure for you.

REFERENCES

Birnbrauer, J. S.; Bijou, S. W.; Wolf, M. M., and Kidder, J. D.: Programmed instruction in the classroom. In L. Ullmann and L. Krasner (Eds.): *Case Studies in Behavoir Modification.* New York, HR&W, 1965.

Hewett, F. M.; Taylor, F. D., and Artuso, A. A.: Santa Montica Project. Evaluation of an engineered classroom design with emotionally disturbed children. *Journal-Council for Exceptional Children,* 35:No. 7, 523-529, 1965.

Kuypers, D. S.; Becker, W. C., and O'Leary, K. D.: How to make a token system fail. *Except Child,* 35:101-109, 1968.

Lovitt, T. C., and Curtiss, Karen, A.: Academic response rate as a function of teacher and self-imposed contingencies. *Journal of Applied Behavior Analysis,* 3:49-54, 1969.

McKensie, H. S.; Clark, Marilyn; Wolf, M. M.; Kothera, and Benson, C.: Behavior modification of children with learning disabilities using grades as tokens and allowances as back-up reinforcers. *Except Child,* 34:745-752, 1968.

---

* Consulting fees paid to the teachers for their extra time commitment, university course credit, daily feedback concerning the behavior of the teacher and the children, frequent discussion with the teacher by the principal investigator, and modeling and rehearsal of appropriate teacher behavior have been especially effective for us in gaining control of teacher's behavior.

Miller, L. K., and Schneider, R.: The use of a token system in Project Head Start. Unpublished Manuscript, Dept. of Sociology, University of Kansas, Lawrence, Kansas, 1969.

O'Leary, K. D., and Becker, W. C.: Behavior modification of an adjustment class: a token reinforcement program. *Except Child*, 33:637-642, 1967.

O'Leary, K. D.; Becker, W. C.; Evans, M. B., and Saudargas, R. A.: A token reinforcement program in a public school: a replication and systematic analysis. *Journal of Applied Behavior Analysis*, 2:3-13, 1969.

Walker, H. M.; Mattson, R. H., and Buckley, N. K.: Special class as a treatment alternative for devaint behavior in children. Monograph Dept. of Special Education, University of Oregon, 1969.

Wolf, M. M.; Giles, D. K., and Hall, V. R.: Experiments with token reinforcement in a remedial classroom. *Behav Res Ther*, 6:51-69, 1968.

Chapter 11

TANGIBLE REINFORCERS: BONUSES OR BRIBES

K. Daniel O'Leary, Rita W. Poulos and
Vernon T. Devine

Objections to the use of tangible reinforcers, such as prizes, candy, cigarettes, and money, are discussed. These objections range from concerns about bribery to concerns about adverse behavioral effects. While the use of tangible reinforcers has been extensively shown to change certain behaviors, their misuse is all too frequent, and attention to the objections to tanglible reinforcers should alert one to these misuses. Treatment programs using tangible reinforcers are recommended as powerful modifiers of behavior to be implemented only after less powerful means of modification have been tried.

T HE USE OF tangible or concrete reinforcers, such as candy or prizes, is often a crucial aspect of behavior modification programs, and the effectiveness of such reinforcers in changing the behaviors of diverse populations has been well documented (Ayllon and Azrin, 1968; Hopkins, 1968; O'Leary and Drabman, 1971; Risley and Hart, 1968). It is noteworthy, however, that the prospect of utilizing tangible reinforcers is frequently met with highly divergent reactions. Parents, teachers, and ward personnel often raise objections to concrete reinforcers which are sufficiently strong to prohibit or seriously jeopardize their use. On the other hand, novice behavior modifiers too often avidly seek the power of concrete reinforcers without considering the possible problems associated with tanglible reinforcement and without searching for more subtle yet equally important factors which may control

From the *Journal of Counseling and Clinical Psychology*, 38:1-8, 1972.

the behavior of the client. In fact, due to an apparent but mistaken simplicity, token programs, which utilize tangible reinforcers, are probably one of the most misused therapeutic procedures developed within the behavioral framework.

Previous attempts to deal with objections to concrete reinforcers have been limited in scope or have dealt with these objections only as a side issue. Because of the frequency and intensity of the objections to tangible reinforcers, further examination of the objections appears warranted. It is hoped that an examination of the objections to tangible reinforcers will prove instructive not only to those people who have a great deal of skepticism about their use but also to those behavior modifiers who use them too enthusiastically. This paper will focus on a number of such objections after first discussing several definitions of bribery, an issue intimately related to the objections to tangible reinforcers.

Concrete Reinforcers and Bribery

Parents and administrators frequently state that the dispensing of concrete reinforcers is tantamount to giving bribes. However, close scrutiny of the definitions of bribery and attitudes toward the use of tangible reinforcers reveals a considerable amount of inconsistency and ambiguity. For instance, as many people have noted, parents who balk at giving concrete rewards to their children for schoolwork on the grounds that such a procedure is bribery do not regard their paychecks as bribery. Teachers who feel uneasy about trinkets or candy as incentives for achievement regard merit raises in salary for themselves as legitimate. Similarly, teachers who feel that the use of trinkets or candy as reinforcers is ill-advised freely use stars for the same purpose. Even in the professional literature, the issue of bribery is cloaked with ambiguity, since such literature contains various definitions of bribery which not only differ from one another but also frequently differ from those definitions used in ordinary discourse. For example, note the following variations in the defintions of bribery taken from recent psychological or psychiatric literature:

> giving a gift to prevent misbehavior [Bakwin and Bakwin, 1967.]
> With adults we talk about bribery where someone is paid to do

something illegal. .. . With children bribery usually refers to the
situation where the child *will not do* something and parents say
"O.K., Mary, I'll give you a dime if you'll do the dishes." Mary
was supposed to do something. When she failed to do it, mother
upped the ante to get her to do it. *That is bribery* [Becker, 1969].
in bribery, pay is given before the act. . . . [In contrast] reinforcers
. . . are only given *after* a desired behavior has occurred [Schaefer
and Martin, 1969].
To bribe means to influence dishonestly, to pervert the judgment
or to corrupt the conduct of a person in a position of trust by
means of some reward [Meyerson, Kerr and Michael, 1967; Ross,
1967]. [This definition used by both Meyerson et al. and Ross is
consonant with Webster's, 1967, dictionary definition of bribery.]

Although some of these definitions of bribery point to important issues concerning the actual *use* of tangible reinforcers,
they are idiosyncratic, with the exception of the latter definition,
and only serve to confuse the issue of bribery. Furthermore, when
one is dealing with the general public, as behavior modifiers are,
one should use definitions consistent with those used by the public.

According to the primary dictionary definition, a bribe is a
"price, reward, gift or favor bestowed or promised with a view
to pervert the judgment or corrupt the conduct, especially of a
person of trust (as a public official) [Webster, 1967]." A tracing
of the word bribery from the sixteenth century to the present
clearly denotes immorality through its historical associations with
stealing and corruption, especially of public officials (Oxford,
1959). This primary definition is clearly not applicable to tangible
reinforcers when they are used in intervention programs for
establishing behaviors such as self-care in hospitalized patients or
speaking and reading in children. That is, unless, one considers
self-help, reading, or speaking as corrupt, one cannot regard
the use of concrete reinforcers for their establishment as bribery.
In short, procedurally, the use of concrete reinforcers is neutral;
only when one considers the social desirability of the behaviors
being changed does the issue of bribery arise.

When the primary definition of bribery is considered, the
distinction between concrete reinforcers and bribes is cogent
and valid. However, this distinction breaks down when the
secondary, more general definition of a bribe is used. A bribe,

according to this secondary meaning is "something that serves to induce or influence to a given line of conduct [Webster, 1967]." One finds the following examples in Webster of bribery given to illustrate its secondary meaning: "Using bribes of candy to get a small child to go to bed" and "bribes offered to new readers ranged from cameras to flannel trousers, E. S. Turner." Thus, bribery when used in its secondary sense is an appropriate label for the dispensing of concrete reinforcers. It should be noted, however, that the acceptance of the similarity of reinforcement to bribery, in the secondary sense, recognizes only that reinforcement is an influencing process. The use of tangible reinforcers to build behaviors such as self-help skills or speech should be regarded as bribery *only* in the sense that there is a definite aim to influence these behaviors which are generally evaluated as beneficial for the client. However, the problem with using the term bribery, even when used in its secondary sense, is that it elicits strong, emotional responses due to its association with the primary definition of bribery and its immoral denotations. Consequently, those persons using tangible reinforcers to build behaviors, such as self-help skills or speaking, should continually emphasize to those who raise the issue of bribery that the use of concrete reinforcers should *only* be regarded as bribery in the sense that there is a definite aim of changing said behaviors.

Objections to the Use of Tanglible Reinforcers

In addition to the strong reactions to the word bribery because of its immoral connotations, there are a number of other attitudes or beliefs which lead to resistance to the use of tanglible reinforcers; they range from philosophical objections to objections based on the behavioral effects of using tangible reinforcers. These objections will now be considered.

(1) *One should not be reinforced for something which is a requirement of one's general daily living.* Thus, reinforcers should not be dispensed to the student for reading or to an adult for making a bed, since reading is a general requirement of a student and since making one's bed is the requirement of most adults. This approach places a strong emphasis on duty and

responsibility, and its flavor was described by Tharp and Wetzel (1969) who quoted a principal as saying, "I will not reward a child for doing his moral duty!" This view is also reflected in the feelings of ward personnel who strongly assert that patients should make their beds without concrete reinforcers because it is the normal, responsible thing to do. Unfortunately, exhortation and preaching has not been effective in treatment, and this plea to one's responsibility provides a relatively weak aid in modifying behavior. The temporary use of extrinsic or "crutch" reinforcers may be called for in those instances where the person has not learned to do his moral duty. Had he, he would not be a subject of our ministrations.

(2) *One should engage in an activity because of intrinsic, not extrinsic, rewards.* When applied to learning tasks, this view is reflected in the assumption that children should engage in such tasks because of the self-satisfaction inherent in their completion. Kilpatrick, a student of Dewey, had contempt for rewards and honors because he felt that extrinsic interests held dim prospects for producing desirable attitudes and ideas (Tenenbaum, 1951). Neil (1959) stated,

> The danger in rewarding a child is not as extreme as that of punishing him, but the undermining of the child's morale through the giving of rewards is more subtle. Rewards are superfluous and negative. To offer a prize for doing a deed is tantamount to declaring that the deed is not worth doing for its own sake. . . . A reward should, for the most part be subjective: self-satisfaction for the work accomplished.

While few would argue against the merit of "intrinsic" satisfaction, unfortunately, for some individuals, completing or even working on tasks is not self-satisfying. Tangible reinforcers have been successfully used to enable such individuals not only to complete educational tasks but apparently to enjoy their completion (O'Leary and Becker, 1967). It is difficult if not impossible to determine when engaging in a task is intrinsically reinforcing, but mastery of certain tasks, satisfaction in finding answers, and discovery of new things are examples of behavior which appear to be reinforcing in their own right. If a teacher or hospital attendant builds certain skills over a long period using tangible reinforcers, he will be able to maintain such skills later by using praise, and finally a behavior, such as reading, may be engaged in without praise from others. The factors responsible for the maintenance of the reading are complex and may not be limited to intrinsic reinforcers. Furthermore, the use of tangible reinforcers is certainly not always necessary. However, for those individuals who find academic tasks, such as reading, only minimally reinforcing, or in some cases actually punishing, the use of tanglible reinforcers may be very valuable in building "intrinsic" reinforcers.

3. *A reinforcement program will teach greed and avarice.* Neil (1959) said that parents who tell their children that when they learn to read they will get a scooter are using a procedure which leads to a "ready acceptance of our greedy, profit-seeking civilization." Ginott (1965) noted that, "some parents have been so conditioned by their children that they do not dare come home from a shopping trip without a present. They are greeted by the children, not wtih a 'hello' but with a 'what-did-you-bring me.' "

Montessori (1967) wrote that, "extrinsic rewards would flatter basic sentiments such as gluttony, vanity and self-love."

These objections to the use of tanglible reinforcers seem well-taken, and they seem to be increasingly important with older children and adolescents. Because of the possible development of greed, it is wise to use natural reinforcers, such as privileges, recess, ward passes, or weekend visits to one's home, wherever possible in a token program, and where extrinsic reinforcers are used, one should withdraw them as quickly as possible.

(4) *The recipients of tangible reinforcers will learn to use tangibles to control others.* Bushell, Wrobel, and Michaelis (1968) mentioned that bright children aged three to six who were in a token program were observed hiring the services of one another, and it seems quite possible that the recipients of reinforcers will model the methods of the token dispenser (parent, attendant, or teacher.) That is, the recipient of the reinforcers may learn to control others by promises of gifts, material goods, and services.

While this concern is not to be taken lightly, it should be noted that most token programs ideally move from positive, concrete reinforcers to positive social reinforcers. Thus, they provide a model for influencing others which is far superior to the aversive control anecdotally observed in classes for disruptive children, psychiatric hospitals, and detention homes (O'Leary and Drabman, 1971).

(5) *Rewarding a child for being good will teach him to be bad.* Baruch (cited in Ginott, 1965) described a boy who said, "I get what I want by keeping mother thinking I'll be bad. Of course, I have to be bad often enough to convince her she is not paying me for nothing." This problem is also reflected in the point made by Becker (1969) who regards bribery as upping the ante or reward for a child who has failed to do something that he should have done. Though the present authors do not accept that definition of bribery, the procedural aspects of that definition are important to note. The present authors have not seen children display bad behavior in order to receive tangible reinforcers, but if reinforcers are repeatedly given *after* disruptive behavior of an individual, it is entirely possible that the individual will learn that his *bad* behavior leads to prizes. Such a procedure would be a misuse of a tanglible reinforcement and clearly should be avoided. This general objection would only occur where a token program is started and stopped repeatedly, and this is generally not the case, or where a parent misuses tanglibe reinforcers by saying to a crying child, "Stop crying and I'll buy you some ice cream." In the latter case, the child might learn to display bad behavior so that when he stops he will receive ice cream.

(6) *The dispenser comes to rely almost exclusively on concrete reinforcers, thereby losing or failing to develop more desirable means to control behavior.* More specifically, it is felt that teachers using token reinforcement will rely on the backup reinforcers instead of focusing on academic programming and their own interpersonal or social skills to establish or maintain appropriate behavior. Similarly, it is possible that if a parent starts a token program in the home without proper consultation, the parent will regard the token program as a panacea and will ignore critical aspects of his or her own behavior and their

effects on the child. The person responsible for the implementation of a program should stress that backup reinforcers are powerful *primers* of behavior which should be paired with and gradually replaced by praise and approval. Supervision is a necessary part of any token program, whether it be to monitor such events as the giving of an insufficient amount of praise by attendants or the changing of the criteria for reinforcement in the shaping process. As Kuypers, Becker, and O'Leary (1968) emphasized, "A token program is not a magical procedure to be applied in a mechanical way. It is simply one tool within a larger set of tools available to the teacher concerned with improving the behavior of children."

Since withdrawal of the concrete back-up reinforcers is usually a procedural goal of token programs, there must be continuing emphasis on variables that will help maintain the behavior when the back-up reinforcers are withdrawn.

(7) *The token program will have adverse effects on other individuals such as siblings, fellow patients, or classmates.* When tangible reinforcers are given exclusively to some but not all individuals in the environment, it is entirely possible that those excluded will feel unjustly treated or even adopt "being bad" as a strategy for obtaining reinforcers. The senior author has seen five-year-old children react negatively when a single child in a class is placed on a token program. Adverse effects on others can sometimes be alleviated by explaining to others that the recipient of the token program needs special help and that an increase in the good behavior of the child on the token program has favorable consequences for everyone. Structuring the program so that others share in the reinforcers earned by the recipient is another possible solution. In the case of a nine-year-old hyperactive boy, the child shared his candy rewards with his classmates thereby prompting interest and help from them in regard to his failure to sit still (Patterson, 1965). The procedure of peers sharing reinforcers must be used cautiously, however, since peers might try to use threat or physical force to coerce the recipient to perform for their benefit. An alternative procedure might be a private contract with the recipient which spells out the behaviors for which he can be privately reinforced.

A home-based program (Bailey, Phillips and Wolf, 1970) in which appropriate behavior is tallied at school but reinforced at home is still another alternative. Such a program would involve having a child carry a card with a note or check about his behavior; the teacher would check the card, and the child would give the card to his parents for receipt of his prize.

(8) *The behavior change will be limited to the situation in which the token and backup reinforcers are given or to the duration of such reinforcers.* In fact, with populations requiring special treatment if reinforcers *other* than the token and backup reinforcers are not made contingent upon appropriate behavior, when the token program is withdrawn, the appropriate behavior *will* decline (Ayllon and Azrin, 1968; Birnbrauer, Wolf, Kidder and Tague, 1965; Bushell et al., 1968; Kuypers et al., 1968; O'Leary, Becker, Evans and Saudargas, 1969). On the other hand, where reinforcers which are natural to the classroom or hospital ward, such as frequent praise and special activities, are substituted for reinforcers extrinsic to the treatment facility such as candy, cigarettes, and prizes, it appears that a token program can be withdrawn without a loss of appropriate behavior (Graubard, Lanier, Weisert and Miller, 1970; O'Leary and Drabman, 1971; Walker, Mattson and Buckley, 1969). While it is likely that the natural consequences of some behavior such as talking (Lovaas, 1966) are sufficiently powerful to maintain these behaviors once they are primed by tangible or concrete reinforcers, in many instances it is necessary to program generalization of behaviors like any other behavior change (Baer, Wolf and Risley, 1968).

(9) *Behaviors in situations not supported by tangible reinforcers will be adversely influenced.* This objection proposes that the recipient of tangible reinforcers will come to expect payoff for *all* appropriate behavior and will not perform without it; for example, a child receiving reinforcers for completing homework assignments may refuse to do chores which he previously finished without concrete payment. In contrast to the ninth objection which states that the beneficial changes in behavior during the token program will decrease or not be influenced at

all when the token program is withdrawn, this objection clearly points to the negative effects a token program will have when the program is in effect for only a portion of the day or for only a few behaviors. A number of studies do not support this contention that behavior in situations not supported by tangible reinforcers will be adversely affected (Kuypers et al., 1968; O'Leary et al., 1969), and it is the authors' opinion that if the problem arises, it is transitory or can be dealt with effectively. In a recent study, Meichenbaum, Bowers, and Ross (1968) found that the appropriate behavior of delinquent female adolescents decreased during the morning when a token reinforcement program utilizing money as a backup reinforcer was instituted in the afternoon. The girls told the *Es*, "If you don't pay us, we won't shape up." As Meichenbaum et al. state, "Clearly the girls were manipulating the psychologists into initiating payment in the morning class and were offering appropriate behavior in the morning class as the possible reward." Consequently, the token program was put into effect in the morning. Clients, such as delinquents and adolescents, deprived of goods or money may attempt to gain as many material reinforcers as they can by various manipulative ploys. Responses to such ploys should be made cautiously, however, lest one simply reinforce manipulative behavior which may be incompatible with the goals of the program, for example, more cooperative and democratic behavior and gradual elimination of backup reinforcers. If one envisioned such problems, one could make participation in the token program contingent upon some level of appropriate behavior during a portion of the day or week when the token program is not in effect. Alternatively one could respond to such a ploy by simply stating unequivocally the behaviors encompassed by the token program. However, if it is likely that the increase in appropriate behavior will be particularly large in a token program encompassing behaivor throughout the day, one may wish to build a token program throughout the day even if it were requested by the clients. In short, one must weigh the likely increase in appropriate behavior that would result if a full-day program were put into existence versus the possible adverse side effects of reinforcing manipulative behavior of the clients or patients.

(10) *The use of tangible reinforcers combined with a system of if-then statements is essentially self-defeating because,* "our very words convey to him that we doubt his ability to change for the better." "If you learn the poem" means "We are not sure you can" (Ginott, 1965). In many cases there is real doubt that an individual can perform certain behaviors, but a token program should be established so that it is very very likely that the individual will exhibit desired behaviors which will eventually result in the requisite skills to perform a terminal behavior, such as reading a poem. Related to this criticism concerning the use of tangible reinforcers is the problem of continual prompting of behaviors with if-then statements. Some people regard the contingent use of tangible reinforcers as a procedure in which if-then statements are repeatedly made to an individual. That is, *if* you do such and such, *then* you will receive a certain thing. In most token programs there are instructions concerning the desired behaviors and their corresponding payoffs, and it is likely that a number of if-then statements are made during the token program. Particularly, since a token program must be constantly changing to be effective, there must be instructions and certain if-then statements concerning these changes. However, these if-then statements should be minimized as the token program progresses, since society will not incessantly prompt the behavior of our clients. Furthermore, it is the authors' opinion that continual reiteration of if-then statements may become highly aversive to the recipient of tangible reinforcers. To appreciate this opinion, one need only imagine himself in a situation in which a person who controls key reinforcers for him (employer, husband, wife, or lover) repeatedly stated that only if certain behaviors were exhibited would affection or material goods be granted.

(11) *The use of token and backup reinforcers interferes with learning.*

> The performance of elementary school children on a two-alternative discrimination task has been found to be significantly poorer under a reinforcement condition in which a material reward (candy) was given for each correct response than under a symbolic reward condi-

tion ('right' spoken by the experimenter or a light signal) [Spence, 1970.]

Though this study by Spence was not related to token reinforcement programs, the results of this study were said to provide some support for the hypothesis that inferior performances of material reward groups in certain experiments are brought about by the distracting effects of the reinforcement procedures. On the basis of pilot work now being conducted with Head Start children, it appears to us that with young children the receipt of tokens and backup reinforcers may initially be distracting, but after the first week of an educational program, the interest of the children receiving tokens is maintained better than those children who simply receive the instruction with praise for correct answers. Thus it appears that the decision to use tangible rewards, particularly with young children, may depend on the length of the particular program. If the educational program is relatively short, lasting only several hours or several days, the use of tangible rewards may be ill-advised. On the other hand, the disadvantages of the distracting effects of the tokens and/or backup reinforcers may be greatly offset by the sustained interest obtained by their use where a program is put into effect for several weeks or more and then gradually withdrawn.

Discussion

The behavior modifier wishing to use concrete or tangible reinforcers to change behavior is challenged frequently by people who assert that the behavior modifier wishes to use bribery. When such objections occur, it is probably wise to emphasize that the use of concrete reinforcers is not bribery in the sense that the reinforcers are used to induce corrupt or immoral behavior. One might also add that tangible reinforcers are definitely intended to influence the behavior of others; in this instance, tangible reinforcers can be regarded as bribery but only according to the secondary definition of bribery. It should be noted that tangible reinforcers, such as food, are used by almost all parents to influence the behavior of young children. Thus, if one regards bribery in its secondary or general influence sense, almost all parents have used bribery to some extent, and it should be emphasized that this latter definition of bribery does not refer to the "immoral" use of tangible reinforcers. It is probably also wise to discuss the natural development of secondary reinforcers with those people who question the use of tanglible reinforcers to change behavior. Most children of school age and most adults have outgrown the need to receive tanglible reinforcers for appropriate behavior. Praise and affection are but two of the strong secondary reinforcers which gain influence over a child's behavior as a result of being paired with tangible reinforcers. Unfortunately, due to poor learning experiences or perhaps biological deficiencies, praise and affection do not acquire reinforcing value for some people. A treatment program in which tangible reinforcers are paired with social approval can be used to build the reinforcers which have become effective for most people as a result of their natural development.

In addition to aiding in the possible development of social reinforcers, tangible reinforcers as primers may have several immediate positive effects. They may serve as a concrete demonstration to the recipient that he can succeed, no small accomplishment to an individual who has experienced persistent failure. Tangible reinforcers may also prompt an individual to engage in behaviors which he previously avoided, thereby creating the opportunity for increased skill or task-related satisfaction. Furthermore, in some situations, an immediate change in behavior may prevent an impending dire occurrence, such as expulsion from school, demotion on a job, or firing. Most important, in order to have long-range effects, a token program should be used to teach people to display behaviors which will be maintained by the natural reinforcers from people in the schools, hospitals, or communities in which they reside.

Despite some of the more apparent advantages of a program using tangible reinforcers, the behavior modifier should seriously face questions raised by skeptics of token programs. Many of these questions have only begun to receive research attention. Attention to such questions should prove helpful not only in considering *whether* a program using tanglible reinforcers should be used, but also *how* to implement such a program. The authors here recommend that token programs using tangible extrinsic reinforcers should be implemented *only after* other procedures of prompting and reinforcing with natural reinforcers have been tried. However, where other methods fail, a token reinforcement program may prove very valuable, and if tangible reinforcers are used as primers of behavior, they may prove a bonus to the mental health personnel who find their clients "unmotivated," "lazy," or "resistant to treatment."

REFERENCES

Ayllon, T., and Azrin, N. H.: *The Token Economy: A Motivational System for Therapy and Rehabilitation.* New York, Appleton, 1968.

Baer, D. M.; Wolf, M. M., and Risley, T.: Some current dimensions of applied behavior analysis. *Journal of Applied Behavior Analysis, 1*:91-97, 1968.

Bailey, J.; Phillips, E., and Wolf, M. M.: Modification of predelinquents' classroom behavior with home-based reinforcement. Paper presented at the meeting of the American Psychological Association, Miami, September 1970.

Bakwin, H., and Bakwin, R.: *Clinical Management of Behavior Disorders in Children.* Philadelphia, Saunders, 1967.

Becker, W. C.: *Teaching Children: A Child Management Program for Parents.* Champaign, Englemann-Becker Corporation, 1969.

Birnbrauer, J. S.; Wolf, M. M.; Kidder, J. D., and Tague, C. E.: Classroom behavior of retarded pupils with token reinforcement. *J Exp Child Psychol, 2*:219-235, 1965.

Bushell, D.; Wrobel, P. A., and Michaelis, M. L.: Applying "group" contingencies to the classroom study behavior of preschool children. *Journal of Applied Behavior Analysis, 1*:55-63, 1968.

Ginott, H. C.: *Between Parent and Child.* New York, Macmillan, 1965.

Graubard, P. S.; Lanier, P.; Weisert, H., and Miller, M.: *An Investigation Into the Use of Indigenous Grouping as the Reinforcing Agent in Teaching Maladjusted Boys to Read.* (Project report) Washington, D.C.: United States Office of Education, Bureau of Education for the Handicapped, 1970.

Hopkins, B. L.: Effects of candy and social-reinforcement, instructions, and reinforcement schedule leaning on the modification and maintenance of smiling. *Journal of Applied Behavior Analysis, 1*:121-130, 1968.

Kuypers, D. S.; Becker, W. C., and O'Leary, K. D.: How to make a token system fail. *Except Child, 35*:101-109, 1968.

Lovaas, O. I.: A program for the establishment of speech in psychotic children. In J. K. Wing (Ed.): *Early Childhood Autism.* London, Pergamon, 1966.

Meichenbaum, D. H.; Bowers, K. S., and Ross, R. R.: Modification of class-room behavior of institutionalized female adolescent offenders. *Behav Res Ther*, 6:343-353, 1968.

Meyerson, L.; Kerr, N., and Michael, J. L.: Behavior modification in rehabilitation. In S. W. Bijou and D. M. Baer (Eds.): *Child Development: Readings in Experimental Analysis*. New York, Appleton, 1967.

Montessori, M.: *The Discovery of the Child*. Notre Dame, Fides, 1967.

Neil, A. S.: *Summerhill: A Radical Approach to Child Rearing*. New York, Hart, 1959.

O'Leary, K. D., and Becker, W. C.: Behavior modification of an adjustment class: A token reinforcement program. *Except Child*, 33:637-642, 1969.

O'Leary, K. D.; Becker, W. C.; Evans, M. B., and Saudargas, R. A.: A token reinforcement program in a public school: A replication and systematic analysis. *Journal of Applied Behavior Analysis*, 2:3-13, 1969.

O'Leary, K. D., and Drabman, R. S.: Token reinforcement programs in the classroom: A review. *Psychol Bull*, 75:379-398, 1971.

Oxford (shorter) English Dictionary (3rd ed.). London, Oxford U Pr, 1959.

Patterson, G.: An application of conditioning techniques to the control of a hyperactive child. In L. P. Ullmann & L. Krasner (Eds.): *Case Studies in Behavior Modification*. New York, HR&W, 1965.

Risley, T. R., and Hart, B.: Developing correspondence between the non-verbal and verbal behavior of pre-school children. *Journal of Applied Behavior Analysis*, 1:267-282, 1968.

Ross, A. O.: The application of behavior principles in therapeutic education. *Journal of Special Education*, 1:275-286, 1967.

Schaefer, H. H., and Martin, P. L.: *Behavioral Therapy*. New York, McGraw, 1969.

Spence, J. T.: The distracting effects of material reinforcers in the discrimination learning of lower and middle class children. *Child Dev*, 41:103-112, 1970.

Tenenbaum, S.: *William Heard Kilpatrick*. New York, Har-Row, 1951.

Tharp, R. G., and Wetzel, R. J.: *Behavior Modification in the Natural Environment*. New York, Academic Press, 1969.

Walker, H. M.; Mattson, R. H., and Buckley, N. K.: Special class placement as a treatment alternative for deviant behavior in children. In F. A. M. Benson (Ed.): *Modifying Deviant Social Behavior in Various Classroom Settings*. (Monograph Series 1) Eugene, Oregon: University of Oregon, Department of Special Education, 1969.

Webster's Third New International Dictionary. (Unabridged) Springfield, Marriam, 1967.

Chapter 12

TEACHER ATTITUDES AS A VARIABLE IN BEHAVIOR MODIFICATION CONSULTATION

RUSSELL M. GRIEGER

This article considers teacher attitudes as an important variable in implementing a behavior modification program in a public school classroom. Six attitudes which, if held by the teacher, tend to undercut the behavioral consultation endeavor, are discussed. These include the child needs fixing; it is wrong to express negative feelings; children must not be frustrated; the "should-ought" syndrome; the "he makes me" syndrome; and, children are blameworthy. Suggestions are offered in dealing with the teacher who possesses them.

T WO MAJOR TRENDS confront the practicing child psychologist today. One is the use of behavior modification techniques as practical and viable methods to bring about behavior change. A second is for the psychologist to function as a consultant in which the focus shifts from the child to those who function as caretakers of the child (e.g. teachers, probation officers, parents). The caretakers, in essence, serve as an extension of the professional and act as a specific mediator of change. For example, Harris, Johnston, Kelly, and Wolf (1964) assisted nursery school volunteers in teaching a regressed preschool crawler to walk, and Wahler (1969) educated parents to function as "change agents" for their own children.

From the *Journal of School Psychology*, 10:279-287, 1972.

In no setting, however, has behavior modification had such an impact as in the public schools where the school psychologist acts as a consultant to assist teachers become the mediators of change. The trend is for the psychologist to remove himself from assuming major responsibility for the child "client" and to equip the teacher with enough behavioral technology so that he may continue to be primarily responsible for the child independent of the psychologist.

As teachers are asked to assume these responsibilities, however, the psychological consultant must first assess whether the teacher has the capacity to cooperate in and effectively engineer a behavior modification program. In many instances strategies developed by the consultant failed because this assessment was not made. If the teacher is found inadequate or in some way inappropriate, education or modification efforts directed toward him must first be undertaken before proceeding to the student.

Tharp and Wetzel (1969) catalog some of the individual and institutional resistences to the employment of a systematic behavioral approach. Grieger, Mordock, and Breyer (1970) discussed teacher behavior as a relevent area in the consultation process. This paper focuses on teacher attitudes about themselves and their students as a major variable in the consultation relationship and the implementation of operant strategies in the classroom. While somewhat speculative and partially based on the author's experience, it is believed that if the teacher possesses one or more of these attitudes, he will tend to resist the use of behavior modification techniques and only reluctantly see himself as being primarily responsible for the child. As a consequence, the specific change program, indeed the total consultation effort, will prove difficult and might even fail.

Positive Irrational Attitudes

The child needs fixing. This is perhaps the basic attitude that interferes with behavior modification problem-solving attempts. It is based on the predominant view that behavior is composed of internal needs and traits that singularly predispose an individual to respond the way he does. In this view behavior is relatively independent of the situation in which the person operates, so that the stimulus for action comes primarily from within. Behavior disorders are thus conceived as "residing" in the child and the emphasis is on fixing him rather than on alternatively attempting to restructure the situation within which his behavior appears (Bersoff and Grieger, 1971).

The author challenges this notion of omnipotent response predisposition and asserts that behavior is jointly determined by previously learned habits and the specific situation the person finds himself in. Thus, personality is seen as learned abilities that, like other abilities, are elicited, maintained, and modified as a result of the press of situational forces (Wallace, 1966). Since behavior is at least partly determined by situational forces, it follows that, in understanding behavior disorders, one must understand the context within which the disordered behaviors are emitted. Thus, behavior disorders are seen as "residing" in a situation comprising the child of concern and all other important people in that situation. The child's behaviors may be deviant, but the situational expectations may be rational or irrational, the behaviors of those in a situation may be complimentary or contradictory, and the rewards may be consistent or inconsistent.

The public school classroom is one extremely important situation for the child. Following the psychosituational logic, the psychologist consulting with a teacher in general or about a particular child should view the total classroom situation deviates from the home situation, the child will be viewed as poorly adjusted or emotionally disturbed. Regardless, either the child or the teacher, or both, may be inappropriate in action, attitude, or expectations, and either the child or the teacher, or both, might need to alter their expectations, attitudes, or behaviors.

The author feels that it is important for any teacher who is enlisted in a behavior modification program to recognize and accept the psychosituational context of any child's objectionable behavior. Teachers who view the child's behavior as solely determined by some hypothetical set of internal predispositions find it difficult to engage effectively in operant programs. This teacher would probably assign major responsibility to the child for his actions and assume that the problem was inside him. Conversely, he would tend to overlook his own behaviors as casual or at least contributing in determining or maintaining the child's behavior.

The goal of the consultant should be to assist the teacher to recognize and admit that his behavior, as well as the behavior of all children in the classroom, has a tremendous eliciting, inhibiting, and altering effect on any one particular child. One plausible means of doing this is to demonstrate the power of operant consequences through a "mini-modification" program. That is, the consultant could alter some circumscribed, perhaps even nondisruptive, behavior that can easily be modified.

It is wrong to express negative feelings. Some teachers hold the opinion that they must not express negative feelings. They think it is inappropriate to show anger to any irritating child or to demonstrate sadness to a pathetic one. Some even carry this to extremes by attempting to inhibit expressions of joy, pleasure, and approval. Not only is this attitude irrational, but it is frequently based on other irrational attitudes, such as a person must be ultimately loved and approved, that one must consistently and thoroughly be on top of all situations, that people are ultimately bad and unworthy when behaving inappropriately (e.g. angrily), and that it is easier to avoid rather than face life's difficulties (Ellis, 1963).

In addition to its irrationality, behaving in accordance with this attitude is impossible. In reality teachers constantly experience both positive and negative emotions toward their students. Not a day goes by without some irritation and exasperation being elicited by the children from the teacher, and, teachers constantly communicate these emotions in some fashion. Feelings, if not directly expressed, are emitted by the tone of voice, by gestures, by withholding of positive feelings, or perhaps by passive-aggressive "accidents." While a teacher might inhibit saying something in anger, he will invariably raise his eyebrow, alter the tone in his voice, or display his anger in some way. Further, the inhibition of anger often causes various negative consequences that interfere with problem-solving attempts. For one, stifling affectional responses is counter productive to establishing trusting relations with those we feel affectionate toward. If one is always concerned with withholding, one can not risk the encounter. Secondly, teachers who inhibit emotional expression typically behave in a stilted, bland way that is counter conductive to appropriate responsiveness of the children. Finally, this bland style eliminates a productive source of behavioral control, the teacher's social reinforcing qualities. The children would be unlikely to find his "personality" rewarding and probably would be unlikely to internalize his (i.e. society) values and goals.

The author disagrees with Caplan (1970), who cautions the consultant not to become involved in the consultee's interpersonal value system. The position held here is that the consultant often has to confront directly the consultee with this irrational attitude and any others that underlie it. Following the techniques of rational-emotive psychotherapy (Ellis, 1963), the consultant can attempt to convince the teacher that he need not always be loved and approved, that he can not possibly "conquer all situations," and that he is not unprofessional if he becomes upset with a child. By so doing, the consultant can convince the teacher that it is appropriate to express his feelings in a reasonable way and even that these feelings, honestly expressed, can be useful to him in shaping desired behaviors.

In conjunction with this the consultant might attempt directly to educate the teacher to express his negative feelings honestly but constructively. Gordon (1970) makes an important distinction between "you talk" and "I talk." "You talk," emphasizes the child and places responsibility for one's own feelings on another. For example, the teacher might say, "You got out of your seat and are bad" or "There you go again." Besides placing tremendous power in the child's hands to rule one's feelings, it invariably involves a put down statement, or, to say it behaviorally, it either punishes appropriate behaviors or rewards with attention inappropriate behaviors. "I talk," on the other hand, emphasizes one's own feelings and perceptions. For example, the teacher who notices that the child keeps leaving his seat might say, "I feel responsible for you to learn this unit and I become upset that I'm not succeeding. Please remain in your seat." This type of statement gives the child feedback as to his objectionable behavior, it tells the child what the expectations for his behavior are, and it gives the teacher an opportunity to vent her feelings without attacking the child. He will then be more likely to give reinforcements for appropriate behaviors and ignore inappropriate ones.

Children must not be frustrated. Some teachers believe that a child's frustration must be avoided at all costs. Probably because of an over-identification with the child, they try to anticipate and avoid all of life's "hard knocks" by placing as few demands on the child as possible. They avoid criticism, reprimand, or punishment, and, in total, attempt to make the child's existence utopian. This is untenable for several reasons. First, frustration is a natural part of life that can not be avoided. Second, children learn to deal with frustrations by dealing with them. Consequently, the teacher's concern might be better placed by helping the child learn to solve frustrating situations and thereby to learn skills he can carry with him into adulthood. Finally, feelings of competence often result directly from dealing with and solving problems, not from avoiding them or having others solve them.

This attitude has direct consequences for the behavioral consultant. A well-organized behavior modification program invariably places demands on the child and often creates frustrations for him. Infrequently or poorly learned behaviors are typically demanded, and, although successive approximation is an operating principle, difficult chores usually await the child. Further, reinforcements are freqeuntly lost and punishments often need to be administered. The teacher who holds this attitude would probably bump headlong into these program realities. The teacher might reason, for example, that he is asking too much of Johnny and that, if he does ask and Johnny can not comply, it will be a catastrophy for Johnny. Even if the teacher makes it past this initial difficulty, he more than likely would experience difficulty maintaining the established consequences to the desired behaviors. He would probably reward Johnny for appropriate behavior, but balk at withholding rewards or dealing out punishment for undesirable behavior. Either way he undercuts the program.

It would certainly be helpful if, preliminary to the behavioral program but as part of the consultation program, the teacher could see that frustration is a part of life that can not be avoided. If he can come to this viewpoint, frustrations on the child's part could be utilized as constructive building blocks to maturity and a teaching opportunity to equip the child with future problem-solving skills (D'Zurilla and Goldfried, 1971). Besides dealing directy with the teacher's attitudes, as Ellis (1963) suggests, most careful attention should be given to demonstrating the efficacy of the operant methodology. To do so, it is helpful to choose a child from the teacher's class who is most amenable to modification, pick a behavior of the child's that is both bothersome to the teacher and relatively easy to change, and choose a behavior that elicits signs of some frustration but is not overwhelming by any means. Following this, careful attention should be given to choosing workable successive approximations to the desired end product, carefully finding *initially* and using the most powerful reinforcers and manipulating all the possible competing reinforcers. Throughout this effort (besides being models of utopian technical skills), the consultant should frequently call attention to the positive results, reinforce the teacher's efforts, and note the satisfaction rather than frustrations of the child.

Negative Irrational Attitudes

The "should-ought" syndrome: Most child psychologists encounter teachers who complain that a particular child should behave better or ought not behave the way he does. For example, the teacher might say that Johnny "should be able to finish his assignments." Statements of this kind and the attitudinal components behind them imply absolutistic, unsupportable, and unreasonable expectations. There is no evidence yet to support the universality of the expectations that children "ought" to behave differently than they do or know more than they do. The underlying assumption is that, without training, children will acquire a behavioral repertoire that will enable them to conform to societal standards. Actually, children behave in certain ways either because they have acquired this behavior through learning or because they have failed to acquire the behavior due to emotional illness, mental retardation, or some situational deprivation.

This attitude, in the author's experience, leads to strong resistences to the behavior modification endeavor. Teachers who hold this attitude frequently blame the child for behaving as he does, feel that he can behave differently if he wishes, and conclude that he deserves no special considerations. The teacher then is likely to refuse the offer of assistance or, if he does agree to a consultation encounter, will probably throw roadblocks to progress. For example, giving rewards of any kind (e.g. candy, smiles) would be thought unethical since the child could do better by himself, and ignoring unacceptable behaviors would be both unfair to the other children and dangerous as an example to the peers. Further, this teacher would find it difficult to understand and implement the concepts of shaping through successive approximations, but would probably demand that the child emit and maintain the desired final performance immediately.

This irriational attitude is most difficult to change. Two ploys, however, have proven successful. One is to think through with the teacher these should-ought statements to their logical conclusions. This involves discriminating between what is desired and what is needed from the child. Teachers might like it better if their students behaved in different ways, but to escalate the wish for better behavior to a demand or need is unreasonable. To want children to work well in school is reasonable, but to need it, thus demand it, and blame them for falling short, is irrational. Except for things that have actual life and death connotations, people arbitrarily define desires as needs (Ellis, 1963). Thus, a self-defined need can be de-escalated with practice back to simple desires.

The second ploy is to capitalize on the teacher's understanding of developmental concepts. The consultant might find it profitable to point out the natural developmental sequence leading to the behaviors that the teacher desires and to note that unfortunately this child is below the developmental level of the other children his age on this variable. Empathizing with the teacher's desires to help the child improve, the consultant would step-by-step outline the program that will lead the child to the desired level of behaving. These successive approximations would then personally reward the teacher and de-emphasize the concept of should-ought.

The "he makes me" syndrome: This irrational attitude is a common one in our society. It follows the logic that other people or events cause us to feel the way we do, "Johnny makes me mad when he talks out," or "Sammy makes me happy when he can answer." In any event, the teacher holds the child responsible (sometimes this means blameworthy) both for the child's actions and the teacher's emotions. Besides putting a great deal of power in a small child, this attitude is based on the irrationality that others determine our own emotions. Actually, our feelings are directly related to the things we say to ourselves. To say it another way, our "silent sentences" determine our feelings by serving as a sieve through which events pass. "He makes me . . . " is really more appropriately conceptualized as, "I react with feelings of . . . to . . . because I think it is awful to have . . . happen to me."

Brophy and Good (1970) have impressively shown that teachers behave differently to children depending on their academic expectations for those children. Accordingly, the author has found that the teacher who believes the "he makes me" syndrome finds it difficult to conduct a behavior management endeavor. Feeling himself to be a passive victim of the child's behavior, he often makes little constructive effort to change his own behavior. Rather, he angrily blames the child both for the child's actions and his own feelings. He consequently finds it difficult to make allowances for the child's shortcomings, finds it awkward to ignore or extinguish his inappropriate behaviors, and finds it difficult to reward him for behaving appropriately. In short, he most likely catches the child being bad rather than good.

Seeing the irrationality of this attitude often serves to turn the teacher's attitudes around; demonstrating how people directly influence their own feelings often serves to defuse the intense feelings toward that child. It is, therefore, quite feasible to directly confront the teacher with this irrationality. In addition, the consultant can train the teacher in the technique of continuously questioning his "silent sentences" by asking, "What did I say to myself just before I became upset that led me to become upset?" When he can honestly and consistently challenge his attitudes in this manner, he becomes more able to accept the responsibility for them, ceases blaming the child, tunes into the child's positive actions, and modifies his behavior in an objective way.

Children are blameworthy for their misdeeds: The belief underlying this attitude is that children freely choose to do bad things. They are malevolent, manipulating, and often take great delight in making others suffer. The reality is that human behavior is determined by an infinite number of events over which people have no control (Bersoff and Grieger, 1971). A whole base of experiences has led the child to this point in his life, and, admitting that the past largely determines present behavior, present situational events quickly and continually become the new past determining a new future. Thus, a child's behavior has, to a large measure, been shaped by past external events and continues to be shaped by present situations.

On a less theoretical level, it is well to note that people behave in inappropriate ways because they "are too stupid, too ignorant, or too emotionally disturbed" to do otherwise (Ellis, 1963). To blame them for their subnormal intelligence, for being ignorant, or for behaving inappropriately will not make children more intelligent, more knowledgeable, or less disturbed. Conversely, blaming the child often exerts a tremendous price. It often serves to perpetuate the behavior we would like to reduce, it often leads the child to believe he is blameworthy, it often reduces attempts on the child's part to try to solve his problem, it often leads the child to resent the blamer, and it often leads the child to avoid the punishing situation.

The teacher who feels that the child should be blamed for his misdeeds is quite often a hostile person prone to anger who punishes children frequently. He frequently either directly reprimands and limits the child or indirectly belittles and derides his behaviors and efforts. Regardless, it is highly unlikely that he would consent to ignoring inappropriate and to rewarding appropriate behaviors.

The author finds the teacher who strongly holds this attitude often is in need of more intense psychological assistance than can be offered through the consultation relationship. It is helpful for this teacher to examine intensely the basis, rational or otherwise, for his anger in an on-going relation geared for this purpose. The consultant can, however, discuss with the teacher the thinking behind the "he makes me" syndrome with the hope that some of the anger can be diffused. The author then finds it helpful to discuss the idea that behavior is determined by the consequences of the environment and that the child who appears to be manipulating us really has been manipulated by us. Finally, efforts can be made to show the teacher how he can systematically control the consequences so that what has just been explained actually operates.

Conclusion

This paper presents six irrational attitudes teachers might hold that could interfere with their successfully learning and implementing behavior modification programs. Holding these attitudes, the teacher would find it difficult to accept the operating principles of behavior modification and act in accordance with them. This does not exhaust the list, however, nor does this discussion imply that only one can be operating at a time. In practice, a teacher who holds one of these probably will hold others. Thus, the consultant must be on the lookout continually for others, even after he has successfully identified and dealt with one or two. In fact, identifying and dealing with this element in a behavior modification consultant endeavor should be a constant, on-going part of the endeavor from start to finish.

The author believes that the attitudes one holds (1) contribute with situational events to the person's behavior and (2) determine to a large degree the person's feelings (Ellis, 1963). These attitudes are learned and since they are learned, they can be unlearned. Following Ellis (1963), identification of the attitude, systematic exploration of the basic irrationality of the attitude, and continued practice in substituting a more rational idea for the irrational one serves effectively to unlearn old and learn new and contradictory ones. This is the basis of rational-emotive psychotherapy, but it also seems to work quite well in teacher consultation. For example, the consultant would point out to the teacher that he angrily blames children for their deeds, helps him see why it is not plausible to blame children for the behaviors, and helps him practice thinking and saying new things to himself that are more plausible.

Finally, this discussion does not imply that the consultant should not be concerned with other areas in a consultation endeavor from an operant standpoint or that this is the area of prime importance. It only suggests that many factors influence that endeavor, and teacher attitudes will have a significant impact on the success of the consultative efforts. Attention must be paid to them at least in the mind of the consultant and perhaps as an important adjunct to the relationship itself.

REFERENCES

Bersoff, D. N., and Grieger, R. M.: An interview model for the psycho-situational assessment of children's behavior. *Am J Orthopsychiatry, 41*:483-439, 1971.

Brophy, J. E., and Good, T. L.: Teachers' communications of differential expectations for children's classroom performance. *J Educ Psychol, 61*:365-374, 1970.

Caplan, G.: *The Theory and Practice of Mental Health Consultation.* New York, Basic, 1970.

D'Zurilla, T. J., and Goldfried, M. R.: Problem solving and behavior modification. *J Abnorm Psychol, 78*:107-126, 1971.

Ellis, A.: *Reason and Emotions in Psychotherpy.* New York, Lyle Stuart, 1963.

Grieger, R. M.; Mordock, J., and Breyer, N.: General guidelines for conducting behavior modification programs in public school settings. *Journal of School Psychology, 8*:259-266, 1970.

Gordon, T.: *Parent Effectiveness Training: The "No-lose" Program for Raising Responsible Children.* New York, Peter H. Wyden, Inc., 1970.

Harris, F.; Johnston, M.; Kelly, S., and Wolf, M. M.: Effects of positive social reinforcement on regressed crawling of a nursery school child. *J Educ Psychol, 55*:35-41, 1964.

Tharp, R. G., and Wetzel ,R. J.: *Behavior Modification in the Natural Environment.* New York, Academic Press, 1969.

Wahler, R. G.: Opposition children: A quest for parental reinforcement control. *Journal of Applied Behavior Analysis, 2*:159-170, 1969.

Wallace, J.: An abilities conception of personality: Some implications for personal measurement. *Am Psychol, 21*:132-138, 1966.

Chapter 13

TEACHER AND STUDENTS AS SOURCES OF BEHAVIOR MODIFICATION IN THE CLASSROOM

J. REGIS MCNAMARA

A treatment approach which separately focused upon behavioral control of teacher and student behavior was presented. Simple information feedback, involving no payoff, was compared to response cost and positive reinforcement procedures which rewarded the teacher for differential attention to disruptive behavior. All three procedures were effective in decreasing teacher attention to inappropriate behavior and increasing it to appropriate behavior.

The removal of attention for inappropriate student behavior did not, however, materially decrease it. Punishment, in the form of negative point consequation, rapidly brought the disruptive student behavior under control. The general effectiveness of punishment approaches to modify oppositional behavior was discussed. Also, the need for the use of data to implement treatment procedures effectively was illustrated by way of the present study.

INTERVENTION IN THE classroom to treat disruptive behavior has frequently relied upon the contingent management of social reinforcement via teacher attention (e.g. Zimmerman and Zimmerman, 1962; Hall and Broden, 1967; Becker, Madsen, Arnold and Thomas, 1967; Thomas, Becker and Armstrong, 1968; Madsen, Becker and Thomas, 1968). With the apparent exception of Madsen et al. (1968), who discussed the technical considerations of gaining stable control over the dispenser of attention, the

---

From *Behavior Therapy*, 2:205-213, 1971.

teacher, no consideration has been given to studying the conditions under which effective teacher control can be obtained. Typical procedures suggested in the above studies for establishing stability in the teacher's behavior have been instruction and exhortation, feedback in the form of graphs, and inspection of self-kept counter records. It would appear that these procedures would be adequate when there is no compelling reason why the teacher should not relinquish or acquire new behaviors suggested by the experimenter. However, when new behaviors required of the teacher compete with high rate preexisting responses, that are being maintained through payoffs in the environment, then it is unlikely that the new behaviors will ever be emitted at an effective rate. One group of investigators (Hall, Lund and Jackson, 1968) have found an instance where instructions, praise, and frequently graphed feedback of the teacher's behavior were totally ineffective in changing the ways a teacher dispensed attention to pupils in her room.

The first part of the present study investigated ways to control the teacher's attention-dispensing behavior. This phase of the study was carried out under conditions where the teacher's attention to inappropriate behavior occurred at a high rate and had acquired functional reinforcement value. The second part of the study empirically began after stable control over the teacher's nonattention to disruptive behavior had been achieved. At this point, no diminution in the disruptive classroom behavior had been accomplished. The lack of deceleration in the disruptive behavior when the teacher's attention to this behavior was removed, paralleled the results Wahler (1968) obtained with younger oppositional children. Therefore, punishment in the form of withdrawal of positive reinforcement (points which bought desired activities) was introduced in continuation with teacher nonattention to modify undesirable classroom behavior.

Method

Subjects and Setting

The study was conducted in a classroom of a special school for behavior problem junior high boys. The age range of the boys was twelve to sixteen with a mean age of fourteen years nine months. Their approximate mean WISC IQ scores were eighty-eight. The average student was functioning at least several grade levels below age expectation in the language arts, reading, and math skills areas. The boys were unable to profit sufficiently from a regular school program and were somewhat immune to adult social influence in the regular school environment. Frequent behaviors the boys engaged in while in the regular school were fighting, trouble making, and underachievement.

Curriculum in the classroom was based on the particular ability level of each student. Within each class there was a preexisting reward system based on a token economy. Students earned points for such behaviors as being on time for class and being prepared to work. The points were exchanged for admission to student-preferred activities, e.g. swimming, pool room, field trips.

Three different groups of boys in three separate classes constituted the treatment groups. There was close correspondence in class attendance for the periods during the intervention program, with average attendance for the periods ranging from 5.9 to 6.1 students per class. A one-way analysis of variance of attendance by class indicated a nonsignificant $F(2,21) = .64$.

Materials

An experimental radio-controlled aversive conditioning system was used in the classroom as a signaling system. The system was composed of a transmitter, a receiver-shock unit, and an arm band. The transmitter was a standard 100-mW walkie-talkie operating on a citizens band control channel. It was modified to transmit a signal directly to the receiver pulse unit. The receiver-shock unit, mounted in a plastic cigarette case, consisted of a commercially available high-sensitivity citizens band receiver and a specially designed electrical shock circuit. Signals in the form of mild electric pulses were delivered through electrodes connected to an arm band worn on the upper arm of the teacher. The teacher selected a shock level which was noticeable but not painful. One pulse signified an appropriate response, while two pulses signaled an inappropriate response to the students' behaviors.

Procedure

After a brief introduction to the principles of behavior modification, the teacher formulated target behaviors that he wished to change in the classroom. The following behaviors were specified and manipulated in the study: Hand Raise (HR)—An HR event occurred only when a student raised one arm above his shoulder while seated; Teacher Attention to a Hand Raise (TAHR)—A TAHR event occurred when, within five seconds of an HR, the teacher gave verbal recognition to it, or directly approached the student who raised his hand; Teacher Call Out (TCO)—A TCO event occurred when a student called out and requested the teacher's attention without having been authorized to do so previously. Remarks, such as "Come here, Mr. . . . .," "Hey, Mr. . . . .," or "Mr. . . . ., look at this," were representative of this class of behavior; Teacher Attention to a Call Out (TACO)—A TACO event occurred, when, within five seconds of a TCO, the teacher gave verbal recognition to it, or directly approached the student who had made the TCO.

Recording

Event sampling was done by one observer for each of the classes of behavior under consideration over a thirty-minute class period. Interrater reliabilities previous to and during base line indicated 90 percent reliability for the procedure, so that only one observer was used during the remainder of the study. This observer both recorded and signaled the teacher concerning his behavior.

Program Operations

A list of the experimental procedures carried out in the classroom is presented in Table 13-I. Descriptions for the procedural labels are as follows:

Base line: The observer recorded the four target behaviors during the first eight sessions similarly for all classes. The behavior was recorded and tabulated without giving the teacher any

TABLE 13-I

MAJOR OPERATIONS IMPLEMENTED OVER SESSIONS

	Session Began	Session Ended	Procedural Label
Class 1	1	8	Base line
Class 1	9	24	Student-teacher instructions
Class 1	9	24	Telemetry equipment used
Class 1	9	24	Teacher feedback
Class 1	17	24	Bonus payoff
Class 1	21	24	Nontarget consequation
Class 2	1	8	Base line
Class 2	9	24	Student-teacher instructions
Class 2	9	24	Telemetry equipment used
Class 2	9	24	Response cost
Class 2	13	24	Bonus payoff
Class 2	17	24	Negative individual consequation
Class 3	1	8	Base line
Class 3	9	24	Student-teacher instructions
Class 3	9	24	Telemetry equipment used
Class 3	9	24	Positive reinforcement
Class 3	13	24	Bonus payoff
Class 3	17	24	Negative group consequation

information concerning the rate of occurrence of the behaviors in the various classes.

Student-teacher instructions: The teacher was reminded each day, by the observer, not to pay attention to the TCO's and attend only to HR student behavior. The teacher in turn, at the beginning of each class period, announced to the classes that he wanted the students to raise their hands if they wanted his attention.

Telemetry equipment used: The telemetry equipment was introduced to all the classes during Session 9. The teacher showed the equipment to the students, told them it was for remote signaling, and stated that the equipment was being used for research purposes in the classes. The telemetry equipment was continuously used in the classes from Session 9 till the end of the study (Session 24).

Teacher feedback: The teacher received immediate electronic feedback contingent on his response to the target student behaviors. He also received delayed feedback. The delayed feedback graphically showed the number of correct and incorrect responses, in terms of points, that he had made during the preceding class period.

Response cost: In the response cost program (Weiner, 1962), the teacher started out with a base of points and then added a point every time he attended to a hand raise and lost a point every time he attended to a call out. Here, of course, the two different telemetry signals indicated a gain or a loss of a point to the teacher. At the end of each class period the teacher was shown the number of points he had accumulated and the number of cans of beer this had earned him. There were two changes in the exchange ratio, between points and beer, made after the initial ratio had been established (Session 9). These changes occurred at Sessions 13 and 17 respectively. For each change made in the exchange ratio the teacher had to double the amount of his correct attending behavior to gain the same amount of reward.

Positive reinforcement: In this program, the teacher did not begin with any points and only earned points for attending to appropriate student behavior. The teacher was signaled for both a correct and an incorrect response but only earned points for a correct response. The way points were exchanged for beer, as well as the exchange ratio schedules, were exactly the same in this program as in the response cost procedure.

Bonus payoff: For every class period that the teacher showed a zero rate of response to TCO's he received two additional cans of beer. This procedure was implemented to stabilize extinction.

Nontarget consequation: Each student received three bonus points at the beginning of each class period. These points were placed next to the student's name on the blackboard. At the start of each class the teacher announced that every time he had to prompt a student to work on an assignment the student lost a point. This procedure was added as a control operation to determine the effect of point subtraction for a nonessential behavior on the target behavior (TCO's) itself.

Negative individual consequation: Each student received three bonus points at the beginning of each class period. These points were displayed next to the students' name on the blackboard. At the start of each class the teacher announced that every time a student emitted a TCO he would lose a point. When a student engaged in a TCO the teacher merely went to the board, erased a mark next to that student's name, then continued on with his activities as usual.

Negative group consequation: The structure of this program was similar to that of the negative individual consequation procedure. However, it differed in that any time a student emitted a TCO every member in the class lost a point. Thus, the whole class was punished for a single student's misbehavior.

There were a number of other procedures carried out that need to be considered also. The particular reinforcer chosen for the teacher, beer, was selected on the basis of the teacher's preference for it. In order to make the reinforcer effective the teacher agreed to drink only the beer that he had earned as a result of his performance in class. This was formalized by having the teacher sign a contract patterned after Pratt and Tooley (1964) which was witnessed by another teacher. This contract was signed immediately after Session 8. After the contract was signed the three programs, Teacher Feedback, Response Cost, and Positive Reinforcement, were then randomly assigned to the classes. With the exception of the daily information (via feedback and points) that the teacher received, he was not shown the cumulative performance of the classes until the end of the project.

Results

Class 1: As can be seen from Figure 13-1 during baseline TCO's occurred at a fairly high rate. The teacher in turn, attended to the TCO's at a moderate rate. Hand raising during baseline was practically nonexistent, as was teacher attention to hand raising. As feedback was provided, TACO's dropped off to zero and remained stable at this level until the end of the study. Procedural extinction for TACO's was already in effect previous to the introduction of the bonus payoffs. Therefore, it seems likely that this procedure was largely noncontributory to the extinction effects observed.

The daily announcement for students to raise their hands in conjunction with a high rate of attention to hand raising

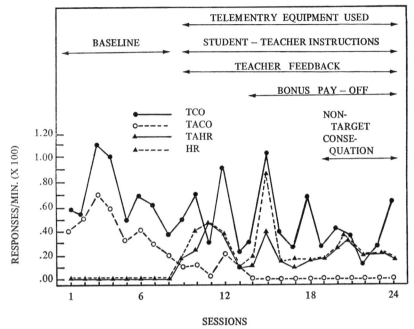

SESSIONS

Figure 13-1.   Responses per minute for Class 1.

produced short-term increases in hand raising (Sessions 9-16). This effect began to diminish during the latter part of the study, however.

A steady decrease in TCO's was noted over sessions. For the last eight sessions the average rate of responses per minute for TCO's was thirty-seven whereas during baseline it was sixty-five. However, even when complete extinction of attention to the TCO's was achieved (Sessions 13-24) there was not a corresponding cessation or rapid deceleration of the TCOs. In addition, a comparison of the last four sessions (when nontarget consequation was in effect) with the preceding four sessions indicated that punishing a nontarget behavior had little effect on the target behavior (TCO's) itself.

Class 2: During baseline (Fig. 13-2) the prominent behaviors were TCO's and TACO's. After the introduction of the Response Cost program and the Student-Teacher instructions, TACO's decelerated rapidly (Sessions 9-12). However, they were not

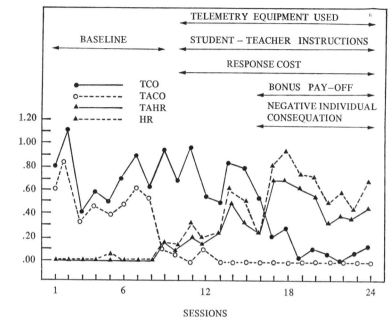

Figure 13-2.   Responses per minute for Class 2.

reliably extinguished until the bonus payoffs were added (Sessions 13-24). Thereafter, a zero rate of responding was maintained.

TCO's still remained at a fairly high rate from Sessions 9 through 12 even though the teacher's attention to the TCO's had been considerably reduced. When the teacher's attention to the TCO's was completely removed (Sessions 13-16) there was a decrease in TCO's. However, rapid deceleration of TCO's was not achieved until negative individual consequation for TCO's was introduced. At this point (Session 17), there was a complete reversal in the relative positions of TCO's and HR's, which was maintained until the end of the study. The effectiveness of negative individual consequation, as an intervention program, is exemplified by a comparison between the first and the last eight sessions in the study. Thus, the average rate in response per minute for TCO's during baseline was seventy; while during the last eight sessions it was only twelve. From Session 9 till the end of the study HR's and TAHR's showed progressive linear increases. However, the topping of TCO's by HR's occurred only after the TCO's were decelerated.

Class 3: Figure 13-3 depicts the fact that the teacher attended to a high rate of TCO's only to a very moderate extent during baseline. The rate of HR's and TAHR's was minimal again. The TACO's decelerated at a rapid rate concurrent with the introduction of the positive reinforcement program for the teacher (Sessions 9-12). However, just as for Class 2, the TACO's were not consistently eliminated until the bonus payoffs were added (Sessions 13-24).

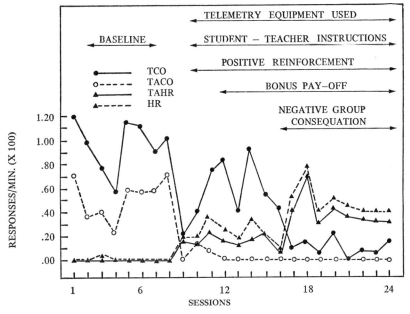

Figure 13-3.   Responses per minute for Class 3.

TCO's decreased considerably from baseline over Sessions 9 through 16. This decrease is associated with the corresponding deceleration in TACO's. Even when complete procedural extinction of the TACO's was achieved (Sessions 13-16), there was little further reduction in TCO's from their rate during the four preceding sessions when TACO's were emitted at a low but noticeable rate.

From Sessions 17 to 24, the same general behavioral pattern occurred for Class 3 that was observed for Class 2. That is, TCO's were rapidly decelerated and maintained at a low rate. This occurred while HR's and TAHR's accelerated rapidly, topped TCO's, and maintained their superiority (in terms of magnitude of effect) until the end of the study. The average rate of occurrence of TCO's for Sessions 17 to 24 was only five, while during baseline the average rate had been eighty-eight. Once again, HR's and TAHR's only became ascendant in the behavioral ecology of the classroom subsequent to the reduction of the TCO's.

Discussion

The results of the present study replicate and extend the findings of Wahler (1968, 1969) to groups. Whereas Wahler used shifts in attention coupled with time out (punishment) for individual children, the present endeavor utilized attention shifts in conjunction with negative point consequation (punishment) for both individuals and groups with essentially similar results. It has been demonstrated that negative group consequances have been effective in modifying "talking-out behavior" in elementary school children(Barrish, Saunders and Wolf, 1969). Thus, the induction of negative outcomes to groups for misbehavior appears to be an important method for changing target behaviors of an oppositional nature across elementary and secondary grade levels.

It seems that immediate feedback was about as efficient as the response cost and positive reinforcement programs in inducing the teacher to attend to the degree of hand raising present in the classes. However, a greater magnitude of effect for TAHR's was clearly evident for both the response cost and positive reinforcement program subsequent to Session 16. The introduction of bonus payoffs produced stable continuous nonattention to TCO's in Classes 2 and 3. However, the same effect was achieved in Class 1, but slightly later in time, merely by telling the teacher not to attend to TCO's and by providing feedback for his behavior.

It seems that merely telling the students to raise their hands, and having the teacher attend to this behavior somewhat frequently, considerably increased the degree of hand raising in the various classes. However appropriate behavior in the form of in the hand raising did not predominate in the classes until the inappropriate call outs were first decreased. Thus in this study no major adjustment in the behavioral ecology was achieved until the inappropriate behavior that predominated at a high rate was reduced to a behavior that occurred at a low rate.

An important principle which guided the treatment procedures was the continuous use of data, as a source, to indicate procedural change. This kind of an approach, when it is not followed, has important ramifications for remediation in the classroom. For example, a school psychologist making initial observations on TCO's and TACO's would likely advise the teacher to stop paying attention to the call outs. He would likely predicate this advice on the apparent relationship between the rates of the TCO's and those of the TACO's. However, without a data source to indicate change, extinction would be inferred to be working effectively with any small report of improvement in the classroom situation. This clearly would not have been the case in the present instance. It was shown that whatever impact extinction had, occurred early. Thereafter, extinction effects were of little practical use in rapidly diminishing the undesirable behavior further.

REFERENCES

Barrish, H. H.; Saunders, M., and Wolf, M. M.: Good behavior game: Effects of individual contingencies for group consequences on disruptive behavior in a classroom. *Journal of Applied Behavior Analysis*, 2:119-124, 1969.

Becker, W. C.; Madsen, C. H.; Arnold, R., and Thomas, D. R.: The contingent use of teacher attention and praise in reducing classroom behavior problems. *Journal of Special Education*, 1:287-307, 1967.

Hall, R. V., and Broden, M.: Behavior changes in brain-injured children through social reinforcement. *J Exp Child Psychol*, 5:463-479 ,1967.

Hall, R. V.; Lund, D., and Jackson, D.: Effects of teacher attention on study behavior. *Journal of Applied Behavior Analysis*, 1:1-12, 1968.

Madsen, C. H.; Becker, W. C., and Thomas, D. R.: Rules praise, and ignoring: Elements of elementary classroom control. *Journal of Applied Behavior Analysis*, 1:139-150, 1968.

Pratt, S., and Tooley, J.: Contract psychology and the actualizing transactional field. Special edition #1 (Theoretical aspects in research). *Int J Soc Psychiatry*, 51-69, 1964.

Thomas, D. R.; Becker, W. C., and Armstrong, M.: Production and elimination of disruptive classroom behavior by systematically varying teacher's behavior. *Journal of Applied Behavior Analysis, 1*:35-45, 1968.

Wahler, R. G.: Behavior therapy for oppositional children: Love is not enough. Paper read at Eastern Psychological Association meeting, Washington, 1968.

Wahler, R. G.: Oppositional children: A quest for parental reinforcement control. *Journal of Applied Behavior Analysis, 2*:159-170, 1969.

Wahler, H.: Some effects of response cost upon human operant behavior. *J Exp Anal Behav, 5*:201-208, 1962.

Zimmerman, E. H., and Zimmerman, J.: The alteration of behavior in a special classroom situation. *J Exp Anal Behav, 3*:59-60, 1962.

Chapter 14

THE EFFECTS OF EXPERIMENTER'S INSTRUCTIONS, FEEDBACK, AND PRAISE ON TEACHER PRAISE AND STUDENT ATTENDING BEHAVIOR

ACE COSSAIRT, R. VANCE HALL, AND B. L. HOPKINS

From the *Journal of Applied Behavior Analysis,* 6:89-100, 1973.
Systematic use of experimenter's instructions, feedback, and feedback plus social praise was used to increase teacher praise for student attending behavior of three elementary school teachers. Experimenter's verbal interactions with teachers, teacher's verbal praise for student behaviors, and pupil-attending behavior were recorded during baseline conditions. As the three successive experimental conditions were introduced first with Teacher A, then with Teacher B, in a multiple baseline design, behaviors of the experimenter, the two teachers, and eight students were measured and recorded. In the cases of Teachers A and B, experimental condition one (Instructions) and experimental condition two (Feedback) produced inconclusive results. Experimental condition three (Feedback Plus Social Praise) produced more teacher praise for student attending behavior. The entire "Package" of Experimenter's Instructions, Feedback, and Feedback Plus Social Praise was introduced

The research was carried out as part of the Juniper Gardens Children's Project, a program of research on the development of culturally deprived children, and was partially supported by the National Institute of Child Health and Human Developmnet, Bureau of Child Research and Department of Human Development, University of Kansas (Grant HD 03 144-04). This research was also supported in part by a grant from the United States Office of Education under the Education Professions Development Act, University of Kansas "T.T.T." program within the Department of Human Development and Family Life, and is identified as an Early Childhood Project, Training Teachers in Behavior Modification.

to Teacher C in a single experimental condition. As in the cases of Teachers A and B, behaviors measured were (1) the experimenter's verbal interactions, (2) the teacher's praise of students, and (3) the student's attending behavior. Introduction of the "Package" also produced more teacher praise for student attending behavior.

A NUMBER OF RECENT studies have investigated the effects of contingent teacher attention on various student behaviors, i.e. attending, instruction following, verbal, and disruptive behavior in the public school classroom (Hall, Lund and Jackson, 1968; Hall, Panyan, Rabon and Broden, 1968; Shutte and Hopkins, 1970; Thomas, Becker and Armstrong, 1968). Results of these studies demonstrate teacher attention in most cases is an inexpensive and effective modifier of student behaviors. While these studies show that contingent teacher attention is effective, few studies have examined procedures for modifying this important teacher behavior. Cooper, Thomson and Baer (1970), used a consistent training procedure to modify teacher attending in preschool settings.

Formal instruction in classroom management procedures has resulted in teachers effectively using contingent teacher attention and carrying out studies with themselves as the observer-experimenter (Hall, Fox, Willard, Goldsmith, Emerson, Owen, Davis and Porcia, 1971).

Articles published by classroom teachers enrolled in a university course on management of classroom behavior (Hall, Cristler, Cranston and Tucker, 1970) demonstrate that formal instruction in operant methods of classroom management, measurement, and application has proved to be an effective way to modify teacher behavior. However, many teachers have no access to such classes.

Principals, teacher supervisors, school psychologists, and consultants often use instructions and demonstrations in attempts to change teacher behavior, sometimes without effect (Hall, et al., 1968). O'Leary, Becker, Evans and Saudargas (1969) used feedback plus social reinforcement of a teacher to ensure that experimental instructions to teachers were carried out. The present study examined the effectiveness of systematic use of instructions, feedback, and a combination of social praise and feedback in increasing teacher praise for student attending behavior; approaches that lend themselves to use by educators responsible for supervising and helping teachers.

The major purpose of this experiment was to study the causal factors in increasing teacher praise by measuring and recording behaviors of all concerned, including the often omitted experimenter's verbal interaction with the teacher. This study featured an examination of the complete chain of behaviors from experimenter through teacher through student.

The basic paradigm of design for this study was the multiple baseline (Baer, Wolf and Risley, 1968) utilizing multiple subjects (teachers). After concurrent baselines of behaviors were recorded, three experimental conditions that included instructions, feedback, and feedback plus social reinforcement were introduced to Teachers A and B at different points in time, providing a means for component analysis within this study.

Procedure

Subjects and Setting

This study was carried out in two elementary schools in a low socioeconomic area of Kansas City, Kansas. Two fourth-grade teachers and one third-grade teacher participated in this study. Teacher A had four years teaching experience, teacher B had two years experience, and teacher C had three years of classroom teaching experience. The three teachers had no knowledge of experimental conditions or hypotheses before these conditions were implemented. All three teachers were effective in controlling their classes and little disruptive behavior occurred in their classrooms as this study was carried out.

Each teacher selected four students of low attending and instruction-following behavior. These students were seated at the same table in the classroom to enable more reliable observation of their behavior. Target students selected for this study included five boys and seven girls.

Experimental Procedures

Data were recorded twice daily as students alternately worked one of two specially prepared math sheets. Each math sheet consisted of five rows of four simple addition and subtraction problems without signs. The problems on the two math sheets remained constant throughout the experiment. General instructions for each math sheet were as follows: "Please, look at me during instructions, keep covers closed when not working problems and use signs on all problems that you work." The specific instructions were changed on each sheet. The teachers read the specific instructions aloud for each row to the class. An example of the specific instructions given is, "Add the first problem, subtract the second problem, leave out the third problem, add the fourth problem, begin." The students then opened their folders and followed the instructions for the first row of problems and closed their folders as they finished. Similar instructions were given for each of the five rows on the math sheet. These math sessions were approximately fifteen minutes in length. Observational data on student attending behavior were taken only during teacher's specific instructions.

One minute of postinstruction time was allowed for the students to work each row of problems. During this post-instruction interval, any comments by the teacher were recorded by the observer. A "+" was recorded for verbal teacher praise for attending. A "1" was recorded for verbal teacher attention for nonattending, and a "0" was recorded for no verbal comment from the teacher. Teacher praise for attending behavior was defined as any positive or praise statement about student attending behaivor. Examples are as follows: (1) "I like the way John is paying attention," (2) "The whole class is doing an excellent job of listening today," (3) "I see Jane is paying attention," and (4) "John and Bill are paying attention today." Teacher attention to nonattending behavior was defined as any (1) verbalization requesting, demanding, or commanding attention, (2) reprimanding for nonattending or disruptive behaviors; e.g. requests or commands, such as "Sit down," "Look here," "Be quiet," "Put your book away," and "You are not paying attention, Jane!" Disruptive behaviors were defined as any behavior that competed or interfered with work on the math sheet or with attending to the teacher during instruction. Talking, whistling, singing, throwing things, making physical contact with other students, and leaving seats during instructions were considered disruptive behaviors. Teacher statements directed toward herself, the observer, the experimenter, and nonmembers of the classroom, as well as any other statements not directed toward class members, were recorded as no verbal comment.

Student attending was defined as student's head and eyes oriented toward teacher for the duration of instruction. The percent of intervals students attended the teacher was computed by dividing the total intervals that students attended to the teacher by the total number possible. The number of intervals of teacher praise for student attending and for nonattending was recorded and graphed as totals and not percentages. During the series of four instructions given per row of problems, the four target students were observed one by one in a clockwise sweep of their table. Each target student was observed for the duration of one instruction. The observation of the first student coincided with the duration of the first instruction, observation of the second student with the second instruction, of the third student with the third instruction, and of the fourth student with the fourth instruction. This method produced good reliability of observation in that both observers were cued by the instructions to look at the same student simultaneously.

During each postinstruction minute, teacher's statements praising student attending behavior were recorded, along with teacher's statements concerning student nonattending behavior. This was done by using observational recording sheets that had a row of squares where intervals of student attending behavior were recorded and a corresponding grid of squares for teacher attention to target students. In addition to the double row of squares provided for each target student, a single row of squares was used to record teacher attention to the class. Due to difficulty in recording these complex multiple statements, reported data indicate only the number of intervals that contained teacher praise for attending, or verbal attention for nonattending, as per the original design.

A second observer periodically made a simultaneous observational record during each phase of the experiment using an identical score sheet. Agreements were based on whether or not intervals contained praise. Percent of agreement of intervals containing praise or attention between observers was computed with the following formula: intervals of agreement divided by intervals of nonagreement plus intervals of agreement times 100.

The experimenter had a postsession conference with the teacher after each session throughout the experiment. The experimenter recorded each postsession conference with the teacher, using a cassette tape recorder. Tapes were played back and the durations of these postsession conferences were recorded, as well as the number of the experimenter's positive comments for teacher praise, on a second recording sheet. The experimenter purposely made separate and complete sentences to facilitate a reliable count of contingent praise statements to teachers.

The experimenter's social praise for teacher praise was defined as any positive any contingent statement about the teacher's use of teacher praise to student attending. Examples of the experimenter's contingent praise statement are (1) "You had the whole class attending to you, Mrs. A.," (2) "John was really responding to your attention, Miss B.," (3) "You certainly have the ability to hold their attention with your praise," (4) "Your praise is powerful. The target students really respond to you."

To determine the extent to which taped data were reliably transferred from tapes to recording sheets, a second observer independently listened to the tape and periodically recorded the duration of the experimenter-teacher conference, along with the number of praise statements by the experimenter, on an identical recording sheet. This was done in each phase of the experiment. Percent of agreements was computed as the number of agreements divided by the number of agreements plus disagreements times 100.

Reliabilities were taken in each phase of the experiment on teacher praise, intervals of student attending, and experimenter's praise. Reliability was checked thirty-four times in Teacher A's classroom, and thirty-three times in Teacher B's classroom. Reliability ranged from 80 percent to 100 percent. The 80 percent reliability was recorded only once during the experiment, and the means of all reliabilities taken was 93 percent.

Experimental Conditions

Baseline Conditions: Baseline conditions for all three teachers consisted of recording: (1) percent of intervals that students attended to the teacher, (2) number of intervals of teacher praise for student attending, and (3) number of intervals of teacher attention to nonattending, as the teacher read the instructions for each math sheet. This was done to determine objectively the operant levels of each of the previously named behaviors before instituting experimental conditions. Baselines for Teachers A and B ran concurrently for the first ten sessions. In Session 11, Teacher A was introduced to condition one (Instructions Condition). Teacher B's baseline was twenty sessions long.

Instructions: The instructions condition consisted of three parts: (1) a brief explanation that positive teacher attention contingently applied is effective in changing student behaviors, (2) instructions to give teacher praise to students who attended teacher instructions, (3) a type-written message reminding the teacher that, "teacher praise for attending instructions sometimes increases instruction-attending behavior." This message was included on each instruction sheet used by the teachers during the instructions condition, whereas, parts one and two were antecedents to the first session of the instructions condition and were presented only once. The instructions condition was in effect with Teach A for Sessions 11 through 28, for a total of eighteen sessions. A substitute teacher replaced Teacher A for Sessions 21 through 26. The substitute was given the same explanation and instructions for the instructions condition that were given to Teacher A. The instructions condition was in effect for Teacher B for Sessions 21 through 36 for a total of sixteen sessions.

Feedback Condition: During the feedback condition, Teachers A and B were given verbal feedback at the end of each session. This feedback consisted of the experimenter telling the teacher the number of intervals during which the students attended her instructions and the number of intervals of teacher praise for student-attending behavior. The feedback condition was in effect for Teacher A during Sessions 29 through 36 for a total of eight sessions. It was in effect with Teacher B during Sessions 37 through 44, also for a total of eight sessions.

Feedback Plus Social Praise Conditions: In this phase, the teachers were given social praise for their praise of student behavior, along with a verbal report of the number of intervals of student attending and the number of intervals of teacher praise. The feedback plus social praise condition for Teacher A was in effect during Sessions 37 through 60 for a total of twenty-three sessions. For Teacher B, it was in effect during Sessions 45 through 60 for a total of fifteen sessions. Both teachers received feedback and social praise during each postsession conference with the experimenter for the first eight sessions of their respective feedback plus social praise conditions. Beginning with Session 9 of this phase, they received only intermittent feedback and social praise for the remainder of the experiment. Thus, Teacher A was put on an intermittent schedule of feedback plus social praise beginning with Session 45 and this intermittent schedule was in force through Session 60. Teacher B's intermittent schedule of reinforcement began with Session 53 and continued through Session 60.

Baseline Condition, Teacher C: Teacher C's baseline was ten sessions long and was carried out using the same procedures as were used with Teachers A and B.

"Package" Condition, Teacher C: All experimental conditions were introduced simultaneously to Teach C as a "package." This "package" condition included instructions, feedback, and social praise plus feedback similar to the conditions introduced separately to Teachers A and B. It was ten sessions in length and included Sessions 11 through 20.

Results

Graphic records of behaviors of Teachers A and B, their target students, and the experimenter are shown in Figure 14-1. Teacher C's praising behavior, the student's behavior, and the experimenter's behavior are shown in Figure 14-2.

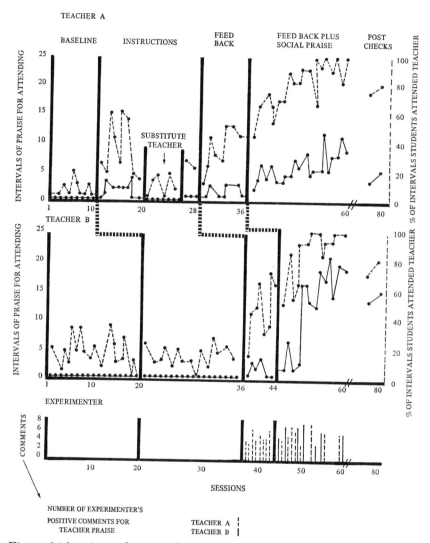

Figure 14-1. A graphic record of praising behavior of Teachers A and B, the percent of students attending each teacher, and the number of experimenter's positive comments for teacher praise.

During baseline, the mean percent of students attending Teacher A was 7 percent, the mean percent of students attending Teacher B during baseline was 16 percent. Neither Teacher A nor B gave any teacher praise for appropriate attending during baseline conditions. The experimenter deliberately did not comment on teacher attention during baseline nor in the first two experimental conditions. After the instructions condition was introduced, Teacher A's rate of positive attention to student attending rose from 0 to a mean of 1.4 intervals for twelve sessions of the instructions condition. The mean percent of intervals students attended Teacher A during the instructions condition increased to a mean of 31 percent from the baseline mean of 7 percent. Graphed data on Figure 14-1 include substitute teacher data, her praise for the student attending, and student attending percentages. All reported means exclude these data and are based on the twelve sessions that Teacher A was present in the classroom. As shown in Figure 14-1, Teacher B's baseline rate of teacher praise for student attending, along with the percent of student attending to her, remained stable through Session 20. The introduction to the instructions condition to Teacher A initially produced teacher praise for student attending. Coinciding with increased teacher praise were higher percentages of intervals in which students attended teacher not noted during concurrent Sessions 10 through 20 of Teacher B's baseline. Instructions to Teacher B produced no significant changes in Teacher B's behavior. Teacher praise for student attending remained at 0 throughout the sixteen sessions of the instructions condition. Intervals of student attending increased from a mean percent of 31 during baseline to a mean percent of 36 during the instructions condition.

The feedback condition showed a decrease in the mean rate of Teacher A's praise from the instructions condition, as noted in Table 14-1. The institution of the feedback condition to Teacher B initially produced teacher praise for attending, which had previously remained at 0 through the baseline and instructions conditions. The mean rate of this behavior was one instance of teacher praise per session for the eight sessions of feedback condition. Intervals of student attending increased to a mean of 47 percent in Teacher B's feedback condition.

Feedback plus social praise resulted in an immediate increase in Teacher A's praise for student attending. Teacher A's mean

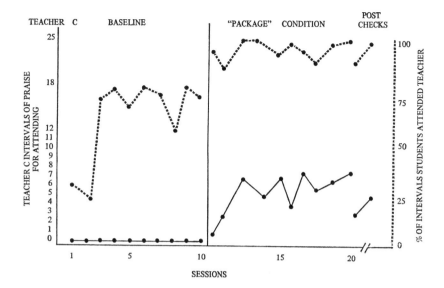

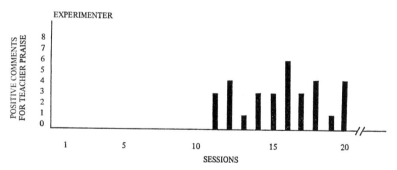

Figure 14-2. A graphic record of praising behavior of Teacher C, the percent of students attending Teacher C, and the number of experimenter's positive comments for teacher praise.

number of intervals of teacher praise rose to five per session during this phase, and intervals of student attending behavior increased from a mean percent of 36 per session in the feedback condition to a mean of 85 percent. The experimenter's mean number of positive comments for teacher praise was 2.6 per postsession conference with Teacher A.

Feedback plus social praise resulted in an increase in Teacher B's praise from a mean of one per session during the feedback condition to a mean of 14.5 per session. The mean percent of intervals students attended to Teacher B increased from 47 percent per session during the feedback condition to 86 percent during the feedback plus social praise condition. The mean

TABLE 14-I

MEANS OF ALL PHASES

Conditions	Number of Experimenter's Positive Comments for Teacher Praise of Teacher Attending Behavior	Number of Intervals of Teacher Praise for Attending Behavior	Percent of Intervals Students Attended Teacher	Number of Intervals of Teacher Attention to Non-Attending Student Behavior
		Teacher A		
Baseline	0.0	0.0	7	0.3
Experimental Condition 1: Instructions	0.0	1.	31	0.6
Experimental Condition 2: Feedback	0.0	0.7	36	0.4
Experimental Condition 3: Feedback + Praise	2.6	5.0	85	0.8
		Teacher B		
Baseline	0.0	0.0	16	0.5
Experimental Condition 1: Instructions	0.0	0.0	11	0.8
Experimental Condition 2: Feedback	0.0	1.0	47	0.8
Experimental Condition 3: Feedback + Praise	2.1	14.5	86	0.2
		Teacher C		
Baseline	0.0	0.0	62	0.9
Experimental Condition 1: "Package"	3.0	5.0	94	0.4

number of the experimenter's positive comments for teacher praise was 2.1 per session.

Teacher C Results

Teacher C's baseline rate of praise was zero, which was identical to the rates of praise by Teachers A and B during their baselines. As in the case of Teachers A and B, the experimenter made no comments about teacher attention during baseline. The mean percent of intervals students attended Teacher C was 62 percent during the baseline sessions. Introduction of the "package" condition of instructions and feedback plus social praise resulted in an increase in teacher praise from zero during baseline to a mean of five times per session during the "package" condition. Intervals of student attending behavior rose during this phase from the baseline mean of 62 percent to a mean of mean number of intervals students attended Teacher A during 94 percent. The experimenter averaged three positive comments for teacher praise per session.

Results of permanent product data (specific instructions followed and correct answers to problems) for all three teachers are shown in Table 14-III.

Postchecks, Teachers A and B

Two postchecks were taken in Teacher A's and Teacher B's classrooms three weeks after termination of continuous observation. The postchecks revealed a decrease in teacher praise for student attending behavior from previous high rates of praise reached by teachers in the later sessions of the feedback plus social praise condition. Teacher A's average praise in two postcheck sessions was 3.5 compared to a mean of five instances per session for all of the prior phase, and the mean of Teacher B's praise in the two postchecks was 13 compared to 14.5. The postchecks one and two was 80 percent; for Teacher B the mean number was 75 percent during postcheck one and 85 percent during postcheck two.

Postchecks, Teach C

Postchecks made two weeks after continuous observation of Teacher C was terminated, produced the following means:

teacher praise, four per session; percent of intervals students attended teacher, 97; thus, it was indicated that high rates of teacher praise and intervals of student attending were being maintained.

Individual Results

The mean percentages of intervals individual students attended teachers per session are shown in Table 14-II. The mean percentages were obtained by dividing the number of intervals in which the students attended the teacher per condition by the total number of intervals possible.

TABLE 14-II

MEAN PERCENT OF INTERVALS STUDENTS ATTENDED TEACHERS
PER SESSION WITHIN EACH CONDITION

Subject	Baseline	Instructions Condition	Feedback Condition	Feedback + Contingent Praise Condition
		Teacher A		
AN	16	40	24	90
PA	10	34	55	88
BR	2	30	31	84
TY	0.4	20	34	78
		Teacher B		
HE	40	10	54	96
LE	28	22	37	83
AL	6	4	17	81
CB	22	8	75	84
		Teacher C		
Subject	Baseline	"Package" Condition		
CU	78	98		
AT	76	98		
TR	46	92		
KE	47.5	88		

These individual mean percentages are generally qualitatively consistent with the group data (see Table 14-I). Three of the four students in Teacher A's classroom showed gains in the percent of intervals they attended with each new condition. Student A. N. displayed a decrease in the percent of intervals she attended during feedback condition.

Students H. E., A. L., C. B., and D. E., in Teacher B's classroom, showed decreases in the percent of intervals they attended from baseline to instruction condition. All four students then displayed concurrent increases in percent of intervals they attended during feedback condition and further increases during feedback plus social praise condition.

All of Teacher C's students clearly revealed higher percentages of intervals of attending from baseline to "package" condition.

Permanent Product Data

Permanent product data in the form of the number of specific instructions followed (correct signs used on math sheets) was compiled daily, and the number of correct answers to the math problems was also recorded. These data were maintained on the target students throughout the experiment. The students' mean permanent product data for each phase of the experiment are shown in Table 14-III.

Individual permanent product means generally increased throughout experimental conditions. All subjects made gains from baseline to instructions condition. There were seven cases in which means decreased from that of a preceding condition. (These decreases are noted with asterisks in Table 14-III.)

Discussion

A major challenge facing principals, teacher trainers, and consultants today is how effectively to promote teacher proficiency to keep pace with the vast and rapidly expanding requirements of the school and postschool environments. Principals are in many cases given much administrative training dealing with school finance and with school plant development and management. Too often, little emphasis is placed on behavioral sciences that would aid them in cultivating adept, effective teachers. The primary role of the principal has been stated to be advancement of the educational processes through guiding his staff members to more skillful performance in their classrooms (Ulich, 1961). In more specific terms, the principal must effect positive changes in the teacher's teaching behavior in the classroom so that teachers can in turn initiate and maintain positive changes in student behaviors.

TABLE 14-III

INDIVIDUAL PERMANENT PRODUCT MEANS OF INSTRUCTIONS
FOLLOWED (IF) AND PROBLEMS CORRECT
(PC) PER CONDITION

Subject		Baseline	Condition 1	Condition 2	Condition 3
			Teacher A		
AN	IF	5.5	9.9	14.3	17.8
	PC	2.5	8.1	12.8	16.8
PA	IF	6.3	8.8	11.4	11.4
	PC	3.6	5.5	9.3	7.7*
BR	IF	7.3	9.9	7.0*	9.2*
	PC	4.3	7.3	5.0*	6.8
TY	IF	12.4	13.8	14.8	14.8
	PC	9.7	12.8	13.8	14.2
			Teacher B		
HE	IF	14.2	17.8	19.1	18.9*
	PC	11.7	15.8	17.3	17.6
DE	IF	12.9	17.5	19.2	19.4
	PC	8.3	15.3	17.5	19.1
AL	IF	16.2	19.0	20.0	19.4
	PC	15.8	18.8	19.7	19.1*
CB	IF	4.1	6.2	6.8	10.8
	PC	2.6	5.1	4.6*	5.8

			Teacher C		
Subject		Baseline		"Package" Condition	
CU	IF	13.2		16.7	
	PC	12.6		15.7	
AT	IF	12.5		18.4	
	PC	12.4		15.7	
TR	IF	10.4		16.5	
	PC	10.1		15.5	
KE	IF	2.3		14.3	
	PC	1.8		11.8	

* Decrease from a previous condition.

Component analysis of three common modes that principals and consultants might use to effect such behavior changes in teachers were examined in this study. As shown in Figure 14-1, the data indicated that instructions (antecedents) produced inconclusive results in increasing teacher praise in that Teacher A was under the experimenter's instructional control and Teacher B was not. Also, even though Teacher A initiated teacher praise, this behavior change was not durable. What occurred in the instructions condition of this experiment may be what happens when teachers receive instructions from principals and consultants who are attempting to change teacher behavior with infrequent visits to the classroom. Further research is needed in that the question of how effective instructions are in changing teacher behavior remains unanswered.

The feedback condition data shown in Figure 14-1 indicates that feedback preceded by instructions may or may not be effective in increasing teacher praise. In the case of Teacher A, the feedback condition produced less teacher praise than did instructions. Teacher B did initiate teacher praise during the feedback condition, but it was not durable in that teacher praise quickly dropped back to zero after only four sesions. As in the case of instructions (an antecedent manipulation), feedback (a consequence manipulation) produced inconclusive results that call for further research.

It was noted that the percent of intervals students attended teachers A and B trended upward through feedback conditions. Ideally, it would have been better to allow both of these dependent variables, teacher praise and student attending, to stabilize before instituting the final condition. However, there were two reasons for instituting feedback plus contingent praise: (1) teacher praise, the major dependent variable, had stabilized, and (2) feedback preceded by the instructions condition without the experimenter's social praise appeared to be aversive to the teachers. Rather than lose cooperation of the teacher or explain the hypothesis of the experiment, which in either case would have terminated the study, the final condition of feedback plus social praise after eight sessions of feedback condition was initiated.

The final condition for Teachers A and B, and the "package" condition for Teacher C, combined feedback and social praise for teacher praise of pupil attending behavior. The increased rates of praise by all three teachers suggest that social praise is a necessary ingredient in changing teacher praise behavior. As shown with Teachers A and B, feedback plus social praise, when preceded by instructions and feedback, effects significant changes in teacher praise. In the case of Teacher C, in which the "package" condition of instructions, feedback, and social praise was introduced as a unit, significant increases in teacher praise were noted.

Data recorded on teacher attention to nonattending student behavior showed that no significant change occurred throughout the study (see Table 14-I).

The results of the permanent product data (specific instructions followed and problems correct on math sheets) for Teachers A and B showed that little significant change took place during the experiment other than a slightly ascending trend (see Table 14-3). This upward trend might be attributed to daily practice. Permanent product data on Teacher C's target students indicated an increase over baseline during "package" condition, but close scrutiny through future research is needed before concrete conclusions can be reached.

It should be noted that intervals of student attending behavior increased with the introduction of teacher praise. Higher means of intervals of teacher praise within conditions generally coincided with higher means of the percent of intervals students attended teacher. These data tend to support the findings of Broden, Bruce, Mitchell, Carter, and Hall (1970). Data on intervals of student attending completed the chain that began with the experimenter and ended with the student, thus indicating that student's behavior was indirectly (through a mediator) sensitive to the experimenter's behavior.

A notable aspect of the study was that teacher praise maintained and even increased when teachers were placed on an intermittent schedule of social praise. This would seem to indicate that the excuse that principals and supportive staff do not have time for the social reinforcement of teacher behavior is invalid. Operant principles of reinforcement systematically applied would, therefore, seem to be functional in helping principals and consultants accomplish their primary goal, which should be improving instruction. It would also seem that this could be done with a minimal amount of time and effort.

REFERENCES

Baer, D. M.; Wolf, M. M., and Risley, T. R.: Some current dimensions of applied behavior analysis. *Journal of Applied Behavior Analysis, 1*:91-97, 1968.

Broden, M.; Bruce, C.; Mitchell, M. A.; Carter, V., and Hall, R. V.: Effects of teacher attention on attending behavior of two boys at adjacent desks. *Journal of Applied Behavior Analysis, 3*:199-203, 1971.

Cooper, M. L.; Thomson, C. L., and Baer, D. M.: The experimental modification of teacher attending behavior. *Journal of Applied Behavior Analysis, 3*:153-157, 1970.

Hall, R. V.; Cristler, C.; Cranston, S., and Tucker, B.: Teachers and parents as researchers using multiple baseline designs. *Journal of Applied Behavior Analysis, 3*:247-255, 1970.

Hall, R. V.; Fox, R.; Willard, D.; Goldsmith, L.; Emerson, M.; Owen, M.; Davis, F., and Porcia, E.: The teacher as observer and experimenter in the modification of disputing and talking-out behaviors. *Journal of Applied Behavior Analysis, 4*:141-149, 1971.

Hall, R. V.; Lund, D., and Jackson, D.: Effects of teacher attention on study behavior. *Journal of Applied Behavior Analysis, 1*:1-22, 1968.

Hall, R. V.; Panyan, M.; Rabon, D., and Broden, M.: Instructing beginning teachers in reinforcement procedures which improve classroom control. *Journal of Applied Behavior Analysis, 1*:315-322, 1968.

O'Leary, K. D.; Becker, W. C.; Evans, M. B., and Saudargas, R. A.: A token reinforcement program in a public school: a replication and systematic analysis. *Journal of Applied Behavior Analysis, 2*:3-14, 1969.

Shutte, R. C., and Hopkins, B. L.: The effects of teacher attention on following instructions in a kindergarten class. *Journal of Applied Behavior Analysis, 3*:117-122, 1970.

Thomas, D. R.; Becker, W. C., and Armstrong, M.: Production and elimination of disruptive classroom behavior by systematically varying teacher's behavior. *Journal of Applied Behavior Analysis, 1*:35-45, 1968.

Ulich, R.: *Philosophy of Education.* New York, American Book Company, 1961.

> Section IV

MENTAL HEALTH CONSULTATION

T HE THIRD TYPE of school consultation presented in this book is mental health consultation, a technique which provides direct service to the teacher rather than the student. Mental health consultation is based, in part, on the principle that factors in the classroom environment are important in the development of classroom problems. Since the teacher is an important part of the classroom environment, changes in teachers will be one important way to produce changes in students. Therefore, school, psychological services programs should focus on teachers' feelings and attitudes about teaching rather than being restricted to individual cases. Mental health consultation can be distinguished from the psycho-educational diagnostic approach and from the behavior modification approach in that the primary goal is to change the teacher's behavior rather than the child's behavior.

Changing the child would be a secondary rather than a primary goal. However, similar to the behavior modification approach, indirect service would be provided to the child since it would still be assumed that the teacher will act as the change agent for the children subsequent to the mental health consultation. On the other hand, the indirect service which the child might receive as a result of mental health consultation would be quite different from that which would result from behavior modification. Rather than implementing specific program recommendations (e.g. behavior modification programs), the teacher might respond to the child with new attitudes or feelings as a result of mental health consultation. For example, after mental

181

health consultation the teacher might become less anxious and more objective in response to classroom problems.

The primary methods employed in mental health consultation are derived from and/or relate to Gerald Caplan's (1970), "consultee-centered-case-consultation." Briefly, sophisticated, diagnostic interviewing techniques would be used by the consultant to determine whether the problem was relevant to any of the four categories of consultee-centered-case-consultation: lack of understanding, lack of skill, lack of self-confidence, or lack of objectivity. The consultant would then use intervention techniques, with the teacher (e.g. decrease anxiety, theme interference reduction, etc.) which would be developed in relation to the problem category.

Caplan's work is given singular emphasis in this book because of the broad influence which his work has had. However, there have been several other important influences in this field. For example, Seymour Sarason (Sarason, Levine, Goldenberg, Cherlin and Bennet, 1966) and Ruth Newman (1967) have each written accounts of school, mental health consultation programs which were established in different cities. In addition, Berlin's work has had some influence, and his position is presented in this book in order to contrast it to Caplan.

One newer approach to mental health consultation will soon be gaining prominence because of the specific skills which can be easily communicated to other psychologists. This relates to the technique which Hyman (in press) has labeled "teacher training," and it includes the use of video-tape or personal observation by the consultant. An observation scale is used which allows the consultant and teacher to examine and consider changing the teacher's style of interaction with students. An example of this new approach was not included since there were no published accounts located in a review of relevant journals.

An examination of the papers presented in this section reveals two important weaknesses with the mental health consultation approach. First, there are not enough clear descriptions of procedures of mental health consultation which could be readily implemented by practicing school consultants. Second, the research in mental health consultation is only beginning to emerge, and greater sophistication of related research techniques is needed.

Mental health consultation can be conceptualized in terms of two distinct approaches. The consultant can work with one teacher in individual mental health consultation, or the consultant can work with groups of teachers in group, mental health consultation. The papers presented in this section can be considered in terms of these two methods.

The first chapter, by Parker, evolved from experiences in group consultation. However, the principles derived from this experience are important for any mental health consultant, and these principles are part of the rationale for each paper in this section. The important point made by Parker is that the mental health consultant should help teachers to express and clarify their feelings. She develops this idea by stressing the important role which anger plays in teaching, and she describes some consultation goals in dealing with teachers' anger. In addition, Parker attempts to categorize problems which have their origin in the personal conflicts of teachers. This categorization provides a framework which can help consultants to understand teachers.

The next three papers were chosen primarily because of their attention to individual mental health consultation. The second and third chapters, provide two different theoretical frameworks for individual consultation, and each can be applied to the examples which follow. The second, by Fine and Tyler, presents Caplan's framework for use in school consultation, and they define the four categories of consultee-centered-case-consultation. Berlin's chapter is third, and he accomplishes two important goals. First, he presents the argument that mental health consultation is an efficient use of limited professional manpower; second, Berlin delineates the types of help which a consultant can offer along with specific steps of consultation.

In the fourth chapter, McGehearty discusses an example of individual mental health consultation in terms of Caplan's theory. In this case, lack of teacher objectivity (1 of Caplan's 4 categories) was part of the teacher's problem. The consultant used "messages" to help increase the teacher's objective approach in dealing effectively with this problem.

The next two chapters presented involve group approaches to mental health consultation, and the fifth chapter, by Altrocchi, Spielberger and Eisdorfer, presents a theoretical framework which forms the basis for the examples which follow. This paper attempts to define the phases, the roles and the techniques of group consultation. In addition, it was selected because of its contrasts with Caplan.

The sixth chapter by Winicki, describes an example of group, mental health consultation. He presents a didactically oriented, case conference approach. Although the teachers' feelings and attitudes were also important, this part of the consultation developed gradually with minimal resistance. Winicki's article is an approach to group consultation which developed from Caplan's theoretical frame of reference.

The final article presented in this section is a research study in which consultees' perceptions were used to evaluate consultation. This study is one of the better examples of research which is beginning to appear. It exemplifies a weakness of research in mental health consultation in that directly observable behavior is not used as a criterion of consultation outcome.

REFERENCES

Caplan, G.: *The Theory and Practice of Mental Health Consultation*. New York, Basic, 1970.

Newman, R. G.: *Psychological Consultation in the Schools*. New York, Basic, 1967.

Sarason, S. B.; Levine, M.; Goldenberg, I. I.; Cherlin, D. L., and Bennet, E. M.: *Psychology in Community Settings*. New York, Wiley, 1966.

Chapter 15

SOME OBSERVATIONS ON PSYCHIATRIC CONSULTATION WITH NURSERY SCHOOL TEACHERS

BEULAH PARKER

IT HAS BECOME increasingly common for community agencies of various sorts to recognize a need for consultation from psychiatrists and trained clinical workers in such related professions as psychology and social work.

Personnel engaged in such professions as the ministry, nursing, and teaching, giving direct service to groups of people, are confronted with a need to recognize abnormal behavior as well as to understand normal human motivation and patterns of emotional expression. Often, however, psychological awareness has received little stress in the curricula of their professional training.

Inservice education or psychologically oriented consultation in connection with practical problems encountered on the job may be used to supplement professional training and greatly increase the effectiveness of workers who are dealing in one way or another with the problems of other people.

In each type of profession, the nature of the work tends to attract individuals who, despite many dissimilarities, may share certain personality characteristics. The type of work itself may also engender specific attitudes and arouse anxieties common to many members of the group, regardless of the personal characteristics or neurotic conflicts of any individual member.

From *Mental Hygiene, 46*:559-566, 1962.

Consultation serves an important function by identifying the ways in which such shared attitudes or anxieties are interfering with the professional functioning of group members.

Individuals in the group may be relieved of anxiety, and may actually achieve considerable insight into their own sources of conflict through improved awareness of reactions common to the group as a whole. Whereas focus on the conflicts of any individual may be extremely damaging to the morale of the group as a whole, a group can almost always accept insight into shared reactions. Consultation focused on problems common to a particular type of group may, therefore, have therapeutic effects upon an individual member of the group, without directly attacking his personal resistances or ego defenses.

Workers trained in psychiatric principles and therapeutic techniques can best act as consultants to a nonpsychiatrically trained professional group if they first familiarize themselves with the attitudes and anxieties specifically related to the work and training of that group and the milieu in which that work takes place.

In previous publications the author has touched upon some of the commonly shared problems of public health nurses and public school teachers (Parker, 1958; 1961). This paper will discuss ideas and feelings frequently encountered in diverse groups of nursery school teachers who were consulted in weekly interviews over a ten-year period. An attempt will be made to clarify the sources and effects of such ideas, and to indicate ways in which a consultant may deal with them in order to prevent their interference with effective functioning of the teachers.

In the vast majority of topics raised by nursery school teachers, ten ideas appeared prominently and seemed to be generally shared.

1. It is unprofessional for a teacher to become angry at a child or his parent(s).
2. If you understand a problem, you should be able to solve it.
3. "Permissiveness" is good, "Authoritarianism" is bad (or vice versa).

4. A really good teacher never dislikes a child.
5. A teacher should be able to help all children who show an obvious need.
6. A prime goal of nursery school is to help all children become "integrated with the group."
7. It is an important part of the teacher's job to help parents develop "healthy relationships" with their children. To do so, the teacher's role is one of counseling with mothers and understanding their personal problems.
8. Disturbed parents and/or family relationships produce disturbed children invariably.
9. Or, a disturbed child will inevitably be found to have a disturbed family.
10. If a teacher does feel anger, dislike, or any other undesirable feeling he must at least control any recognizable expression of that feeling.

Some of these ideas are entirely erroneous, and some are true under certain conditions but not under others. Some of these ideas set up stereotypes which make it difficult for teachers to use their trained perception of observable behavior in order to make a correct evaluation of individual situations. These ideas are involved in many of the conflicts that impede the ability of teachers to deal adequately with the problems of children and parents in their schools.

In a large number of the situations with which nursery school teachers were having difficulty, there was evidence of guilt among the teachers for having feelings that, although perfectly normal and understandable, they felt they should *not* be having. Frequently this guilt made them feel they should act in such a way as to hide or counteract these feelings. Whenever they did so, they became uneasy and lost objectivity toward the problem. In the vast majority of cases they had all the knowledge necessary to handle the problem successfully, but they were unable to use it effectively because of their guilt.

The author will attempt to indicate some of the ways in which these ideas create difficulties and some of the ways in which these difficulties may be prevented.

First of all, the feeling that anger on the job is unacceptable has seemed to me to be nearly universal among nursery school teachers. Often they cannot admit even to themselves that they feel angry at, or dislike, any child. No matter how much provocation they have had, if they get angry they feel guilty. They frequently try to hide the anger by being especially patient and understanding with the child.

It is an empirical fact, however, that when a person tries to hide an attitude or feeling, the impact of the hidden attitude upon the other person is apt to be even greater than it would have been if the attitude had been openly expressed. The person who is trying to hide the attitude is hampered in his capacity to resolve the problem, and the reaction of the one exposed to the hidden attitude is one of either confusion or mistrust. Such distortions in the interaction between teacher and child can be prevented in various ways if the source of the guilty emotion is clarified and the guilt reduced.

The commonest causes for anger at, or dislike of, a child fall into two categories. One of these cannot be prevented and should be faced realistically. The other may be prevented if the real sources of the feeling are recognized. Into the first category fall what the author consider to be *realistic reasons for anger*:

1. The child behaves in a way that creates immediate danger to himself or others. No matter how "understanding" one may be as to why he acted that way, such behavior is frightening to everyone and evokes instantaneous, spontaneous anger. This cannot be avoided. Also, it is actually useful to the child to recognize that people react in that way when he endangers himself or others.
2. The child makes a painful personal attack e.g. kicks a person hard in the shins. Everyone gets mad under these circumstances, and it is unrealistic not to show it.
3. A child is purposely naughty in a way that he could very well control, and disrupts group activity. If the teacher tries to act as though he is not angry, he usually is not helping the child to learn acceptable ways of behaving. He can control the *way* in which he shows his feelings, but if he tries to cover them up, his own ability to handle

the situation may be damaged; the child is not fooled, and as a result his ability to come to grips with realistic demands may be impaired.

The second category of situations in which teachers get angry at children may be more preventable. This includes cases in which anger which has origins elsewhere is displaced onto the child. The commonest *causes for displaced anger* are as follows:

1. Feelings about the parents. If a teacher does not like the child's father and/or mother for any number of conscious or unconscious reasons, the feeling may rub off on the child.
2. Frustration with the child's problem. If the needs of the child makes a teacher feel helpless, he may dislike the child.
3. Competitive or hostile feelings toward other teachers. If, for instance, there is some disagreement between two teachers and a particular child is attached to one of them, the other may dislike him.
4. Reaction to not being loved by a child. This is exceedingly common. Everyone who chooses to work with little children tends to respond to a child who responds to him and vice versa. All adults find certain children more appealing than others, although the type of child they find appealing varies greatly among individuals. If a child has the kind of personality that makes him hostile, cold or indifferent to adults, many teachers will not care for him, although they will all feel very guilty about it. They believe that an understanding of his problems should make them immune from reacting to his hostility.

In all of these cases, when a teacher recognizes what his feelings really are and why, he often has a marked change of feeling toward the child; he is able to see the child clearly, without impairment of his objectivity. When it is not possible for him to like a particular child, he should be helped to overcome his guilt. It is seldom possible for every teacher to like every child in a school. There is often one teacher in any group who likes a particular child better than another teacher does, and if there is a problem, there is no reason why the one who likes the child should not be allowed to assume the major responsibility in his case.

No matter what the administrative set-up in the school, the author has seldom encountered a situation in which this could not be easily arranged when the advisability of making a change was accepted without guilt or recriminations. The author has seen a number of cases in which an intense need to "work through" the negative feelings for which a teacher felt guilty resulted in a prolonged struggle in which neither the child, the teacher, or the rest of the group profited.

Teachers are commonly made angry by certain kinds of parents:

1. Parents who "mistreat" their children. Individual teachers vary in their opinions as to what constitutes mistreatment, but if a teacher feels a parent is being cruel, he invariably has strong feelings about it (as do most people).
2. Mothers who put their relationships to husbands and boy friends ahead of their responsibility to the child. Almost all teachers consulted seemed to feel some resentment toward a mother who is relatively neglectful of the needs of her child when they conflict with her pursuit of a husband.
3. Parents who value system differs markedly from that of the teachers. Rigid, dirty, careless, irreligious people, for instance, will have different effects upon different teachers depending upon whether the teachers themselves value religion, conformity, etc. and what their own standards of cleanliness are.
4. Parents who, for any reason, seem to "look down" on the teachers, or do not recognize their professional training. Skilled nursery school teachers are frequently very defensive against any implication that they are "glorified baby-sitters."
5. Parents who, for any reason, criticize the school. The need for good public relations has been a very real problem,

particularly in agencies whose support from public funds has to be renewed periodically. Anyone who is critical becomes a threat to the existence of the school, even if the teachers recognize the hostility as a neurotic problem in the parent.

Whenever anger arises for any of these reasons, the teacher is apt to create a reaction formation against it and to become unusually understanding and patient. He feels he has to do this because to admit anger is unacceptable. Unfortunately, the real feeling usually creeps through somehow and damages his effectiveness.

Consultants can help teachers to admit anger by emphasizing its normality under certain circumstances, and the universality of some displacement in all professional workers. Teachers can be encouraged to discharge their anger either to supervisors, among themselves, or in the consultation group.

Support and reassurance from administrative levels is important in keeping down the anger that arises from fear for their jobs. An understanding of the needs of parents as well as children may cut down on resentments that arise from the "child-centered" attitudes that are *normal* among people who choose to work with children.

Unavoidable anger simply has to be discharged, although not necessarily toward the "cruel" parent (who sometimes is not nearly as cruel by the parent's own standards as he is by the standards of the teachers). In any case, a teacher must get rid of his anger, not pretend he does not have it. This is necessary if he is to avoid displacing it onto the child.

The feeling that teachers should be able to help all children according to their needs, and that understanding a problem inevitably leads to its solution, is another source of guilt. Often after some experience with consultation, a myth will begin to arise among the teachers to the effect that "talking a problem over" will inevitably make it disappear. Sometimes this does happen, through relief of the tension-creating anxiety of the teacher group, but sometimes the teachers develop an almost magical expectation that it will, and are filled with guilt and disappointment if it does not.

Often the needs of an individual child conflict with the needs of the group as a whole, and a teacher is thrown into conflict over the nature of his responsibility. He may have to choose between damaging the morale of the group, or taking a course that is less than ideal, from the standpoint of the individual child.

There are times when an individual child has such overwhelming emotional needs that they cannot possibly be met fully, no matter how hard the teacher tries. In such cases, the teacher feels helpless, and a vicious cycle may occur. The feeling of helplessness makes him angry at the child who evoked it, but the anger makes him guilty, and the need to counteract that anger makes him still more helpless.

Anger is a normal reaction to a feeling of helplessness. The need to deny the feeling leads to displacements and reaction formations that interfere with a clear view of what is happening in an interaction, and impedes realistic resolution of the problem.

In situations of this kind, it is important to help the teacher realize that some children just cannot be helped as much as he would like to help them. Recognition of this fact reduces the teacher's own feelings of helplessness and frustration, and cuts down on the personal sense of threat which makes him angry at the child. When he begins to feel irrational anger or dislike of a child whose intense needs are obvious, he should be encouraged to recognize his own need to be infallible. He can best be helped to face it if he realizes that, to one degree or another, it is shared by everyone in his line of work.

Certain problems arise directly from confusion in the application of knowledge about psychodynamics and emotional development. Psychoanalytic principles have become increasingly well-known in the last twenty years, and their misapplication in practical situations has done a lot of damage to both parents and teachers.

One particularly destructive misconception is the idea that it is good to allow a child completely free expression of aggression and/or hostility whenever he feels angry. "Permissiveness" in regard to feelings is, of course, not synonymous with lack of limits on a child's behavior, but nursery school teachers often seem to think they will be criticized or thought "old-fashioned" if they put any restraints upon the way in which a child expresses rage and frustration. The big problem that arises under these circumstances is again apt to be development of the "hidden attitude." It results in what can be called "rule by indirection."

Teachers, as well as parents and many other people today, think they *ought* to feel permissive, but in reality they do not. They really feel they should have some control over a child's choices, but they feel guilty about it. Therefore, they frequently offer the child a choice that turns out to be no choice at all. They want to make the child self-reliant by permitting him to choose between various alternatives, but if the child chooses something they cannot accept as wise, they try to make him change his mind without letting him know that they are trying to manipulate him. They want him to think the choice is his own. This makes for much confusion in the child's mind.

However, hidden authoritarianism is very prevalent in our culture today, creating emotional disturbances that range from mild to exceedingly serious. A consultant can help teachers to recognize their own tendencies to indulge in this very common practice and to avoid it. A teacher must determine the degree of permissiveness with which he feels comfortable and act accordingly. Even if some teachers are too strict and others too lenient, they will be successful, on the whole, with most of the children in their charge if they act according to the way they feel and do not try to hide an opposing attitude.

Psychiatric knowledge has also had a tendency to create conflict over the concept of need for "integration with the group." Recognition that a withdrawn child may have emotional problems that need attention tends to make teachers feel that any child who prefers to play alone is maladjusted. An individual child may be quite normal and still prefer at times to be outside the group. Whether or not this tendency is an indication of maladjustment can be evaluated on the basis of the child's *total* observable behavior and attitudes.

However, acceptance by teachers of a stereotype, regarding the need to be "adjusted to the group," may impair their ability to make such an evaluation according to their experience and knowledge of behavioral signs. When a consultant senses that a stereotype has developed, he can help reorient the teachers to focusing on total observable behavior.

Emphasis during a nursery school teacher's training on the importance of his role as a parent-counselor has opened up another source of guilt for the teacher. In frequent cases a teacher's desire to be helpful to a mother in improving her relationship to the child has caused the teacher to become more deeply embroiled in the personal affairs of the mother than both he and the mother feels comfortable about.

Anxiety about the degree of involvement may lead to guilt and insecurity in handling the problem. The teacher may become confused and the mother angry. If the mother accuses the teacher of being intrusive, the teacher's own guilt may be expressed in retaliatory punitiveness toward the mother.

Here again, it is important to help teachers set limits on a counseling relationship, at the point where they feel comfortable and secure. If a mother needs more than the teacher feels he can offer, the mother can be directed toward the kind of facility available for further pursuit of the problem, with someone specifically trained in the techniques of psychotherapy.

Counseling by nursery school teachers is most useful to mothers if it is directed toward increasing the mother's understanding of the child's behavior, and the feelings reflected by that behavior. The teacher can make use of his trained observations of the kind of behavior observable at school, and help the mother to be more tolerant and understanding of normal developmental stages. The mother's anxiety will thereby be reduced without the application of any specific therapy for her internal conflicts.

Even though a teacher may have a clear understanding of the reasons for emotional tensions in a child and may feel them to be connected with a mother's own neurotic problems, the teacher is not trained in the techniques for making interpretations to a mother about disturbed family relationships. When he tries to do so, he often gets into situations which arouse anxiety in himself and anger in the mother. His effectiveness in helping the mother is reduced. A consultant can help teachers determine the best level for their interventions.

Another misconception promoted by training is the assumption that a child is disturbed just because his family is upset, or that a family must necessarily be pathological because a child has symptoms of emotional unrest. These conditions often go together, but not *always*. Sometimes a child from the most highly disturbed background remains relatively healthy for a number of reasons that are not always apparent. Sometimes, too, a child's aggressive behavior results from inner conflicts that persist in spite of a relatively benign current family situation. A teacher may misperceive the child if he has a tendency to accept the stereotype. The consultant can encourage him to avoid this pitfall by focusing on the child's observable behavior.

A relatively small, but also significant, number of problems presented by nursery school teachers have their origin in the personal conflicts of the individual teachers. Whatever the variations may be in individual source or expression of such conflicts, they seem to fall into four general categories:

1. Projection of own childhood hurts onto a child. The teacher reacts to a child's difficulty as though it were identical with something he had suffered as a child. He often cannot see that the child's reaction has a different explanation, because he is overidentified with one aspect of the child's problem. For instance, a minority group teacher may interpret a fight between two children as evidence of racial prejudice when actually it has a quite different explanation.

2. Projection of own relationships with authority onto other relationships. If a teacher has difficulty with a supervisor or consultant, he may need to counteract his own feelings of helplessness by acting toward one of the mothers as he feels the supervisor is acting toward him. Or the converse; he may act toward the mother as he wishes the supervisor would act toward him, even though the actual basis of interaction may be quite different.

3. Projection of problems a teacher has with his own child on the problems another parent has with his child. Here, the teacher cannot perceive the differences, again because of identification with one aspect of the mother-child relationship.

4. Rationalization or reaction formation to personal feelings of repugnance to dirt, racial prejudice, professional rivalry or any other "unacceptable" feeling.

A consultant does not need to go into the individual's personal reasons for such feelings. He may be most helpful by demonstrating the universality of personal conflicts even in "well-adjusted" people and by exploding misconceptions regarding the need for perfection in teachers.

One of the misuses of psychodynamic knowledge that is becoming increasingly widespread among people who deal with other people's problems professionally is propagation of the concept that all such professional people are supposed to be perfectly well-adjusted and without evidence of any personality problems. Nothing could be farther from the truth. The myth of the "perfectly analyzed analyst" is no sillier than the myth of the "perfectly loving and understanding" nursery school teacher.

A consultant can point out that certain kinds of built-in attitudes and personality characteristics are frequent in all people who choose to work professionally with children, just as the same is true for people who choose other kinds of professions. Such attitudes and feelings are always reflected to some degree in their interactions with others on the job. Training can teach that certain ways of expressing feelings are more, or less, useful than other ways.

Knowledge and experience help to overcome certain feelings that may have antedated entrance into any field, and most professional workers hopefully continue to change their attitudes throughout their careers. Some feelings, even unacceptable ones, however, we will always have with us. The important thing is to bring them into awareness and create realistic interpersonal relationships. This is most important for people who are working with children and hoping to help them build sound emotional attitudes.

REFERENCES

Parker, B.: Psychiatirc consultation for nonpsychiatric professional workers. *U.S. Department of Health, Education and Welfare Public Health Monograph No. 53,* 1958.

Parker, B.: The value of supervision in training psychiatrists for mental health consultation. *Mental Hygiene,* 45:94-100, 1961.

Chapter 16

CONCERNS AND DIRECTIONS IN TEACHER CONSULTATION

MARVIN J. FINE AND MILTON M. TYLER

Teacher consultation is viewed as a vital part of school psychology. The use of reports in lieu of teacher contacts and the programs are examined in terms of the problems they present for implementation of prescriptive teaching and behavior modification consultation. Caplan's consultee-centered case consultation is discussed as a viable framework for teacher consultation. Related problems of training and system expectations are also reviewed.

T HE ROLE OF the school psychologist as a consultant has not been ignored in the literature. Newman (1967), for example, presented a strong and illustrative treatise on effective consultation, arguing the need for continuous and on-the-spot contacts and for the development of a trusting relationship among the people involved as being central to effective consultation. Gray (1963) also treated consultation extensively, presenting the early consultation model of Caplan (1956) as a viable framework. Other recent publications (Fischer, 1969; Mannino, 1969; Berkowitz, 1968; Losen, 1964; Farnsworth, 1966; Handler, Gerston, and Handler, 1965; Reger, 1964; Capobianco, 1967) have examined the parameters of psychological and psychiatric school consultation, and it would be accurate to conclude that almost all models or conceptions of school psychology view the

From the *Journal of School Psychology*, 9:436-444, 1971.

psychologist-teacher relationship as the pivotal point for effective service.

Despite this apparent plethora of attention to consultation, many school psychologists seem unresponsive to the interpersonal dimensions of their functioning, preferring to operate out of a narrow, insulated tester-reporter model, or substituting technological knowledge for human relations skills. It is hoped that the ensuing discussion of concerns and directions in consultation will prove helpful and stimulating to the practicing school psychologist who is struggling to mediate the demands of his position with the existing needs of teachers and children and with theoretical advances in the fields of psychology and education.

Current Concerns in Consultation

Several areas of the psychologist-teacher relationship have been identified as having special pertinence to the consultation process; these areas need examination. The substitution of written reports for *vis-a-vis* teacher contacts has been and still is of concern to school psychologists. Additionally, the more recent thrusts by school psychologists into the realms of behavior modification and prescriptive teaching, though potentially quite productive, possess some inherent dangers for the psychologist-teacher relationship.

Psychological Report

The school psychologist's report historically has been quite enigmatic; psychologists have debated what should go into it, who should read it, and what it accomplishes, and yet many school psychologists still seem content for the report to represent their main communication with the teacher. The image of the "hit and run" school psychologist who tests and weeks later sends a jargonish or abbreviated report to the schools is only too prevalent.

The psychological report, however descriptive and prescriptive, is highly subject to individual teacher interpretation. By itself, a report may suffice for the disseminating of objective data; it is questionable, however, how effective an unaccompanied report would be in leading to some significant behavior change in teacher or child.

Similar thoughts prompted Bardon (1963) to query, "Instead of testing a child and writing a report with recommendations for the teacher to follow, what would happen if a psychologist tested or observed a child and then sat down with the teacher to exchange views?" Bardon's question was tentatively answered in a study of school psychological services in an Ohio county (Baker, 1965), "Results suggested that a teacher's willingness to carry out recommendations and the psychologist's willingness to make specific recommendations was directly proportional to the quality of face-to-face relationship existing between these two professionals."

The excessive use of written reports as substitutes for personal contacts may be tied in with the pressures for handling many cases. Also, the demand for the testing and retesting of retarded children with the emphasis on obtaining scores seems to be another logical culprit in this situation. The probability that reports alone may be a highly ineffective way of helping individuals should prompt school psychologists to reconsider the function of reports.

Prescriptive Teaching

This orientation places extensive and somewhat esoteric data in the hands of the school psychologist, who must translate this information into educationally relevant concepts. The psychologist's attempts to communicate the existence of specific language or sensory motor deficits to a teacher and then to develop an appropriate in-class program may meet considerable resistance from the teacher. The teacher may hold an opposing rationale for the child's lack of achievement (the child is just being lazy, or "he could succeed if only he would try"), or the teacher may accept the definition of the child's problem but then protest that there is not enough time to work with the child.

A rhetorical question can be raised regarding the teacher's right to his own beliefs about the child and whether or not he can program for the child in his classroom. However, in many situations the teacher's position is a reflection of anxiety or threat, and a phase of the school psychologist's consultant role should be to deal with these feelings. The curricular emphasis upon prescriptive teaching can represent a source of threat to the teacher. Curriculum know-how is supposedly the teacher's area of competence, but now the teacher finds himself confronted by a nonteacher who is very knowledgeable about unfamiliar curricular concepts and materials.

The prescriptive teaching recommendations should be in terms that the teacher can understand and accept. The psychologist may be impressed by elaborate terminology and concepts, but the teacher will only be threatened or disgusted if the psychologist's recommendations are unfathomable.

If the psychologist is unable to obtain the teacher's support for the prescriptive teaching program, then diagnostic testing time has been wasted, the child remains with his problem, and the teacher has not been assisted in broadening his skills and understanding his students. It is important that the psychologist attempt to introduce his recommendations in a sensible way and be prepared to deal with the teacher attitude variable. The psychologist should assume an approach to consultation that reduces the likelihood of threat and that includes provisions for helping teachers become more sensitive to themselves and to their relationship with the child.

Behavior Modification

The procedures encompassed under the rubric of behavior modification represent an effective technology for changing behavior, and the literature abounds with testimonials to this observation. But the zeal and certitude of the behavior modification oriented psychologist may not be matched by the teacher's readiness to participate in a program. As with the area of prescriptive teaching, the teacher might be threatened by the newness and technical aspects of this approach. Also, the ethical questions pertaining to actively manipulating behavior via reinforcement, resolved by the psychologist, might still concern the teacher.

In some cases the psychologist may erroneously interpret the absence of verbalized resistance as meaning that the teacher endorses a behavior modification approach. In order to satisfy the psychologist, the teacher may have selected certain behaviors for modification that really were not the vital ones. Not only does a teacher usually have ambivalent feelings about a misbehaving child, he also may not clearly recognize which behaviors or combinations of behaviors constitute the problem.

In planning a modification program there can be a great deal of teacher-psychologist communication, but these contacts might be primarily in terms of the teacher being used as an observer, recorder, and contingency manager. The perceived insensitivity of the psychologist to the teacher's feelings and concerns over the child may prompt the teacher to reject the psychologist and the modification techniques. A paradox lies in the frequently found contrast between the amount of attention given by the psychologist to the easily objectified classroom variables, compared with limited attention to the teacher's feelings about himself in relation to the child.

Directions in Consultation

The components of a successful consulting relationship have been discussed by a number of writers and common themes are easily detected. Rogers (1959) suggested that a productive and satisfying relationship between teacher and school psychologist will ensue when (a) the teacher perceives himself as having a problem (e.g. a child with whom he has been unable to cope successfully); (b) the school psychologist is a congruent, genuine person in the relationship; (c) the school psychologist feels a high degree of positive regard for the teacher; (d) the school psychologist experiences an accurate, empathic understanding of the teacher's experiences, and communicates this; and (e) the teacher, to a degree, experiences the psychologist's congruence, acceptance, and empathy.

In a similar vein, Lippitt (1967) described a fruitful, helping situation as one characterized by, "(1) mutual trust, (2) recognition that the helping situation is a joint exploration, (3) listening, with the helper listening more than the individual receiving help, and (4) behavior by the helper which is calculated to make it easier for the individual receiving help to talk."

The psychologist's sensitivity, ability to communicate, and non-dominative attitude were valued in both orientations. The two orientations also appear to have a common goal to consultation, that of strengthening the teacher personally and professionally. Magary (1967), while generally supporting Rogers' orientation, cautioned that the skills of diagnosis, assessment, and evaluation are also needed by the school psychologist along with the psychologist's characteristics described by Rogers.

Caplan's (1964) discussion of consultee-centered case consultation is extremely germane to the school psychologist. This approach focuses on the teacher and his relationship with the child. Caplan is concerned that, as a professional person, the teacher may be impeded in working effectively with children. The school psychologist's entree into the situation will probably be through a teacher's referral, but if the psychologist "listens" carefully to the teacher he may conclude that a major portion of the difficulty lies in some way with the teacher's perceptions or handling of the situation. This approach to consultation does not preclude the possibility that the child may be experiencing a "real" problem; it simply emphasizes how a better classroom adjustment might be affected for the child through a change in teacher understanding and behavior, and through the teacher altering aspects of the classroom environment.

The four major categories of difficulty identified by Caplan as potentially interfering with a teacher's ability to deal effectively with a child were lack of understanding, skill, objectivity, confidence, and self-esteem.

Lack of Understanding: The teacher may have drawn erroneous conclusions or may simply lack the psychological skill to draw any conclusion regarding a child's behavior that he finds unusual or disturbing. Caplan (1964) illustrated this point by describing how a teacher believed that a child was going "bad" or delinquent as a result of his beginning to steal. The clarifying information the teacher received was that the boy's mother was pregnant and that his stealing was associated with feelings of loneliness, loss of love, etc. This information gave the teacher a new understanding of the child, and the teacher changed his behavior accordingly.

The psychologist's insights into the teaching-learning process as well as his understanding of child development can be shared with the teacher. The problem situation may exist simply because the new teacher is unaware of what constitutes normal behavior for a group. Or a teacher may have misinterpreted some data from a child's cumulative folder, such as the IQ score. Or perhaps a teacher is using noncontingent reinforcement with a child, in which case a simple explanation of systematic, contingent reinforcement would be sufficient to increase the effectiveness of the teacher. In such situations, when the teacher lacks basic psychological insights, the consulting relationship could carry a needed didactic dimension.

Lack of Skill: In this instance the teacher has adequate insight into the child's behavior but lacks specific skills or information pertaining to a course of action. For example, a teacher may be aware that a child has visual-perceptual problems but is unaware of how to program for the child within the classroom. Another teacher might be working with a socially alienated child and may not know how to "break the ice" and establish communication. Or the teacher may have an adequate awareness of the complexity of a child's problem and the child's need for psychotherapy, but may be unfamiliar with the community's psychiatric resources.

As with "lack of understanding," the psychologist's approach can be almost of a supervisory or didactic nature, "telling" the teacher would be the effective consultative strategy.

Lack of Objectivity: Caplan gave relatively more emphasis to this category of difficulty, and school psychologists attempting teacher consultation will probably agree with this emphasis. The teacher through training and experience may have the understanding and skills necessary to work with a particular child, but he is in some way inhibited from using his professional skills. Caplan used the term "theme interference" to describe how certain problem themes interfere with a person's professional functioning. An illustration of this phenomenon (Fine, 1970) involved a psychologist advising a teacher to positively reinforce specified behaviors of a child and ignore other behaviors. The teacher's reluctance to accept this program was subsequently discovered to be based on her moralistic beliefs about the need to punish misbehaving children. She believed that the recommended program was the reverse of what it should be on moral grounds.

Some anxiety and fautly stereotyping can be expected from a teacher who has been unable to cope satisfactorily with a child. Examples of faulty stereotyping would be statements, such as "his older brother had the same problem, no one in that family can learn" or, "you have to expect retarded kids to get in fights, they just don't know any better." In each of these examples the objective of the teacher's rationalization was to allay the threat and anxiety associated with being unable to cope with the child's behavior, and with the symbolic meaning that the child's behavior held for the teacher.

Caplan emphasized that the separation of the teacher's personal life from the work difficulties should be respected by the consultant. The consultant's concern should be with reducing the theme interference by focusing "on defining the nature of the theme by a careful examination of its manifestations in the work context. The consultant then reduces the theme interference by influencing the consultee to adopt a reality-based expectation for the client" [1964].

The psychologist must be careful not to provoke teacher compliance through his inferred authority. The earlier discussed difficulties in implementing behavior modification and prescriptive teaching programs are sometimes brought about because, to use Kelman's (1958) terms, the teacher feels he must "comply" but has not really "identified" with or "internalized" the basic rationale of these programs.

Interpersonal sensitivity, ability to communicate, and a non-dominative attitude, already mentioned in the context of Rogers (1959) and Lippitt (1967), would be vital for the school psychologist working with a teacher who lacks objectivity. Teacher trust in the psychologist should increase as it becomes apparent that they are working together toward common goals, rather than trying to dominate or control each other. As the psychologist and teacher discuss the child, simultaneously unveiling the teacher's distorted perceptions, the psychologist can periodically highlight and reflect the teacher's feelings and comments, giving the teacher a conscious opportunity to reevaluate them. The psychologist can also introduce reality variables through looking objectively at the child's strength and limitations and at how the educational environment psychologically matches or mismatches the child. This kind of interaction is likely to dissipate the teacher's distorted stereotyping, and he can be expected to contribute ideas for altering his own behavior or altering classroom variables. The psychologist can also introduce possible avenues of change, but these too should grow logically out of the shared analysis of the situation and agreement as to the basis of the child's problem. This kind of teacher-psychologist interaction will usually not be obtained in just one visit, but will require several sessions and occasional follow-up.

Lack of Confidence and Self-esteem: Teachers who are challenged daily by the disparate personalities of their children, bombarded with literature describing technological advances in curriculum materials, and subjected to mass media criticisms of education, periodically experience a lack of confidence and self-esteem. Consequently, in some consultant situations the teacher may be seeking ego support rather than specific help with a child.

The ego support can be offered just through the consultant's willingness to sit and listen while the teacher describes his approach to dealing with the child. An approving and admiring comment, such as "that sounds like a great idea" or, "I'll have to remember to suggest that to another teacher" can be a tremendous ego booster. In other situations the consultant may need to allude to the progress the teacher has made or to the value of the teacher's efforts under difficult circumstances. Overly sympathizing with the teacher's despondency may tend to reinforce these feelings, while focusing on the teacher's strengths and accomplishments with the child, without sounding artificial, can energize the teacher.

Some consultants are ever-ready to contribute a suggestion or a totally different program even when this kind of advice is not needed, and in this way they further weaken the teacher's self-concept. These consultants seem in need of reaffirming that they are the expects who give final approval on a course of action and that the teacher cannot independently arrive at an accurate perception of a situation or a viable solution. Such people lower the teacher's self-esteem and sense of adequacy. The ideal consultative experience should leave the teacher feeling more capable and confident.

Postscript to the Consultative Process

The structure and content of consultation are going to vary from situation to situation, and in this regard Caplan's (1964) consultee-centered case consultation, including the four categories of teacher difficulty, seems to represent a viable framework. In some situations, giving specific clarifying information to the teacher will suffice, while in other situations reduction of theme interference or teacher ego boosting may be required. Sensitivity to the teacher's feelings, flexibility, and an ability to establish a trusting relationship are tremendously important in consultation. Under most circumstances the school psychologist would be naive to believe that he could analyze and remediate a child's problem without the cooperation of the child's teacher.

In an ideal situation, all teachers would be able to respond to school psychological consultations as this one did. "Although my feelings were mixed and varied, they were all vital to my growth as a teacher. They made me more sensitive and aware of my role. They gave me direction and, perhaps most important of all, the conviction that I was a good teacher" [Williams, 1967].

Conclusions

The intent of this paper was to examine some problems and directions in teacher consultation with school psychologists. Writing reports and implementing behavior modification and prescriptive teaching programs were identified as potential problem areas. Rogers (1959), Lippitt (1967), and especially Caplan

(1964) were seen as offering meaningful insights into the consultative process.

Though there is general agreement that teacher consultation is important, this seems to remain a questionable area in the practice of school psychologists. One frequent defense against extensive teacher consultation has to do with the time factor. Other demands being more pressing, there simply is not enough time for adequate teacher contacts. This position is often suspiciously viewed as being a self-imposed limitation by those who would rather not spend the time with teachers. Related to the disinclination toward consultation is the possibility that many practicing school psychologists, master's level trained, have not been adequately prepared in interviewing and counseling skills or the consultation process. As Gray (1963) observed,

> Consultation, when broadly interpreted, is one of the major roles of the school psychologist today. It should even be a larger role in the future. Yet unfortunately there is little available published material that treats this topic directly in relation to the school psychologist's functioning; there is little direct teaching or practicum experience in consultation current in training programs for school psychologists.

Her observations are still generally accurate; curricular changes are needed in school psychology training programs.

As to the time factor argument, Starkman's (1966) discussion of the decision-making paradox in school psychology is most apt. If school psychologists value teacher consultation and consider it a viable avenue for reaching many children, they should communicate this professional posture to the appropriate administrators and begin a program of educating administrators as to what constitutes effective service. Constructive changes in the nature of school psychological services cannot realistically be expected to emanate from the "top." The importance of teacher consultation needs to be articulately expressed to administrative people, with as much documentation as is available, including the results of surveys of teacher opinions on psychological services and the testimonials of teachers who received satisfactory consultation.

Ideally, the school psychologist should be one of the most

competent consultants in the schools in terms of his skills in interpersonal relations and his understanding of human behavior. Most of the other school consultants (speech clinicians, remedial reading teachers, guidance counselors, etc.) tend to focus on the child and usually work with him independently of the teacher and classroom. In a period of increasing role diffusion among these various consultants, when testing, counseling, and remedial skills are claimed by different professional groups, perhaps the school psychologist can establish himself as the person concerned about the teacher and the classroom and enthusiastically available to consult with the teacher.

REFERENCES

Baker, H. L.: Psychological services: From the school staff's point of view. *Journal of School Psychology*, 3:36-42, 1965.

Bardon, J. I.: Mental health education: A framework for psychological services in the schools. *Journal of School Psychology*, 1:20-27, 1963.

Berkowitz, H.: The child clinical psychologist in the schools: Consultation. *Psychology in the Schools*, 5:118-124, 1968.

Caplan, G.: Mental health consultation in the schools. In *The Elements of a Community Mental Health Program*. New York, Milbana Memorial Fund, 1956.

Caplan, G.: *Principles of Preventative Psychiatry*. New York, Basic, 1964.

Capobianco, R. J.: Psychologist collaborates with other school staff. In J. F. Magary (Ed.): *School Psychological Services*. Englewood Cliffs, P-H, 1967.

Farnsworth, D. L.: Psychiatric consultation in secondary schools. *Psychology in the Schools*, 3:17-19, 1966.

Fine, M. J.: Some qualifying notes on the development and implementation of behavior modification programs. *Journal of School Psychology*, 8(4):301-305, 1970.

Fischer, H. L.: School consultation in a special education setting. *Psychology in the Schools*, 6:12-17, 1969.

Gray, S. W.: *The Psychologist in the Schools*. New York, HR&W, 1963.

Handler, L.; Gerston, A., and Handler, B.: Suggestions for improved psychologist-teacher communication. *Psychology in the Schools*, 2:77-81, 1965.

Kelman, H. C.: Compliance, identification, and internalization, three processes of attitude change. *Journal of Conflict Resolution*, 2:51-60, 1958.

Lippitt, G. L.: The consultative process. *The School Psychologist, 21*:72-74, 1967.

Losen, S. M.: The school psychologist-psychotherapist or consultant. *Psychology in the Schools, 1*:13-17, 1964.

Magary, J. F.: Emerging viewpoints in school psychological sources. In J. F. Magary (Ed.): *School Psychological Services.* Englewood Cliffs, P-H, 1967.

Mannino, F. V.: *Consultation in Mental Health and Related Fields. A Reference Guide.* Chevy Chase, National Institute of Mental Health, 1969.

Newman, R. G.: *Psychological Consultation in the Schools.* New York, Basic, 1967.

Reger, R.: The school psychologist and the teacher: Effective interpersonal relationships. *Journal of School Psychology, 3*:13-18, 1964.

Rogers, C. R.: Significant learning: In therapy and education. *Educational Leadership, 16*:232-242, 1959.

Starkman, S.: The professional model: Paradox in school psychology. *Am Psychol, 21*:807-808, 1966.

Williams, M. E.: Help for the teacher of disturbed children in the public school: The use of consultation for problem solving and personal growth. *Except Child, 34*:87-91, 1967.

Chapter 17

PREVENTIVE ASPECTS OF MENTAL HEALTH CONSULTATION TO SCHOOLS

IRVING N. BERLIN

T HE VAST NUMBER of emotionally disturbed children, adolescents, and adults is dramatically illustrated by swelling numbers of nonlearners in schools, unabating delinquency, violence, and pregnancies among adolescents, and increased divorce rates and decreased job and interpersonal satisfactions among adults. All these have made society increasingly conscious of psychological problems and the need for treatment.

Studies have indicated that there will never be sufficient mental health professionals to give treatment to the children who need it, not to mention the disturbed adult population. Prevention must concern us as one attack on this overwhelming problem.

In the schools we are concerned primarily with secondary prevention (Eisenberg, L. and Gruenberg, E. M., 1961). The prenatal and early infancy and childhood problems antedate school, that is, problems that may stem from mothers' depression, from parental conflicts that affect the infant and small child, from mother-infant and mother-toddler alienation, resulting from mothers personality problems or inexperience in the mothering process, or problems caused by the unhappy child's reaction to his environment, to neurophysiological dysfunction, or to socio-

---

From *Mental Hygiene*, 51:34-40, 1967.

cultural deprivation, which increases the child's turmoil and thereby increases family troubles, in a vicious circle. All these have already had their effects by the time the child enters kindergarten or first grade. There are, however, a few areas of primary prevention in which educators do play a vital role, especially in cases of crisis in a child's life, in which an educator's sensitivity to the child and his response may be of crucial importance.

Secondary prevention centers around the early identification of emotional disturbance due to interpersonal, neurophysiological or sociocultural factors and early intervention by the educator, through the mental-health consultation process. In many instances this process includes involving the parents; in a few instances referral must be made to community resources. However, preventive work centers essentially around learning to recognize and to use the potentially healing or therapeutic aspects of the educative process. Prevention also depends on the alertness of educators to "normal" maturational and school crises that may affect the vulnerable child adversely if they are not recognized, understood, and reacted to helpfully.

Our concern here is with some general aspects of prevention in schools, the role of mental health consultation as a means of facilitating and enhancing prevention, and a specific technique or method of mental health consultation found effective by some mental health specialists and educators.

The School's Role in Prevention

Most teachers are capable of early recognition of behavioral disturbances due to emotional factors, or of a child's inability to learn because of maturational lag, sociocultural deprivation, or manifestations of brain dysfunction. Bowers (1960) and others have compared the reliability of teachers' concerns and evaluations of a child's functioning in school with later diagnostic studies by mental health professionals and have found teachers' observations very trustworthy. Thus, the early recognition of a child's problems in school is possible.

The central problems are subsequent assessment of the disturbance by educators and others in terms of the child's socio-cultural background, neuromuscular maturation, emotional instability, and possible organic retardation. Once a tentative diagnosis is made, the experienced educator can begin to make some prognoses and attempt to verify them by observations in the classroom. He may then be better able to decide whether a youngster needs further, prompt evaluation. Inherent in the process of early identification of problems is contact with the parents to obtain their observations on the child and his development and to assess any evident troubles in and between parents that may be affecting the child.

It needs to be stressed and restressed that, even when evaluation and treatment are undertaken by outside agencies, the school still has the challenging problem of determining how educative methods and classroom experiences can be used to take maximal advantage of the early recognition of disturbance and to enhance the therapeutic process. Since treatment is a slow process, it requires all the additional help possible in the everyday life of the child. Mental health consultation is often helpful in developing collaboration between the educator and the psychotherapist. The consultant is also able to help educators recognize that learning expectations are often supportive to the sick child's ego.

Maturational Crises of the School-age Child

Leaving the protection of home and mother at age five or six represents a crisis for some children. How the school deals with the child and parents and with the child's fears of school and desire to stay home can affect the prevention of future disability.

Restriction of gross motor activity, learning to attend and to begin to learn may precipitate a crisis, especially for slowly maturing boys who are not yet able to contain large muscle activity in favor of the pleasures to be obtained from increased fine motor co-ordination. The recognition of these problems, and of the crises that may result from pushing a child and not providing frequent outlets for large muscle movement and suitable rewards for sitting still, using small muscles, and acquiring fine motor coordination, is important to the learning future of the child.

The use of imaginative stimulation of all the senses and of special educational techniques to help the socioculturally deprived child achieve learning readiness is among the educator's most important preventive activities. The third grade, in which learning commences with real seriousness and most children are maturationally ready to learn, may find many children still unable to read, poorly motivated to learn, and unable to sit still, yet wanting to learn and to experience the fun of learning and the excitement of acquiring knowledge so evident in their classmates. The educator's failure to recognize increased hyperactivity, truculence, and opposition to learning as evidence of possible acute conflict about the desire to learn and the inability to find the means of learning may aggravate this crisis and alienate the child from the learning process and its potential satisfactions.

Similarly, it is often difficult for educators to keep in mind the fact that, for most youngsters, any sudden spurt in growth means that energy is being mobilized for the growing process and that there may be less energy available for learning. Thus, the correlation of growth spurts with falling-off in grades points to a need for increased understanding of the youngster rather than pressure for performance, but without permitting a serious drop in performance. Usually, vigorous engagement in learning returns in a few weeks.

In early adolescence, the development of secondary sexual characteristics, growth spurts, and flowering of social activities, especially for girls, often result in reduced energy for learning.

The shift from elementary school to the middle school or junior high school, in which the child has many teachers instead of one, may present crises for particular children who emotionally need the support, the firm expectations, and the rewards of a single parental figure. These children may begin to do badly in the larger and more impersonal junior high school, and may need to form a tie with a central person to facilitate their adaptation.

If the situation is correctly assessed and dealt with, each of these potential crises offers the educator opportunities to help a youngster mobilize his integrative capabilities and learn to cope more effectively with the external world.

Preventive Implications of Students' Life Crises

Many children, in the course of their school experience, undergo serious crises in their family situations that may require alert aid from the teacher to prevent serious impairment of the child's mental health. For example, death or divorce of parents, death of siblings or other family members, unemployment of the father, instability of the parents' financial or emotional support, serious illness of or accident to the student or another member of the family, with its potentially ominous import, all may have a marked impact on the child.

Perhaps the best single indicator of a serious crisis in a child's life is an abrupt change in behavior, such as a sudden lose of interest in learning, withdrawal from social interaction, explosive behavior (i.e. "blowing up" or crying), or silence and isolation on the part of a hyperactive child. Such changes should be a signal for inquiry. In these instances, the continued interest and support of teachers and others may be a vital factor in the child's ability to deal with the home crises. All experienced teachers can cite examples of how their support and, sometimes, intervention have been important to a child's emotional survival during a crisis in which the child feels alone and helpless. Here, also, the mental health consultant may be helpful in finding the best ways for a teacher to approach a difficult and nonrelating child.

The Therapeutic Effect of Learning

In order to be an effective adult in our technical society, the child must master ever more difficult and complex subject matter and acquire a variety of increasingly more refined skills. Mastery of academic materials depends on the satisfaction, pleasures, and rewards of the learning process. These often have not been acquired in the preschool years if the child has lived with deprived, troubled, not very effective, and not very nurturant or supportive parents. The school's efforts to help a child learn through a variety of sensory experiences and pleasurable early learning experiences, may begin to help him to develop habits and successes in learning that can be critical to his future living as an effective adult.

Thus, inherent in the learning process itself are preventive and therapeutic implications that the mental health consultant may be able to help the teacher make more explicit for particular children.

The Role of Mental Halth Consultation in Schools

The mental health consultant in a school is usually a social worker, clinical psychologist, or psychiatrist employed by the administration. This consultant may be helpful in the school in a variety of ways, depending upon the needs of the school, its personnel, and the skill and experience of the consultant himself (Berlin, 1962; 1964).

First, he may be of factual help. He may provide information about growth and development, the impact of certain socio-cultural experiences, diagnostic implications of a particular type of behavior of child or parents, or the community resources available for diagnosis or treatment of particular children.

Second, he may be of interpretive help. His knowledge of interpersonal dynamics and the developmental process may permit him to piece together the data gathered by the teacher, administrator, school nurse, and others and to give some picture of the origins of, and reasons for, the child's difficulties. He may be able to draw implications from the child's present behavior and past experiences for corrective classroom experiences. He may be able to delineate what the child may need from an adult that the teacher can give as part of his job as educator.

Third, the consultant may be of help in clarifying the integrative part that learning may play in the child's life and in the reduction of the child's troubles. He may be able to help teachers recognize that emotional disturbance, and even severe mental illness, may be benefited by the teacher's firm expectation that a child can learn and, through learning, feel more effective and intact. He may also be able to trace the nonintegrative experiences of the distractible, hostile, hyperactive child, so that the teacher can begin to recognize the kind of attitudes, the personal investment, stimulation, concerned firmness, persistence, and rewards required to help a particular child begin to learn. He may also be able to help the educator become alert and sensitized to certain aspects of a child's behavior that indicate, often through negative and challenging behavior, the child's increased readiness for certain expectations, for increased tolerance of closeness, or for more firmness, required by the child to take the next step in learning and personality integration.

Fourth, the consultant may be in a position to help the educator preserve his own mental health in the face of the many pressing mental health problems of his students and the students' parents. He may be able to aid the educator with his own self-expectations, which are often inconsistent with the harsh realities. Thus, he may assist the teacher who feels a failure if his youngsters are not up to grade or if he is unable to generate in his students responsive pleasure and excitement in learning. By enabling the teacher to recognize the obstacles to learning and the therapeutic function of learning for certain children, the consultant may encourage him to find satisfaction in the bite-size increments of learning that occur as children begin to work through the initial turmoil of the learning process. He may help the teacher recognize, with more and more genuine pleasure and satisfaction, the learning and consequent changes that occur as the teacher provides the appropriate milieu for change. He may also be in a position to interpret the pressures of the community and administration for heroic action so that the teacher sees the realities of his day-to-day job in terms of accumulation of tiny increments of learning and behavior change.

Hopefully, the consultant can also aid the teacher, under the trying conditions of very difficult classrooms, to recognize his human feelings of despair, anger, and even hate, as well as a sort of general guilt at not being able to love all the children and work miracles for them. When she or he understands these as common human feelings, the teacher often feels less frustrated and is able to work more effectively bit by bit and day by day. A not-so-incidental result of this is that the teacher provides an example to his students of what they need to do, showing that achievement comes not with wishing, but with hard and unremitting work. As the teacher evaluates the reality of his situation more objectively and scales down his self-expectations, he begins to try to clarify where each student is and what he needs to learn. He also then begins to expect realistic increments of learning from each student. And, as his students do learn more under these conditions, he feels better about himself and his job.

Inherent in all this is a serious problem. Mental health consultation is designed to help educators deal more effectively with disturbed children in their schools rather than get rid of them. The reality of the situation is this: there is nowhere to refer all the problems and no way to wash one's hands of them since there are so many problem children. Educators must understand the function of consultation, to help teachers learn to work with more children more effectively so that only the most seriously disturbed youngsters will require referral.

A Method of Mental Health Consultation

There are four or five steps in the process of mental health consultation, often not consecutive steps, but all important to successful consultation (Berlin, 1964). Perhaps the most important guideline is that the process is designed to promote collaboration between educator and mental health specialist, with the goal of helping the former to do a better job with students who have mental health problems.

The first step is the consultant's efforts to become acquainted with the organization, structure, and problems of schools in general, the usual burdens of the teacher, and the special problems of the particular school. The consultant must become sufficiently immersed in the school setting so that he can understand the teacher's comments in the context of the special milieu in which the teacher works.

The second step centers around the consultant's efforts to facilitate the educator's acceptance of the mental health consultant as a potentially helpful person rather than one who is concerned with analyzing the educator and uncovering character problems and unconscious motivations. In short the consultant's concern is the educator's work problems, and not his personal ones. The educator should experience the mental health consultant as a fellow human being whose task is to engage him as a collaborator, *not,* in any way, as a patient or client.

This phase of the work may take some time. The working-through is focused on the consultant's trying to indicate, in a variety of ways, that he can understand the teacher's feelings about the particular students he teaches in his particular setting. The consultant's projection of empathy with, and acceptance of, the teacher's feelings as both human and understandable should lead to collaboration in the service of the student.

The third stage of consultation is concerned with relieving the anxieties, self-recriminations, and feelings of failure that result from attempting to teach difficult and disturbed children. The reduction of teacher anxiety is a prerequisite to being able to explore methods of working with the child. Unless the educator's self-blame, tension, and feeling that he should be able to handle such problems without help are dealt with, he is not able to listen to and consider alternative courses of action. Teacher anxiety is best reduced by the consultant's discussing similar problems that he or others have been confronted with, which clearly demonstrates his understanding of similar feelings and moments of impasse.*

The fourth step is an effort to increase the teacher's distance from the problem and his objectivity by using all the data provided to draw a picture of the etiology of a particular child's problems, showing how experience with the important adults in the child's life have affected him and resulted in his present

---

* The teacher who has to deal with hostile, aggressive, hyperactive children know the author understands these problems when some harrowing experiences of my own in the playroom, with a child who had similar problems, are described; but the author has had to contend with only one youngster for one hour once or twice a week, rather than with thirty-six children daily for six or seven hours. Since we both have experienced the kind of wounds that come from being rendered "temporarily" ineffectual by a child, we can understand each other's feelings.

behavior. This not only helps the teacher feel less responsible for the child's problems and for his immediate cure, but also indicates the conditions in which the child's problems developed and where it may be necessary to take hold, or what adult behavior is required to alter the child's view of the adult and of himself. In instances of sociocultural deprivation, it may also help the teacher to understand that, as a teacher, he has an important function in the community. Not only does he help children become more effective persons, but also, by participating in community activities, he may enhance his access to parents in the service of their children.

The fifth step is considering alternative methods of dealing with the child's behavior that, in the consultant's experience or that of other educators, have been effective. Often the consultant's understanding of the origin of the child's problems can be restated to the educator so that, from this, certain attitudes, attentions, and expectations seem to evolve for mutual consideration. Alternative possibilities congruent with the teacher's experience and ideas need to be explored. The consultant who makes a recommendation or gives a prescription instead of fostering a consideration of alternatives usually learns that the teacher has already tried what he proposes and found that it did not work; or, if the teacher tacitly accepts a recommendation to which he has not contributed, he is apt to report back the next time that it has not worked. Thus, the consultant needs not only to help the educator consider alternatives, but also to suggest that these be *tentatively* tried and reported on the next time for mutual reconsideration.

The sixth step is the follow-up of consultation, in which sustained interest, concern, and supportive help provide a recurrent opportunity for the teacher to learn to deal with his problems more effectively.

Inherent in all of these phases of consultation is the probability that much of the effect of the process results from the identification of the educator with the consultant, his attitudes, and his methods of interaction. The consultant's attitudes, which are based on respect for the teacher as a potentially effective collaborator who can learn to use teaching and learning as a means of helping disturbed students, are often adopted by the teacher. Very clearly, teachers often act toward their difficult students as consultants have acted toward them.

It is important that the administrator be present as the key person in the school who not only needs to agree that the ideas to be tried are consonant with his own philosophy, but also to mediate between teacher and consultant. In addition, the administrator can learn from observing the consultation process what aspects of it he can use to make his own work more effective.

Each successful consultation not only reduces the child's present learning and behavior disturbance, but also prevents future learning disability and personality disorder. The youngster's increased learning ability and effectiveness in school may change his view of himself and his functioning in the world. The teacher is frequently able to apply what he has learned in consultation about one child to other children in the classroom. The consultation process thus helps the teacher to feel ever more effective and successful as a teacher and furthers the goal of prevention through both pupil and teacher.

REFERENCES

Berlin, I. N.: Mental health consultation in schools as a means of communicating mental health principles. *J Am Acad Child Psychiatry, 1*:671, 1962.

Berlin, I. N.: Some learning experiences as psychiatric consultant in the schools. *Men Hyg, 40*:215, 1956.

Berlin, I. N.: Learning mental health consultation history and problems. *Men Hyg, 48*:257, 1964.

Bowers, E. M.: *Early Identification of Emotionally Handicapped Children in School.* Springfield, Thomas, 1960.

Eisenberg, L., and Gruenberg, E. M.: *Am J Orthopsychiatry, 31*:355, 1961.

| Chapter 18 |
| CASE ANALYSIS: |
| CONSULTATION AND COUNSELING |
| Loyce McGehearty |

Consultation, as has been noted before in this column, needs to bring about change in the teacher's viewpoint toward particular kinds of cases in order to be most effective. This change, which is expected to be long-range, is additional to the function of the consultant, i.e. the counselor acting as an agent enabling the particular teacher to cope more effectively with the problem. The consultant needs experience in order to detect the central theme that may be interfering with the most effective functioning of the teacher. The following case is presented as an example of a combination of themes revolving around a particular teacher.

The School

This situation occurred in an essentially lower-middle-class neighborhood with a mixture of levels of ability among the children. The student body had a large turnover, partly because a military installation was nearby, and many of the children had problems brought about in part by frequent family moves. Those whose parents exhibited less stability in homeowning tended to exhibit less stability in terms of personal family adjustment. While the correlation between frequency of moves and stability is not demonstrated, there seems to be some relationship. The

---

From *Elementary School Guidance and Counseling*, 4:54-58, 1969.

faculty in the particular school had been together for some time with few turnovers. The principal had been with the school for some time. He was trusted by his teachers and was very helpful in most instances.

The Teacher

Mrs. Ford was middle-middle-class, as is typical of most teachers. She was an attractive woman in her middle thirties and was the mother of a boy and a girl in early adolescence. She had been divorced from their father for about two years. She was very concerned about their levels of achievement and about their general success in the academic world. She was well liked by the other teachers and by her principal.

The Child

Robbie was in the fifth grade. His family's income was above that of most of the community; the father was the last member of a family of early community residents and had been clinging to the old family home rather than selling while the neighborhood was deteriorating. Robbie had been retained in school the previous year. He had tremendous difficulty with writing and with most of his other school work, although test results indicated that he was of normal intelligence. He had one brother, just older, who also had had some difficulties but who had not been retained and was currently in the junior high school. The parents were in the process of obtaining a divorce.

Initial Consultation

Mrs. Ford had contacted the consultant in the teachers' lounge early in the school year about a minor problem with another child, and she had been very friendly and talkative since that time. Several of the teachers who shared the conference period were also quite lively and the conversations were free-flowing and easy. Whenever possbile, the consultant used the period as an informal teaching session. The teachers appeared quite willing to go along with this and encouraged the process by bringing up cases that puzzled them. Only after three months or so did Mrs. Ford ask for a private consultation about Robbie, although he and his brother had been mentioned casually in the lounge.

The Problem as Presented by the Teacher

According to Mrs. Ford, Robbie was being seriously neglected by his mother. The parents were living separately, and Mrs. Ford had been attempting for several weeks to contact the mother, with no success. She reported that one of the boys would answer the phone in the evening and say that their mother was not at home. Mrs. Ford had heard that the mother spent her time with men in various bars around the community. Mrs. Ford felt that she herself had been showering Robbie with special attention to help him with his problems but that he, while affectionate and friendly, did not seem to be learning anything at all. He failed to improve his handwriting, he seemed incapable of paying attention, and while apparently not unhappy, he was not doing any work. The teacher felt the problem was that the mother had consistently neglected the children from birth, that they were never required to do anything, that they had no responsibilities at home, and that the mother needed counseling assistance. During the early part of the year, Mrs. Ford spent most of her time urging Robbie to do better.

Consultant's Analysis

The consultant felt that there must be some connection between the teacher's recent divorce and this mother's impending divorce but was uncertain at first about what it might be. Using the technique of *hooking* as defined by Caplan (1959), she expressed interest in the case and agreed that the child did need help, ending with the comment that perhaps they could both think about the case until the next week. This procedure enables the consultant to help the teacher focus on the relevant parts of the situation without suggesting any specific cure, thus reinforcing the independence of the teacher but encouraging her to think through and analyze her problems while giving the support of a future conference.

Additional Consultations

Roughly eight sessions were held covering a period of nearly four months. The consultant was available only every two weeks unless the teacher made some special arrangement. The teacher's personal needs in some ways actually seemed to be met by the situation since she continued to be rather preoccupied by Robbie and his problems, almost to the exclusion of the other children in the class. This is an unfortunate trap many teachers unconsciously fall into, allowing themselves to become so emotionally involved with one child that they neglect the rest of the class for the sake of the one disturbed child. She would relate each new occurrence, each new effort on her part with a certain degree of relish, although her words expressed her concern and her frustration at being unable to help him. During this period she did manage to contact the mother and insisted that the child be seen by a psychiatrist. Following the initial examination, the psychiatrist saw him regularly for the rest of the year.

The psychiatrist's report indicated some slight neurological impairment with strong emotional problems intertwined. He saw the mother and father once each. The teacher was disappointed that he did not choose to work with the mother. In her opinion, the mother was the one who needed the help. Another interesting facet of the situation revolved around the triangle of the teacher, the child, and the mother. The teacher related some of her conversations with the child in which she tried to persuade him to get his mother to help him with his school work. The feeling communicated to the consultant was that the teacher simply could not understand how the child could possibly be so fond of his mother, could love and admire her so much, when she was so obviously neglecting him.

Additional Analysis of Teacher

The consultant felt that the situation involved four problem areas:

1. Because of her guilt feelings about her divorce and because of her sense of responsibility toward her children, the

teacher wanted to make herself feel better by being highly critical of the other mother. In a way she seemed to be saying, "See, I could be like that one, but I am sacrificing everything for my children, teaching them to be responsible, staying at home at night, and in general, being a good mother even at the sacrifice of my own pleasure."

2. The teacher felt the child's lack of response to her teaching as a threat to her competence. One of the most common reactions to a lack of response is to become angry with the cause of one's frustrations. In this case, however, Mrs. Ford developed a type of reaction formation in which she was determined to help this child. ("Nobody is going to defeat me! I won't give up.")

3. The rather helpless dependence of the child and his affectionate nature appealed to the maternal side of the teacher. She wanted to help the "poor little fellow." This pattern of response was especially strong since she had recently gone through a difficult period with no one to help *her,* and she could identify very strongly with the helpless feeling. Moreover, helping him made her feel stronger.

4. Related to the first area were her own feelings of lack of love, lack of fun, and probably an unconscious desire on her part to be like the mother in the case. She would have enjoyed getting out and having fun, too; hence, all the stronger was her resentment of the mother who did have fun and whose child continued to love her in spite of her irresponsible behavior.

Messages Given in Response to Problem Areas

During the period of the consultations the consultant experienced some frustrations of her own. Messages, comments made to the teachers, concerning the need we all have to feel important (and how this can sometimes cause us to react in illogical ways) were only partially heard. "Needing to feel important" was translated as needing to help the child feel important. As a result, Mrs. Ford moved Robbie up to her desk in the front of the room and she continued to reinforce his dependency by helping him with all his work. Certain other environmental situations came about, however, which helped resolve the problem to a degree and which the consultant could use as excellent material. The teacher began to go out again and to have some fun herself. She needed support from the consultant concerning this kind of activity. Indirect reinforcement was given through comments about parents being better parents when they enjoyed life, about the amount of time spent with children not being as important as the quality of time, about self-sacrifice leading to unconscious resentment and later to retaliation, etc.

The concern about Robbie's love for his mother was handled through communications about parents being one of those things we cannot order in particular models and that even in the worst parent there might be some good. Gradually, additional messages were added that attempted to bring about a more sympathetic feeling toward the mother. Perhaps she was so hurt by the divorce that she was trying to escape the hurt by seeking an active social life. Perhaps she really did care about her children but was not intelligent or educated enough to know what to do to help them (implying, of course, that the teacher was superior). Perhaps she had been frustrated long ago in the same way the teacher was being frustrated by Robbie's apparent inability to learn (compare 11 years exposure to the pattern of behavior with 1 years exposure). Finally, some children need to fall on their faces before they can learn to be independent.

While gradual, the changes desired took place in the teacher's attitude. Hopefully, these changes will enable her to work more effectively with the next child of divorced parents or with the next dependent child she encounters. By the end of the year, she seemed to be more able to accept her role as teacher, not therapist, and she was more willing to agree that there are some children upon whom we could spend all our time and still help them only a very small amount.

These children are the ones we would do well to help just a bit and then refer them to outside help. The law of parsimony indicates that we are most efficient when we spend time with the children who can benefit most by our help.

Chapter 19

MENTAL HEALTH CONSULTATION
WITH GROUPS

JOHN ALTROCCHI, CHARLES D. SPIELBERGER, AND
CARL EISDORFER

A case-seminar method of group mental health consultation is
presented and differentiated from group supervision, seminar teaching, sensitivity training, and group psychotherapy. The group consultant employs roles and techniques of a teacher, a group leader,
a clinician, and a communication facilitator. Analysis of the process
of group consultation suggests that several phases are discernable
and that each phase offers opportunities for fruitful, problem-solving
discussions of the personal reaction of clients and consultees. Group
discussion of consultees' reactions to and feelings about their clients
and the active use of group processes by the consultant most clearly
differentiate this method from Caplan's approach to mental health
consultation with individual consultees.

T HE GROWING INTEREST in prevention of psychological disorders and promotion of mental health has led mental health
professionals to engage in a wide variety of activities which may
be collectively labeled mental health consultation. Developments
in consultation theory, however, have not kept pace with practice
and have been concerned with interactions between a consultant
and an individual consultee (Bindman, 1959; Caplan, 1964),
with only a few exceptions (Kevin, 1963; Parker, 1958; Rieman,
1963). The aim of this paper is to describe mental health consultation with groups of consultees.

From the *Community Mental Health Journal*, 1:127-134, 1965.

Mental health consultation generally refers to one aspect of a program for the promotion of mental health and the prevention and treatment of psychological disorders. More specifically, mental health consultation is "a helping process, an educational process, and a growth process achieved through interpersonal relationships" (Rieman, 1963). The goals are to assist the key professional workers of a community to carry out their professional responsibilities by becoming more sensitive to the needs of their clients and associates and more comfortable and adept in their relationships with them. Members of certain professional groups, such as ministers, teachers, public health nurses, and welfare caseworkers are likely to be called upon by their clients in times of personal and interpersonal crises; it is assumed that such crises provide particularly opportune times for influencing the clients' emotional growth (Caplan, 1964).

Group mental health consultation is similar in some respects to group supervision, seminar teaching, sensitivity training, and group psychotherapy; but it is also discriminably different from each of these other methods, all of which may have a role in a comprehensive mental health program. While this form of consultation closely resembles group supervision in its emphasis upon the consultees' understanding of the general principles and technical procedures essential to working effectively with their clients, group mental health consultation differs from group supervision in that the consultant typically enters the consultees' social system from the outside and is often from another profession, and each consultee's supervisor retains the usual administrative control.

In its educational goals and emphasis on discussion methods, group mental health consultation resembles seminar teaching, but goes beyond it in attempting to make use of group processes and the consultees' affective involvement in their work problems. Group mental health consultation resembles sensitivity training [when applied to groups of co-workers (Bradford, 1964)] in its use of group process and consultees' personal involvement; it diverges in its greater degree of structure and the limitation of content focus to work-related problems of the consultees.

A group method of consultation is similar to group psychotherapy in its attempt to increase personal growth, sensitivity, and effectiveness by applying group processes to individual affective and intellectual learning but is distinct in several important ways: (a) the implicit psychological contract in consultation (Caplan, 1964; Parker, 1958) involves a relationship between professionals in which the consultee is free to apply what he learns or not as he sees fit; (b) the relative emphasis is on educational goals rather than on the modification of a disorder; and, especially, (c) the content focus is on the professional rather than the personal problems of the consultee. The consultees' affective involvements with clients are considered only in their relation to current work problems. For example, as Parker (1958) has suggested in reference to group consultation with public health nurses, "When an emotional reaction of the nurse destroys her objectivity about some aspect of her job, that reaction is a suitable subject for group discussion, but the intrapsychic conflict which may have helped to generate the reaction should not be considered. . . ." Nevertheless, many of the mechanisms observed in group therapy, acceptance, universalization, intellectualization, reality testing, interaction, spectator therapy, and ventilation (Corsini and Rosenberg, 1955), may also be observed in group mental health consultation. Thus, while the primary goals of mental health consultation are educational rather than therapeutic, some phases of group consultation resemble some kinds of group psychotherapy and corrective emotional experiences do take place. Although group consultation is not therapy, it may have therapeutic effects.

A CASE-SEMINAR METHOD OF GROUP
MENTAL HEALTH CONSULTATION

For varying periods since 1958, each of the authors has been engaged in part-time group mental health consultation in one of two North Carolina counties. One of these is rural and the other is a small metropolitan seaport area. The absence of mental health facilities and the considerable interest of a large number of key professionals in each community made group consultation more appropriate for scrving the needs of these communities than working with individual consultees or attempting to work directly with clients. Moreover, time restrictions (only one to three scheduled days a month were spent in these distant counties) rendered "on-call" response to individual consultee crises impractical. For these reasons, we focused on group consultation and selected a case-seminar approach as the principal consultation procedure.

For each case-seminar meeting, a member of the group was asked to present a problem case for which he (or she) had responsibility, and was encouraged to select one of general interest to the group. In order to obtain first-hand contact with the client (patient, student, or parishioner), the consultant, whenever practicable, either interviewed or observed the client interacting with the consultee. This served as a safeguard against missing crucial diagnostic information (e.g. suicidal tendencies) of which the consultee was as yet unaware. Observation of the client also provided the consultant with a better basis for discussing the case with the consultee and for helping the consultee prepare the case for presentation in the group. Actual contact with some clients, when used, permitted the consultant to demonstrate interviewing techniques. In such contacts, the consultant's impact on the client was typically supportive and often therapeutic.

We have used the case-seminar method with public health nurses, ministers, welfare caseworkers, probation officers, policemen, public housing authority personnel, elementary and secondary school teachers, principals, school guidance counselors, and school speech therapists. In these meetings, the etiology and dynamics of the case are discussed in relatively nontechnical terms. The interpersonal relations between client, consultee, and other persons involved in the case, such as the client's family and professional workers from other disciplines, are considered in detail, as is the relevance of the specific case to the roles of the consultee group in the community. Although there are individual differences among our consultation techniques, the general approach which developed is coherent and communicable.

Group Processes

The processes that we have observed in the case-seminar method are similar in a number of respects to those more generally observed in the behavior of small groups. During a single session, there are recognizable phases: an introductory phase, a warming-up phase, a problem-focused phase, and an ending phase (Kevin, 1963). Over a series of sessions, we have repeatedly observed a number of characteristics peculiar to the group consultation process, each of which offers opportunities for fruitful problem-solving discussions involving the reactions of clients and consultees.

1. In the early stages of group consultation, when group members are unsure about consultation and are testing the consultant, bizarre or "impossible" cases are often presented (Rieman, 1963). After discussing such cases, reassurance that the consultee is doing all that is reasonably possible (if this is true, and it usually is) helps to establish rapport with the group and provides considerable support for group members, each of whom has some impossible cases. Indeed, an important facet of the consultant's role is helping consultees to recognize impossible cases and the guilt and anxiety associated with them. When a consultee understands that the investment of inordinate amounts of time with such cases is often unwarranted, he is enabled to make better use of his professional time.

2. Consultees tend to present clients from minority or impoverished groups, especially in the beginning stages of consultation. Because they are different and distant from himself, such cases help the consultee avoid examining his own attitudes and behavior (Rieman, 1963). This tendency, like resistance in psychotherapy, needs to be handled carefully. The discussion of attitudes toward minority or impoverished groups, however, often provides an appropriate and useful entree for more specific understanding of the personal reactions of consultees toward their clients (Parker, 1958; Parker, 1962).

3. Those members of professional groups who initially volunteer to present cases, or who are the first to share their reactions, frequently are the least defensive and most competent members of the group. They can be counted on to help move the group into problem solving. Although it is often tempting to move eagerly ahead with them, the consultant must wait until he perceives that the majority of the group can move forward together so as to avoid subgrouping and fragmentation.

4. There are important differences between groups with respect to initial cohesiveness, resistance, and the rapidity with which they proceed from one phase of consultation to the next. Groups with strong cohesiveness and high morale proceed rapidly into the problem-solving phase where they work productively and creatively toward the solution of the problems of individual consultees and their clients. Other groups are simply collections of professionals with similar jobs who may never move beyond the introductory stage of the group consultation process.

Dynamics of Group Influence

In the case-seminar method of group mental health consultation, the consultant attempts to arouse and channel peer influences. Peers have close mutual identifications, share sources of data not available to the consultant, and often provide excellent feedback to each other (Bradford, 1964). If the consultant has been successful in stimulating the development of a group atmosphere which is generally supportive and nonjudgmental, then group members will feel inclined to share problems, anxieties, and guilt. Sometimes this occurs very quickly, sometimes only after a long testing-out period. The sharing of problems establishes meaningful rather than superficial communication between group members and gradually assures each consultee that his problems are not unique. This reduces the consultees' feelings of isolation and inadequacy, permits a more objective evaluation of problems, and leads to the formation of helpful alternative courses of action. The feedback provided at continuous case seminars also enables group members to observe the practical results of various suggestions made during former sessions.

We have observed that the work requirements of a professional group may dispose group members to develop similar attitudes toward their clients and similar anxieties concerning their professional competence. Also, each profession tends to attract individuals with similar personality characteristics. These factors increase the probability that the problems which come up in group mental health consultation will be shared and work-oriented. In gaining increased awareness of reactions common to the group as a whole, the individual consultee is helped to achieve insight into his own conflicts (Parker, 1962). Occasionally, when there is sufficient group cohesiveness and confidence in the consultant, a nonshared, but still work-connected, personal problem of an individual consultee may be introduced into the discussion. (For instance, discussion of a child who has been neglected by a working mother may stimulate a public health nurse to share her personal guilt about leaving her young children to be cared for by someone else.) When this occurs, we have observed that the group usually deals with it in an understanding and appropriate manner. With regard to the sensitivity of consultee groups in handling the personal problems of group members, our experiences with a number of different professional groups are consistent with Parker's observation, "In the ten years of my experience as a mental health consultant, not once has a nurse succumbed to the pressure of anxiety and brought before the group personal matters that were inappropriate in kind or degree" (1958).

Our observations that group members usually handle personal problems with sensitivity and appropriateness contrast markedly with those of Caplan and his colleagues who have focused on mental health consultation with individual consultees. Caplan states,

> The techniques of theme-interference reduction as practiced in case consultation are often hazardous in handling an individual member in the presence of the group. If the consultees are psychologically sophisticated, one of the individual's colleagues may realize his subjective involvement and make a defense-destroying inter-

pretation before the consultant can stop it. Such a situation may rapidly slide into group psychotherapy, in which the separation of personal and work problems is set aside, with the usual arousal of anxiety and resistance. In order to avoid this, the group consultant must structure the group rules to prevent the airing of personal problems and must maintain a tight control over the direction of the discussion, so that he can avoid a focus on theme interference in an individual member [1964].

We believe that the forces of group influence in mental health consultation, like other social forces, either can be feared and restrained, or can be put to use.

Roles and Techniques of the Group Consultant

The mental health consultant who uses the case-seminar approach must function simultaneously in several different roles: teacher, group leader, clinician and facilitator of communication between community groups. As a teacher, the consultant does not necessarily attempt to transmit specialized technical knowledge; but he does convey general principles and knowledge about those techniques which can be used within the range of the consultees' particular professional background. In this capacity, the consultant may function as a seminar leader, a resource person, and a lecturer; the specific techniques will naturally depend upon his own professional background as well as the qualifications, experiences, and needs of the consultee group. In early sessions formal lecturing on personality development and psychopathology, as well as suggestions on interviewing technique, are often appropriate. In later sessions he is more apt to function as a resource person and seminar leader. In the early sessions it is particularly important that the consultant be careful to clarify the limits of his ability to resolve questions raised by the consultees and to dispel any omniscience or omnipotence which may be imputed to him. Since the consultant's primary goal is to help the group and the individual consultees to learn to be able to derive meaningful solutions for work problems on their own, he should gratify demands for him to provide solutions only enough to keep the consultation sessions from becoming unduly frustrating to the consultees.

As a group leader the consultant acts as a catalyst to stimulate members of the group to share experiences and to explore together the problems of their clients, and helps to clarify problems, focus discussion, and conceptualize solutions suggested by consultees. In the role of group leader and teacher, we have also found it useful to relate the case under discussion to our own clinical experience and to expose to the group our own limitations and continuing efforts to broaden our understanding of human problems. Such personal reflection typically fosters identification with the consultant and emphasizes his humanness and lack of omniscience and omnipotence (Berlin, 1962).

An important technical issue has arisen involving the consultant's teaching and group leader roles. Caplan (1964) has suggested that consultants should employ supportive reassurance and praise with great caution in order to avoid implying that the consultant is judging the consultee and to avoid emphasizing status differences between consultee and consultant. Members of professional groups, however, are aware that they are constantly being judged by their supervisors, colleagues, and clients, and that there are implicit judgments in all interpersonal relationships. Furthermore, consultation implies unequal knowledge and skills in specific areas, and to ignore this is unrealistic. A very crucial task for the consultant is to demonstrate clear respect for the consultee. Only genuine respect, communicated in many subtle ways, can establish a productive working relationship and is, in our judgment, more important than the avoidance of specific kinds of verbal statements.

The mental health consultant's role as group leader often merges with his role as a clinician, especially during the discussion of the feelings of a consultee toward a client. Considerable clinical sensitivity may be required in deciding when to slow down or, instead, to deal directly with affective expression by a consultee. However, as indicated above, we do not concur with Caplan (1964) that the consultant should consistently avoid any direct discussion of the consultee's feelings and should interrupt such discussions if they arise spontaneously in a consultation group. Members of professional groups are not as fragile as patients and, therefore, do not require the same degree of protection, given the existing protection of the work-group setting. We do draw the line when aspects of the historical development of the consultee's personal feelings enter the discussion. On rare occasions, a brief excursion into a consultee's personal problems may be deemed appropriate because of the centrality of the problem to the role of the particular professional group. Such invasions of the consultee's private life should only be pursued if the consultee has the requisite strength to deal with his problems, commands the respect of the group, and provides the initiative for discussing his personal problems as "a case at point."

As a clinician, the consultant must always be prepared to use his clinical skills and his knowledge of referral resources and procedures in cases of client emergencies. The consultant's experience and ability as a clinician is a particular asset when consultees are interested in "practical approaches" and not merely theoretical approaches to their problems.

Finally, an additional important role of the consultant becomes clear in his interaction with different community agencies. Case presentations often reveal the frustrations of consultees who must work with personnel from other agencies. Complaints range from individual ineptitude on the part of other professionals to red tape, gross obstructionism, and glory seeking. On more than one occasion, workers from two agencies competing for the management of a client presented the same case in their respective seminar groups. This presents the mental health consultant with an ideal opportunity for facilitating interagency communication by helping members of different professional groups to appreciate the role of other professionals. Thus the mental health consultant who works with groups on a community-wide basis has the role of a facilitator of communication between various community caretakers and the professional groups they represent.

A central feature of this method involves clarifying the relationship between the feelings and attitudes of consultees and their work with clients. As Kevin (1963) has pointed out, there are three different foci which the consultant may take in working toward such clarification. If the consultant focuses on the mutual interchange of affectively involved problems and solutions by consultees, group movement and breadth of learning are likely to occur; but this focus can be very frustrating for inexperienced group members who feel that they have little to contribute. If the consultant focuses on the interaction between himself and individual consultees, or if the consultant focuses primarily on the feelings and reactions of individual consultees in response to clients, individual learning at depth is possible; but the consultant must be especially alert to the possibility that such procedures may be sufficiently threatening to some group members to cause them to withdraw from group discussions and he must be constantly aware of the important differences between consultation and psychotherapy. Either of these latter two approaches may provide more direct help with specific problems but also tend to increase the dependency of an individual consultee upon the consultant and to generate competition among the consultees. Some consultants may prefer to use one of these three approaches as a primary approach, despite its potential disadvantages. We have found that the use of all three techniques at appropriate times tends to result in meaningful and rapid progression by the group from the early phase of consultation to the later problem-solving phase. Any approach or combination of approaches, however, can be overused and carried so far that it is disadvantageous to the successful growth of the group and the individual consultees who comprise it. The consultant must always appreciate the difference between consultation and meddling in the affairs of the consultee. Not all of the consultee's work problems are appropriate for discussion in group consultation and not all of the client's problems are the business of the consultee. It is important that the consultant remember that his long-range goal is to help the consultee to be more self-reliant and independent; the consultee in turn learns to help his clients to become more able to help themselves. In ther words, what works for the consultant-consultee relationship ought to work for the consultee-client relationship.

CONSULTATION WITH GROUPS AND CONSULTATION WITH INDIVIDUALS

The choice of group or individual methods for consultation will depend on many factors. Group methods have the advantage of efficiency; they provide more cues and hypotheses for the consultant and more support to group members. A group focus musters the forces of group influence on individual members and helps to break through intragroup and intergroup communication barriers. In group consultation, members of different agencies can be included in the same group; this often serves to bring about a more complete understanding of a case while contributing to better cooperation between agencies.

On the other hand, group consultation may have a number of disadvantages: (1) attendance at group sessions takes members of the group away from performing their usual services (Kevin, 1963) and requires more coordination of consultees' schedules; (2) problems that involve delicate personal matters, or in which the confidentiality of case material is critical, may be more appropriately dealt with in individual consultation; (3) insecure consultees are often unwilling to expose to their peers work problems which they might discuss alone with the consultant; (4) group consultation is not as adaptable as individual consultation for meeting individual consultee-client crises; (5) if group cohesiveness is lacking, the case-seminar method of group consultation may not be effective. For example, in group consultation with the principals of schools scattered over a large rural county, there was a defensive tendency on the part of some group members to regard the problems presented to the group as idiosyncratic to other schools and not characteristic of their own. Consequently, it became necessary for the consultant to focus upon specific informational content rather than on the cases introduced by the group members. Although this resulted in requests for consultant visits to a number of the schools and opened the door for individual consultation with several principals, such initial nongroup or antigroup spirit might well present a technical limitation to the case-seminar consultation technique.

Individual and group consultation each appear to have particular advantages and disadvantages. A combination of approaches, such as was noted above with school principals, may prove to be optimal for some professional groups. In group sessions, the individual consultee becomes familiar with the professional competence of the consultant, develops respect for him as a person, and learns to trust him. Subsequently, the consultee may seek consultation on problems that he might feel reluctant to discuss in the group. As a function of such individual consultation, the consultee may ultimately become more comfortable in bringing up his special problems within the group context. Creative exploration of a variety of consultation techniques with many different professional groups by consultants with diverse backgrounds is needed.

While there is as yet no objective evidence of the effectiveness of mental health consultation either with individual consultees or with groups, there is impressive agreement concerning many aspects of group consultation by those who have compiled and recorded their observations (Maddux, 1953; Berlin, 1962; Parker, 1958; Parker, 1962; Rieman, 1963). Our own experiences have indicated that group consultation consistently improves communication, group cohesiveness, and morale among consultees, and gives the consultees increased sensitivity to the dynamics of interpersonal relations. We have also been impressed with consultees' reports of the beneficial influence of consultation on their relationships with their clients. However, objective data, derived from carefully controlled research, will be required to evaluate the effectiveness and usefulness of group consultation procedures and to establish consultation theory.

REFERENCES

Berlin, I. N.: Mental health consultation in schools as a means of communicating mental health principles. *J Amer Acad Child Psychiat,* 1:671-679, 1962.
Bindman, A. J.: Mental health consultation: Theory and practice. *J Consult Psychol,* 23:473-482, 1959.

Bradford, L. P.: Membership and the learning process. In L. P. Bradford, J. R. Gibb, and K. D. Benne (Eds.): *T-Group Theory and Laboratory Method: Innovation in Re-education.* New York, Wiley, 1964.

Caplan, G.: *Principles of Preventive Psychiatry.* New York, Basic, 1964.

Corsini, R. J., and Rosenberg, Bina: Mechanisms of group psychotherapy: Processes and dynamics. *J Abnorm Soc Psychol, 51*:406-411, 1955.

Kevin, D.: Use of the group method in consultation. In Lydia Rapoport (Ed.): *Consultation in Social Work Practice.* New York, National Association of Social Workers, 1963.

Maddux, J. F.: Psychiatric consultation in a rural setting. *Am J Orthopsychiatry, 23*:775-784, 1953.

Parker, Beulah: Psychiatric consultation for nonpsychiatric professional workers. *Public Health Monograph No. 53.* Washington, D.C.: Department of Health, Education, and Welfare, 1958.

Parker, Beulah: Some observations on psychiatric consultation with nursery school teachers. *Ment Hyg, 46*:559-566, 1962.

Rieman, D. W.: Group mental health consultation with Public Health Nurses. In Lydia Rapoport (Ed.): *Consultation in Social Work Practice.* New York, National Association of Social Workers, 1963.

```
┌─────────────────────────────────────────┐
│                                         │
│             Chapter 20                  │
│                                         │
│   THE CASE CONFERENCE AS A              │
│   CONSULTATION STRATEGY                 │
│                                         │
│           SIDNEY A. WINICKI             │
│                                         │
└─────────────────────────────────────────┘
```

A MAJOR EMPHASIS of Caplanian mental health consultation is the development of resources already present in an organization (Caplan, 1970). The model leads to the formulation of interventions that develop and refine the indigenous yet latent strengths of teachers. The Caplanian consultant differs from the traditional "expert" who conveys knowledge, but makes no provisions for sustained development of the consultee. Consultation-based strategies seek to involve the school personnel in an active manner. This approach strives to increase the probability that an initial intervention will become an on-going program that will have significant effects.

The ultimate goal of consultation is to increase the competencies of the consultee by freeing of his latent abilities and resources. This goal requires a different kind of psychologist-client relationship. The consultation model involves a collaboration between a psychologist with his expertise in behavior and the teacher with his expertise in education. The two work together to cope with problems of mutual concern.

Most schools utilize only a small part of the resources present in their staffs. These resources are comprised of the variety of experiences found in a group of teachers as well as their personalities. All of these resources have a great potential to help a school cope with the problems that typically arise. The

From *Psychology in the Schools*, 9:21-24, 1972.

challenge for school psychologists thus becomes how to design experiences that foster the utilization and continued growth of these latent capabilities.

Open communication in the faculty is necessary before teachers can begin to work together on school-related problems, but such a condition typically does not exist in most schools. Teachers often feel isolated and under constant scrutiny by the administration. Inexperienced teachers often feel threatened at the prospect of sharing school-related problems with colleagues. Circumstances such as these prevent the staff from using its resources to focus on problems. Experiences that facilitate and promote this communication process must be provided to encourage the utilization of the latent capabilities of the staff in problem-solving situations.

THE CASE CONFERENCE

This paper will describe a case conference intervention strategy. The purpose of these conferences was to provide groups of teachers with the experience of working jointly on school-related problems. During the initial sessions of the conference the goal of increased problem-solving competence was explained clearly to the teachers. The faculties were divided so that each group contained no more than eight teachers who taught similar grade levels (primary, intermediate, junior high). The groups met once a month, and the conferences were led by a person associated with the school who was a counselor-in-training.

The primary role of the consultant was as a facilitator to the communication process. The consultant encouraged teachers to utilize their collective resources in problem-solving situations. His work involved such activities as asking questions to help define the problem and explore its dimensions. The consultant often focused on understanding the behavior that was being discussed, the possible dynamics involved, and the interaction between classroom and home environments. Two important characteristics of these conferences were their nonthreatening nature and their emphasis on the teacher's ability to generate ways to cope with these problems. Therefore, the consultant did not dominate the interaction or take the responsibility to conduct the meetings.

The consultant remained alert to persistent themes that appeared to interfere with the teachers' ability to deal effectively with a problem. For example, one teacher appeared to overreact to children whom she perceived as outsiders to the class group. In such a situation, the consultant gave a "message" that was minimally threatening but that clarified the situation for the teacher and thereby reduced the theme and its interfering effect. For example, "kids who are isolates can sure make a person feel uncomfortable." Later during the same discussion, the consultant may add, "It's surprising how quickly isolates can fit in when they feel valued."

The consultant also provides data or psychological principles when necessary. The need for this type of substantive input arises when a lack of knowledge is making it difficult for the group to formulate interventions. When he is providing this type of input, the consultant must be alert to the tendency on the part of the teachers to view him as the "expert," a categorization that would tend to minimize his effectiveness because the teachers would tend not to rely on themselves, which is contrary to the goals of consultation.

The consultant shares the teacher's frustration when very difficult cases that often involve a chronic condition are being discussed. The consultant's behavior provides the teachers in the conference support and a model for problem-solving in difficult situations. This approach often leads to the surprising discovery of tenacity in some teachers that eventually results in viable suggestions.

The Development of the Case Conference

During the school year in which this program was conducted, the resources in the groups of teachers gradually emerged. Common developmental patterns became apparent in the eight groups of teachers. In order to help the strengths of the groups evolve the consultant persistently had to keep from being cast as the "expert." He encouraged contributions from group members. The consultant respected and valued the insights and reactions of the staff; through him, they became aware of their own strengths. As a consequence of the consultant's interaction, the groups gradually evolved as autonomous problem-solving groups.

The consultant continually had to monitor his interaction with the group. He constantly was faced with the dilemma of how and whether to intervene in a discussion. This decision had to be based on the consultant's assessment of the current developmental status of the group and what intervention would help them progress most effectively.

In the beginning stages of the case conferences the anxiety level was high and interaction was inhibited. Participants did not know what to expect and probably had fantasies with regard to group therapy. During these initial stages, two general topics typically were discussed. The first involved questions to the consultant designed to clarify the situation. The consultant used this opportunity to discuss the theory of mental health consultation (Caplan, 1970; Plaut, 1961). The second topic discussed was children. In these early sessions the problems were either innocuous, such as how to handle children with offending odors who have an obvious hygiene problem, or a series of long-standing insoluble problems. The former functioned as "smoke screens" to prevent any meaningful discussion of significant problems. The latter represented attempts to test the consultant on cases for which there is no solution nor any expected. The consultant refused to become involved with these initial problems. The rationale for inaction was that these are not soluble problems, and discussion of them would have been an exercise in futility.

In the intermediate stage, the teachers actively began to discuss problems, but needed help to learn how to use each other. For example, Mrs. Smtih indicated that she has found it difficult to correct Tommy and then to avoid a subsequent temper tantrum, while Miss Gold indicated that she had had no difficulty with the child. At this stage, the consultant may intervene to ask Miss Gold how she handled these difficult situations with Tommy in order to give Mrs. Smith some ideas about how to handle him in a more salutary manner. In a sense, the consultant was acquainting the teachers with each other and their resources. The meetings at this stage also tended to be less threatening, and much of the anxiety had subsided.

In the advanced stages, the groups appeared to function almost autonomously. The consultant had become just another member of the group. He was no longer needed as a mediator. Teachers spontaneously volunteered suggestions and explored situations together. There also was an emerging concern and awareness of children discussed, which was expressed in such ways as a desire to communicate to subsequent schools that they will be attending. Interventions are proposed and implemented. The self-confidence generated in the case conferences is reflected in greater effectiveness in the teachers' individual classrooms.

Issues in Case Conference

An important issue is whether to include the principal in the meetings. This issue should be evaluated by the consultant in terms of the dynamics of the relationship between the principal and the faculty. At first, it did not seem desirable to include him because of a stifling effect that he might have had on the interaction. In retrospect, it appears that he should have been included. Inclusion of the principal would have given him a better idea of what was going on in the school, and his participation also would have helped to diminish suspicions he might have had with regard to his possible betrayal in the meetings. These fears on the part of the principal eventually could have led him to sabotage the meetings. The case conference also would give him an opportunity to make valuable contributions as well as to learn. The principal could use the consultant's model to learn how to tap the initiative and strengths of the faculty.

The case conferences can be upsetting; at times they uncover administrative problems that can be difficult and sometimes involve pathology. These discoveries are emotionally upsetting. The consultant is faced with helping teachers to sort out their feelings and specifically define the problem. It then becomes possible for the participants to cope more adequately with the situation. This coping includes decisions as to how and when to intervene.

One difficult issue involves the individual teacher. In some instances, it seems to be appropriate to focus on a theme of a particular teacher who has a neurotic need such as an overwhelming desire to be nurturant. The discussion can make the teacher feel threatened and exposed, and it is not clear whether it is fruitful to work on such problems in the group setting or whether they ought to be reserved for individual consultation. Probably most sensitive issues of this sort can be approached in relatively nonthreatening ways, and all participants can grow through the group discussion.

Issues that can pose problems for the consultant cannot be avoided. These problems, however, are not insurmountable and do not detract from the usefulness and general applicability of the consultation strategy described above.

REFERENCES

Caplan, G.: *Theory and Practice of Mental Health Consultation.* New York, Basic, 1970.

Plaut, T. F. A.: Techniques and problems of mental health consultation. Paper presented at workshop on Consultation in Community Mental Health, Chapel Hill, North Carolina, April 26, 1961, sponsored by the North Carolina State Board of Health.

```
┌─────────────────────────────────────────────┐
│                                             │
│              Chapter 21                     │
│                                             │
├─────────────────────────────────────────────┤
│         STUDENT CONSULTANTS:                │
│       EVALUATIONS BY CONSULTEES             │
│                                             │
│              PHILIP A. MANN                 │
│                                             │
└─────────────────────────────────────────────┘
```

Elementary school teachers in five schools participated in a mental health consultation program. All teachers, both users and nonusers of the program, were asked to evaluate it by means of a questionnaire. A comparison of questionnaire responses by twenty-five users and twenty-five nonusers of consultation indicated that less experienced teachers of the upper three grades used consultation more often, and more experienced teachers of lower grades used consultation less often than did teachers in the remaining two combinations of experience and grade level. Teachers using consultation gave more specific definitions of the consultant's function than did nonusers. Teacher-consultees who rated consultation high in usefulness reported that the consultant's behavior was in line with their expectations more often than did teacher-consultees who gave low ratings. High raters also perceived more changes in children's behavior or their perceptions of children. Implications for consultation training and practice are discussed.

T HE SCHOOLS ARE A prominent potential locus of intervention for preventive mental health programs since schools have both widespread and prolonged influence on the development of children. Mental health consultation has been identified since the inception of the community mental health programs as one of the required services. Although mental health and educational personnel have developed working relationships in the past,

From the *American Journal of Community Psychology*, 1:182-193, 1973.

those relationships have probably been more restricted, and undoubtedly less numerous, than those envisioned in the programs of community mental health centers (Newman, 1967; Sarason, Levine, Goldenberg, Cherlin, and Bennett, 1966).

The expansion of these efforts has created strains at several levels. Paradoxically, although consultation was seen as one means of easing the professional manpower shortage, there were insufficient numbers of trained mental health consultants available and few persons and programs to provide such training. Many would-be consultants have had to learn from experience or to rely on previous modes of functioning often inappropriate to the task.

In addition to a shortage of manpower, there is a knowledge lag in the field of consultation which has impeded the development of coherent strategies for training consultants. Theories, anecdotes, and case reports began to appear during the 1960s, the most prominent of which has been Caplan's (1963; 1970) model of consultee-centered case consultation. There has been precious little material in the literature, however, which a student of consultation could look to as a substantive guide to practice. Conspicuously lacking have been detailed descriptions of consultants at work and evaluative data on effective techniques.

Moreover, in the particular case of the schools, some noticeable difficulties have arisen in developing workable relationships between mental health consultants and educational personnel. Unlike the relationships between mental health consultants and, say public health nurses who share a somewhat similar professional heritage, mental health, and educational personnel often come out of different operational patterns associated with their respective institutional bases (Rhodes, 1972). Developing shared expectations, which is thought to be an important precondition for successful consultation work (Glidewell, 1959), has often been difficult and frustrating (Glidewell and Stringer, 1967).

A few attempts have been made to evaluate the effectiveness of consultation, and these have shown mixed results (cf. Mannino and Shore, 1971). Changes in consultees are reported more often than changes in clients, and the results tend to be inconsistent.

Virtually no effort has been devoted, in even the most well-controlled of these studies, to attempt to relate consultation effectiveness to features of specific consultant-consultee relationships. Such data might yield knowledge on which to build models of effective training and practice.

Learning to become a consultant is an ambiguous, frustrating experience which is apparently not made easier by seasoning in other professional roles (Berlin, 1965; Signell and Scott, 1972). If trainers of consultants are to have at their command material which can provide more specific guidelines for consultant activity, more detailed examination of consultation processes and evaluations of individual consultant's work is needed.

A promising beginning has emerged recently in several reports of consultee impressions of consultants and the consultation process. Eisdorfer and Batton (1972) surveyed public health nurses who had received consultation and constructed descriptions of successful and unsuccessful consultant characteristics. Norman and Forti (1972) and Mannino (1972) matched reports of both consultants and consultees on activities in the consultation process with ratings of the success of consultation. These studies provide an opportunity to examine more details of the consultation process as it is seen by its immediate consumers. Despite the difficulties of interpreting impressionistic data, this approach can be useful to the development of more effective mental health consultation until such time as more objective measures are developed or, indeed, are deemed more valid.

The current study attempts to extend the understanding of effective consultant behavior by examining the evaluative comments of consultees. Unlike the studies just cited, the consultee sample consists entirely of elementary school teachers, the use of open-ended response formats for some questions instead of preconstructed checklists, and includes both users and nonusers of consultation to whom the services were equally available. The study is exploratory in nature and seeks to elicit an understanding of consultation practices from an analysis of the relationships among teacher perceptions and expectations of consultants, their use of consultation services, and their ratings of its usefulness.

Method

Consultants

The consultants were graduate students in clinical and school psychology who were enrolled in a seminar-practicum in mental health consultation taught by the author, who also provided individual supervision. The students attended a 3-hour weekly seminar during the first semester and a one-hour weekly session the second semester, together with several other students who were placed as consultants to other agencies. The orientation of the seminar was a combination of social systems and Caplanian concepts. The author and the students met with school administrators and principals to discuss the consultation service and make assignments to specific schools. The principals then arranged to introduce the consultants to the school faculty in a group meeting, at which time the student-consultants explained the purpose of consultation, their role, and procedures for scheduling consultation sessions. Thereafter, each consultant was present in the school for one-half to one full day each week. At the end of the second semester, the author and the consultants met with the administrators and principals to review the program.

Consultees

The potential consultees were sixty-eight elementary school teachers in the five schools receiving the consultation service. No school included in this study had received mental health consultation before. Following the program, each teacher was asked to complete a questionnaire anonymously and mail it to the author in an attached, stamped envelope so as to guarantee confidentiality. There were fifty questionnaires returned, a rate of 73.5 percent.

Questionnaire

The questionnaire consisted of seventeen items. One set of items was concerned with identifying information: the name of the school, grade level taught, years of teaching experience, and class size. A second set of items dealt with familiarity with the consultant: whether the teacher knew a consultant was available, whether he had met the consultant individually or in a group, and whether he had used the consultant's services. Those who did use the consultant were asked to indicate what they had talked with the consultant about and to rate the usefulness of consultation on a Likert-type scale, ranging from 1, "Extremely Useful," to 5, "Not at all useful." They were asked to indicate what the consultant did, what they had expected the consultant to do, whether their expectation was different from what the consultant did, and whether having the consultant available made any difference in the behavior of children in the class. A fourth set of items asked all teachers about their general impressions of consultants: whether the consultant was readily available, whether they would use consultation again if it were offered, what they thought a mental health consultant did, and how a consultant could be more helpful. Two open-ended items asked teachers to indicate what the best and worst things were about the consultant. Finally, they were asked to indicate what they felt were the most pressing problems in the school, whether they felt the school would be willing to pay for consultation, and if so, whether they would approve of such payment.

Analysis of Data

Teacher-questionnaire responses were analyzed to determine relationships among teacher characteristics and perceptions of consultants on the one hand, and use and evaluation of consultation services on the other. Among the fifty responding teachers, users and nonusers divided themselves evenly into two groups of twenty-five each. Since most data is nominal in form, the Chi-square statistic was employed to analyze differences in the frequency of responses to the various questionnaire items.

Results

All fifty teachers responding indicated that they knew the consultant was available and that they had met the consultant. Among those teachers who used consultation, the average rating of usefulness was 2.96, with a range from 1 to 5. Six teachers said consultation had made a difference in the behavior of children in their class, four teachers said the change had come from a difference in their perception of the children, twelve said it had not made any difference, and three did not respond to this question.

Twenty-seven teachers said they would use consultation in the future. Two teachers, one of whom used the consultant, said they would not use the service again, and twenty-one, all nonusers, failed to respond. Twenty-five teachers (all users) felt the school would pay for the service if funds were available, three felt it would not, and twenty-two did not answer. However, twenty-eight said they would approve of such payment, with twenty-two again not responding.

Factors Associated with Consultation Use

Both grade level taught and years of teaching experience were significantly related to use of consultation when viewed separately. Teachers of grades four through six used consultation more often than teachers of grades one through three ($X^2 = 6.57$, $df = 1$; $p < .02$); and teachers with five years or less of teaching experience used consultation more often than teachers with six years or more of experience ($X^2 = 8.12$; $df = 1$; $p < .005$). The range in the more experienced group was from six to forty years. These distributions are presented in Tables 21-I and 21-II respectively.

TABLE 21-I

FREQUENCY OF CONSULTATION USE BY GRADE LEVEL

	Consultation		
Grade Level	*Used*	*Not Used*	*Total*
1-3	9	18	27
4-6	16	7	23
Total	25	25	50

TABLE 21-II

FREQUENCY OF CONSULTATION USE BY
YEARS OF TEACHING EXPERIENCE

Years of	Consultation		
Experience	*Used*	*Not Used*	*Total*
0-5	19	9	28
6 or more	6	16	22
Total	25	25	50

Closer examination of this data revealed that there was a statistically significant interaction effect, between grade level and years of experience, on the use of consultation. When grade level and years of experience were combined with use and nonuse of consultation to produce a 2 x 2 x 2 table, the overall X^2 was equal to 13.51 ($df = 3$; $p < .005$). This distribution is shown in Table 21-III. The table was then partitioned according to a procedure described by Castellan (1965), which resulted in a barely significant component within less experienced teachers ($X^2 = 4.12$; $df = 1$; $p < .05$); a nonsignificant component within more experienced teachers ($X^2 = 1.27$; $df = 1$; NS); and a significant component for interaction between years of experience and grade level ($X^2 = 8.12$; $df = 3$; $p < .05$). Table 21-III indicates that less experienced teachers of grades four through six used consultation more often, while more experienced teachers of grades one through three used consultation much less than did the other two grade-level and experience groups, whose distributions of use and nonuse paralleled those in the sample as a whole.

TABLE 21-III

JOINT FREQUENCY DISTRIBUTION OF CONSULTATION USE BY YEARS OF TEACHING EXPERIENCE AND GRADE LEVEL

Years of Experience	Grade Level	Consultation		
		Used	*Not Used*	*Total*
0-5	1-3	7	7	14
	4-6	12	2	14
Subtotal		19	9	28
6+	1-3	2	11	13
	4-6	4	5	9
Subtotal		6	16	22
Total		25	25	50

Responses to the question, "In your opinion, what does the consultant do?" were then analyzed to determine if users and nonusers had different perceptions of the consultant function. Teacher responses were coded into six categories. These categories and the distribution of teachers who used and did not use consultation are shown in Table 21-IV. The overall X^2 of 11.03 for this table is very nearly significant ($df = 5$; X^2 .05 =

11.07). Most of this effect, however, is contributed by the number of nonusers who indicated they did not know what the consultant does, or did not respond. When the first four rows of Table 21-IV are combined to form a single category, and the last two rows are combined to form another, the resultant X^2 of 8.42 ($df = 1$; $p < .005$) is very significant; while the difference between the number of users and nonusers who attributed some specific function to the consultant was not significant ($X^2 = 2.2$; $df = 1$; NS). Thus, the difference in perception of the consultant function between users and nonusers is due mainly to the failure of nonusers to provide any description, and it is impossible to determine from the data available whether this results from a lack of information or from ignoring the question.

TABLE 21-IV

FREQUENCY OF CONSULTATION USE BY PERCEIVED
CONSULTANT FUNCTION

	Consultation		
Perceived Consultant Function	*Used*	*Not Used*	*Total*
Gives advice, expertise	4	2	6
Discusses, listens	6	3	9
Helps teacher	9	4	13
Helps child	4	5	9
Don't know	1	3	4
No response	1	8	9
Total	25	25	50

Neither school size nor classroom size were significantly related to use of consultation among teachers or to rated usefulness of consultation among teacher-consultees.

Rated Usefulness of Consultation

Among users of consultation, the distribution of rated usefulness was explored to assess what factors were associated with the ratings. There was no difference in the average ratings given by teachers of the upper and lower grades, but there was a significant difference in ratings according to years of teaching experience. In contrast to the distribution of use of consultation, the average rating of usefulness by more experienced teacher consultees ($N = 6$) was 2.17, while the average rating of usefulness by less experienced teachers ($N = 19$) was 3.21 ($t = 3.25$; $df = 23$; $p < .01$, two-tailed). Thus, while the more experienced teachers as a group used consultation less often, than did the less experienced teachers, the more experienced rated consultation as more uesful when they did use it.

The responses of the group of teacher-consultees were divided according to the ratings, with those rating the usefulness consultation high (1 or 2) and those rating it low (4 or 5) forming two groups. Those giving a rating of 3 were omitted. Responses of the teachers in the high- and low-rating groups were compared with respect to the following questions: "What did the consultant do?" "What had you expected the consultant to do?" Both questions were specific to their consultation experience. Responses to the question of what a consultant does in general were also compared. Responses were coded according to the same set of categories presented in Table 21-IV. There were no significant differences in the distribution of responses across the categories for the high- and low-rating groups on any of these questions.

When the high- and low-rating groups of teacher consultees were compared on their responses to the question, "Was this (what the consultant did) different from what you expected?" proportionately more of the high-rating group answered, "No" and proportionately more of the low-rating group answered "Yes" ($X^2 = 5.14$; $df = 1$; $p < .025$). The distribution of ratings of consultation and congruence with expectation is presented in Table 21-V. Consultant behavior perceived as being consistent with what the teacher-consultee had expected the consultant to do was associated with higher ratings of consultation usefulness, while perceived consultant behavior alone was not related to rated usefulness. Congruence with expectations or its absence was not related to grade level or experience.

Of the ten teachers who said that having the consultant available had made a difference in the behavior of children or in their attitudes toward them, all but two rated the consultant 1 or 2. The two exceptions gave a 3 and a 4, respectively. One

TABLE 21-V

FREQUENCY OF CONGRUENCE OF CONSULTANT BEHAVIOR
WITH TEACHER EXPECTATION BY TEACHER-RATED
USEFULNESS OF CONSULTATION

Consultant Different From Expectation?	*Rating of Consultation*		
	1, 2	4, 5	Total
Yes	3	7	10
No	6	1	7
Total	9	8	17

of them expressed ambivalence about focusing on his own feelings in the consultation, while the other expressed concern that he had begun to perceive more disturbance in the lives of children than he had realized was present.

Discussion

Compared with the total potential sample of teachers (assuming that those not responding did not use consultation), the proportion of teachers using consultation is consistent with that reported by Iscoe, Pierce-Jones, Friedman, and McGehearty (1967) in a similar program conducted earlier in different schools in the same city. The finding that less experienced teachers used consultation more often also agrees with their results, although they did not report an interaction between grade level taught and years of experience in the use of consultation. In fact, their report suggests that consultation may have been sought more often about younger children.

These results may be interpretable with reference to a crisis framework. The most frequent problem for which teachers reported seeking help was a behavioral disturbance, the next most frequent was a learning problem, and neither were related to variables associated with use or rating of consultation. Assuming there is no difference in the existence of problems across grade levels, behavior problems appear to cause more concern among teachers in the upper grades, particularly among less experienced teachers. In the lower grades, and especially among more experienced teachers, such problems either do not cause as much concern or are not seen as creating a need for consultative help. This interpretation would be consistent with the crisis basis for consultation proposed by Caplan (1963).

Most teacher-consultees who reported behavioral changes in children gave high ratings for usefulness. Such responses suggest that the ratings are backed up in part by perceived results. All but two teachers reporting behavioral changes, however, had less than five years of experience. Since the more experienced teachers gave generally higher ratings of usefulness, perhaps they are more patient in expecting results, an expectation which is realistic for a program of this type. In addition, they possibly are more critical in judging change or are more charitable in rating consultants than are less experienced teachers.

The finding that perceived congruency between consultant behavior and teacher expectation was associated with higher rated usefulness of consultation supports Glidewell's (1959) emphasis on the importance of developing shared expectations in consulting relationships. Additionally, one might expect that this congruency would be associated with more perceived change in children's behavior. Although the data on behavioral changes are limited to perceived changes, they suggest some qualifications on the relationship between congruency with expectations and successful consultation.

Teachers who reported behavioral changes were evenly divided in saying that the consultant's behavior was or was not in line with their expectations. Nearly all teachers who reported unexpected consultant behavior indicated that they expected the consultant to be more active, to observe the children, to give specific advice, or to work with the children individually. Teachers for whom the consultant did not fulfill expectations were divided into two further groups: those who reported behavior changes in the children and those who did not. Teachers reporting behavioral changes indicated in other responses that they now perceived their expectations as inappropriate or that they accepted the incongruity of the consultant's behavior. Those reporting incongruity and no behavioral changes tended to insist that the consultant should have met their expectations. Thus, where teacher expectations were initially incongruent with the consultant's role, successful consultation included resolving the incongruity or its effects, while unsuccessful consultation did not.

Further qualitative evidence amplifies this difference. The open-ended items asked for the "best" and "worst" things about the consultant. Teachers who gave high ratings listed positive, specific qualities of the consultant, which imply that the consultation had an effect on the consultee, "He listened, offered suggestions, but he always had nice things to say about things you had previously tried." "He lets you tell your problems, get this off your chest." "Offers new perspectives to problems where apparent stalemate has arisen." Teachers who gave low ratings indicated more vague, unspecific qualities that imply passive availability but not particular utility: "He's there for you to go see." "He was a sounding board." "He was there in case I needed him." In listing the worst thing about the consultant, teachers who gave high ratings indicated more than anything else the limited time the consultant was available, although one teacher responded, "The threat he poses to some people." Teachers who gave low ratings listed as the worst thing the fact that, "he didn't have the right answer" when the teacher expected it, or that he did not observe the classroom. One of these teachers said, "I felt he was here under false pretenses. I distrusted him, although I felt like he was a nice person. I suppose I felt more threatened since I am a beginning teacher." Another said, "Gave advice suited to a one-to-one relationship. No time or proper place to do this."

Implications for Consultation Training and Practice

The finding that grade level and teaching experience interact to effect the use of consultation provides information that may be helpful to beginning consultants in adjusting their expectations concerning the demand for their services. If one follows Caplan's assumption that crisis situations are a basis for seeking consultation, then it would seem from these data that the less experienced, upper grade teachers were more often in crisis.

The findings here and in other studies suggest an explanation other than a crisis situation. That younger teachers use consultation more often is consistent with a social-power explanation. Assuming that the less experienced teachers could be ranked lower in organizational power within the school social system, the data are similar to a finding by Mann (1972) and widely encountered by experienced consultants. Mann found that elements of a social system lower in organizational power are more accessible to the consultant. Interpreting differential use of consultation as a response to the innovation represented by the consultant, rather than to some characteristic of the teacher stimulated by a particular child, suggests that nonusers of consultation might make more use of the service as it comes to be more accepted as part of the school program.

The initial response of the less experienced teachers as a part of the organizational dynamics of the school is not incompatible with a notion of individual consultee experience of a crisis situation; it merely focuses on a different level of analysis of social forces. Similiarly, the interaction between teacher experience and grade level may be viewed as a reflection of the school organization's definition of critical behavior as well as a product of individual teacher's perceptions. Older children may present a greater sense of urgency than do younger children; the upper grade children may have been problematic for the school for a longer period of time, and there is less time remaining to resolve their behavior problems.

If the consultant is to emphasize the importance and potentially greater payoff of earlier intervention, it is clear that some more deliberate efforts will be required, such as the employment of objective surveys of potentially problematic behavior among younger children, to bring their needs to the teachers' attention. As the data indicated, teachers who did not use consultation did not give as many specific definitions of the consultant's function as did those who were consultees. Thus, the consultant cannot rely sufficiently on an initial definition of the consultant role at a teacher's meeting.

An especially important aspect of defining the consultant's role is shown here as the congruency between perceived consultant behavior and teacher expectations. While this is an important dimension to most interpersonal relationship, including counseling and psychotherapy relationships, this effect has not been demonstrated clearly before in the consultation literature. Seeking out the consultee's expectations would seem to be an important working dimension of the consultant's job. Consultant and consultee perceptions of each other and the effects of these perceptions on the process and outcome of consultation should be studied more extensively to establish a more systematic basis for consultative intervention.

REFERENCES

Berlin, I. N.: Mental health consultation in the schools: Who can do it and why? *Community Ment Health J, 1*:19-22, 1965.

Caplan, G.: Types of mental health consultation. *Am J Orthopsychiatry, 33*:470-481, 1963.

Caplan, G.: *Theory and Practice of Mental Health Consultation.* New York, Basic, 1970.

Castellan, N. J.: On the partitioning of contingency tables. *Psychol Bull, 64*:330-338, 1965.

Eisdorfer, C., and Batton, L.: The mental health consultant as seen by his consultees. *Community Ment Health J, 8*:171-177, 1972.

Glidewell, J.: The entry problem in consultation. *Journal of Social Issues, 15*:51-59, 1959.

Glidewell, J., and Stringer, L.: The educational institution and the health institution. In E. M. Bower and W. G. Hollister (Eds.): *Behavioral Science Frontiers in Education.* New York, Wiley, 1967.

Iscoe, I.; Pierce-Jones, J.; Friedman, S. T., and McGehearty, L.: Some strategies in mental health consultation: A brief description of a project and some preliminary results. In E. L. Cowen, E. A. Gardner, and M. Zax (Eds.): *Emergent Approaches to Mental Health Problems.* New York, Appleton, 1967.

Mann, P. A.: Accessibility and organizational power in the entry phase of mental health consultation. *J Consult Clin Psychol, 38*:215-218, 1972.

Mannino, F. V.: Task accomplishment and consultation outcome. *Community Ment Health J, 8*:102-109, 1972.

Mannino, F. V., and Shore, M. F.: Consultation research. *Public Health Monogr, No. 79,* 1971.

Newman, R. G.: *Psychological Consultation in the Schools: A Catalyst for Learning.* New York, Basic, 1967.

Norman, E. C., and Forti, T. J.: A study of the process and outcome of mental health consultation. *Community Ment Health J, 8*:261-270, 1972.

Rhodes, W. C.: *Behavioral Threat and Community Response.* New York, Behavioral Publications, 1972.

Sarason, S. B.; Levine, M.; Goldenberg, I.; Cherlin, D. L., and Bennett, E. M.: *Psychology in Community Settings.* New York, Wiley, 1966.

Signell, K. A., and Scott, P. A.: Training in consultation: A crisis of role transition. *Community Ment Health J, 8*:149-160, 1972.

```
┌─────────────────────┐
│                     │
│     Section V       │
│                     │
└─────────────────────┘
```

ORGANIZATION DEVELOPMENT
CONSULTATION

T HE FOURTH LEVEL of consultation presented in this book is the
organization development approach. This approach has expanded
in recent years, and fortunately has resulted in detailed descriptions of consultation procedures. On the other hand, research
on these techniques is only beginning to appear, and like all
approaches to consultation, further research is needed in order
to develop methods of proven effectiveness.

In contrast to the preceding three types of consultation, a
major feature of this approach is that change in the behavior
of children or individual teachers is not the consultant's primary
focus. On the other hand, a change in the functioning of the
organization is the primary goal. The organization would be
defined as including any of the many subgroups associated with
the school (e.g. administrators, teachers, students, parents, etc.).
The organizational aspects of the school system include some
of the environmental factors which influence children's behavior,
and a secondary goal of this approach is to change children's
behavior indirectly through these environmental agents.

Organization development attempts to change the school's
functioning by improving communication in the system. In order
to accomplish this, the consultant tries to discover whether there
are any impediments to communication, whether there is confusion as to the organization's goals, and whether there is any
weakness at problem solving. Diagnostic skills are needed in
order to help the organization to develop effective intervention
strategies. Rather than using traditional individual psychological

tests, organizational diagnosis is carried out with interviews, surveys, and questionnaires. Generally, the focus of intervention strategies is to facilitate communication between relevant subgroups. The techniques used might include role playing, direct feedback between teachers and students, and a variety of T-group techniques.

The articles selected for this section are organized into three groups. The first group includes two theoretical articles which form a conceptual framework for the organization development approach to consultation. In the first chapter, Gallessich discusses three important integrating themes which are found in the following articles presented in this section: (1) the system is the client; (2) the goal is to facilitate organizational growth; and (3) the focus is on impeded communication, confused objectives, and decisions made with insufficient staff contribution. Next, Broskowski discusses many of the same theoretical themes discussed in the first chapter.

Two types of organization development consultation can be conceptualized. These include either a focus on general problems or specific problems of the organization, and they determine the second and third groups of articles selected for this section. Following the theoretical discussion noted above, the second chapter, by Broskowski, describes a consultation attempt to improve the general problem solving in a school. To accomplish this, consultants assisted in developing specific teacher projects which involved self-assessment and change. In addition to the projects themselves, group discussions of the projects served to increase communication between the faculty. The third chapter, by Schmuck, Runkel, and Langmeyer describes another attempt to improve the general functioning of a school. Positive aspects of this paper include a description of the procedures derived from T-Group techniques which could be useful to practicing consultants and date evaluating the effectiveness of the intervention.

The last three chapters provide examples of programs whose goals were to improve organizational functioning regarding specific problems. In Chapter 25, Berlin focuses on confrontation by rebellious students. He describes techniques which help to open communication between faculty and students and between administration and students. These include role playing and group discussion followed by individual consultation with some teachers and administrators.

Chapter 26 by Snapp and Sikes focuses specifically on racial tension. The techniques attempt to open communication channels between students and students and between students and faculty. The open communication was expected to improve problem solving by students and faculty resulting in less fighting between racial groups. Perhaps the most important contribution which this paper makes is that it provides clear procedures which could be implemented by practitioners. The program included an encounter group for teachers and one for potential student leaders. From these two groups, a teacher and student were paired so that they could be co-leaders of student discussion groups which focused on racial disturbances.

In the last chapter, Levin and Stein focused on a problem involving relations between the community and the school during a teachers' strike. The techniques were oriented towards increasing communication between these two groups in order to reduce the existing tension. While the other chapters in this section described programs which were developed in order to improve present functioning and to avoid future crisis, this paper describes a program which was implemented during a crisis. The procedures included a forum in school community relations. Parents, teachers, and students were invited and given a task. Subsequent discussions involving the task were designed to increase communication between the three subgroups.

Chapter 22

A SYSTEMS MODEL OF
MENTAL HEALTH CONSULTATION

JUNE GALLESSICH

The Model

THE MENTAL HEALTH consultation model developed by Caplan (1970) for use with individuals (teachers, nurses, and other professional workers) is adaptable to a systems-consultation approach to schools and school districts. The staff or faculty are the consultees; the focus of the consultation is upon the total system or components of the system. The primary assumption of this model is that the system, whether it is a small unit, such as a team of two or three teachers or a larger unit, for example, a school district, contains the basic resources for effective problem-solving; the consultant enters the system with the goal of facilitating organizational growth through more effective use of indigenous resources. He maintains a coordinate posititon with the consultees; rather than give them diagnoses and recommendations, he helps them work out their own assessments, decisions, and implementations. The systems model of mental health consultation is a useful strategy for the introduction of behavioral science concepts to traditional organizations (Argyris, 1962; Bennis, 1969; Lawrence and Lorsch, 1970; McGregor, 1962; Schein, 1969).

Prior to the consultant's entry into the system, he should dis-

From *Psychology in the Schools*, 9:13-15, 1972.

cuss with organizational representatives an informal, tentative "contract" that outlines the services expected. Then his immediate tasks are to learn the organization's formal and informal structures and processes and to build relationships with staff. He needs a substantial amount of time, observation, and informal contacts to understand the overt system; an even larger investment is required to identify the covert structure, the complex norms, processes, and social patterns that shape and direct the staff's energies. As the consultant studies the system, he concurrently begins to build relationships. As he inquires about organizational features, he explains and demonstrates his function as consultant. With time and free access to all personnel, the entry task is facilitated.

Consultation with the System

Scanning the System

The consultant who uses this model follows a systems-analysis paradigm (Churchman, 1968) to help the staff study its organization. Organizational difficulties are predictable in several areas (Lippitt, 1959). Typically the staff lacks clear, mutual understanding of objectives and priorities. Communication within the system usually is obstructed. Decisions often are based on inadequate data and involve only a small fraction of staff creativity and expertise. Inertia, simple resistance to change, is sometimes the most obstructive force. The consultant's most significant input may take place during the early exploratory period, often a time of unsettling "eye-opening" for the consultees. The consultant's questions as to the purpose, functioning, and relationships of the various elements of the system encourage the staff to scrutinize its policies and procedures.

Organizational Objectives

As the staff members explore their system with the consultant, they begin to clarify the objectives that presumably form the rationale for the organization's existence. Important areas for consideration include (1) goal specificity (Parsons, 1951), the clarity with which intermediate as well as ultimate goals are explicated and arranged in order of priority; (2) the degree of staff concensus as to goals; (3) the congruence between the organization's structure and processes and goal attainment; (4) the integration of specified goals into the organization's reward system; and (5) goal-flexibility, the ability of the organization to modify its objectives in order to adapt to environmental changes.

Communication Problems

The study of goals usually leads to the discovery of communication breakdowns that are preventing the development of common goals as well as inhibiting the full utilization of the system's problem-solving and decision-making resources. To function optimally, the system needs a free interchange of ideas and reactions. The consultant can help the staff study their communication patterns: vertical and lateral flows, directionality, content, and form of communication processes. Location of barriers is especially important. For example, a faculty may discuss only pleasant subjects and thus avoid controversial issues. Often there is no meaningful interaction between curriculum and guidance staffs in a district office or between primary and intermediate grade teachers within a school. Communication downward in the hierarchy may consist of memos which discourage the dialogue that could clarify areas of misunderstanding. The consultant who is alert to these common failures can help the staff discover ways to create and maintain an open system of communication.

Implementation of Objectives

The consultant then works with the staff to study the organization's effectiveness to implement goals. Usually the staff discovers that traditional patterns of management, including centralized decision-making, are preventing full use of resources (Haire, 1962). Most administrators have been trained in traditional institutions and are unaccustomed to relinquish control. Often they are motivated by strong power needs. A common administrative pitfall is to delegate authority and then recall it arbitrarily. Staff members then become demoralized and immobilized by feelings of inadequacy and powerlessness; they may react with passivity, dependency, or open rebellion, reactions that prevent a climate of cooperativeness. The consultant can help his consultees perceive and evaluate the many implications of alternative power arrangements so that they can select the most appropriate decision-making patterns to implement their goals (Beckhard, 1969; Schein, 1965).

Evaluation and Adaptation

Each system needs continual evaluation of its effectiveness in relation to goals, strategies, and the changing environment. No structure or process will always be optimally useful to a system. The consultant can help his consultees set up mechanisms for feedback (Argyris, 1962) to facilitate on-going evaluation and adaptation. He can help them determine the best balance of stability and change for any given period of their organization's life, in terms of their common goals.

Conclusion

The Caplanian model of mental health consultation (Caplan, 1970) can be adapted to a system approach designed to increase the coping skills of an organization. This paradigm is useful to help the staff of a school or school district define objectives and develop communication patterns and problem-solving techniques that facilitate the attainment of these objectives.

REFERENCES

Argyris, C.: *Interpersonal Competence and Organizational Effectiveness.* Homewood, Dorsey, 1962.

Beckhard, R.: *Organization Development: Strategies and Models.* Reading, A-W, 1969.

Bennis, W. G.: *Organization Development: It's Nature, Origins and Prospects.* Reading, A-W, 1969.

Caplan, G.: *The Theory and Practice of Mental Health Consultation.* New York, Basic, 1970.

Churchman, C. W.: *The Systems Approach.* New York, Dell, 1968.

Haire, M.: The concept of power and the concept of man. In C. Argyris, *et al.* (Eds.): *Social Science Approaches to Business Behavior.* Homewood, Dorsey, 1962.

Lawrence, P. R., and Lorsch, J. W.: *Organization and Environment.* Homewood, Dorsey, 1969.

Lippit, R.: Dimensions of the consultant's job. *Journal of Social Issues, 15*:5-12, 1959.

McGregor, D.: *The Professional Manager.* New York, McGraw, 1967.

Parsons, T.: *The Social System.* Glencoe, Free Press, 1951.

Schein, E. H.: *Organizational Psychology.* Englewood Cliffs, P-H, 1965.

Schein, E. H.: *Process Consultation: Its Role in Organizational Development.* Reading, A-W, 1969.

Singer, D.; Whiton, M. B., and Fried, M.: An alternative to traditional mental health services and consultation in schools: A social systems and group process approach. *Journal of School Psychology, 8*:172-179, 1970.

Chapter 23

CONCEPTS OF
TEACHER-CENTERED CONSULTATION

ANTHONY BROSKOWSKI

In applying process consultation and open systems theory, the school consultant strives for active participation by all in the problem-solving process, leading to self-assessment and self-directed change.

Education, like psychology, is something many persons feel free to criticize by virtue of having had firsthand experience as students. Psychologists may be prone to compound this error by applying some principles of psychology within a school without first developing some models of schools as organizations and models of consultation tailored to fit such systems. Too often we may use the familiar doctor-patient model in trying "to help the school" (the patient) and then experience frustration when our attempts are resisted or fail.

The purposes of this article are (a) to present a model of the school as an organization, (b) to present a model of consultation suited to such an organization, and (c) to describe and evaluate a program of consultation to an inner-city, junior high school faculty based on these two models.

Schools as Open Systems

Using general systems theory (Katz and Kahn, 1966; Miller, 1955; von Bertalanffy, 1968), the school is viewed as a complex

From *Professional Psychology*, 4:50-58, 1973.

organization with permeable boundaries residing within a larger environment (including the larger school system) that exerts pressures on the boundaries and with which it must interact. As an open system, the school receives inputs across its boundaries, operates on these inputs within the boundaries, and transfers outputs back into the environment. The inputs may include such physical factors as money, personnel, materials, and pupils, as well as such abstract entities as community values and goals. Within the boundaries there exists a hierarchy of status and authority, governing rules and normative systems, and differentiation of roles based on various task functions. The outputs include the graduates and some less obvious factors called ideas, values, attitudes, and skills.

The model becomes increasingly complex when it focuses on the internal operations of the system and their reciprocal relationships with the external environment. The goals of the school are partly determined by the environment which has control of the necessary supporting resources. The school's assigned goals, moreover, are multiple and are often vague and mutually conflictual. For example, not only must the school *teach* new facts and problem-solving skills to children, it is also expected to *socialize* them to fit the prevailing norms of the community and to help promote their physical and emotional health. Given the ambiguity and frequently conflicting nature of these goals (Miles, 1967), the system must develop an elaborate method of operation to insure continual support from the environment.

Another vital function for open systems is to monitor the environment for information regarding the output and to feed this information back into the organization at various points in order to make any necessary internal corrections in the production of the output. This feedback functions to keep the system in a quasi-stable equilibrium with its environment. To maintain equilibrium the feedback should be *negative* in the sense that it should operate to subtract from the internal processes that are producing errors or deviations in the output. In systems terms, positive feedback is that feedback which *amplifies* deviance, leading to a spiraling increase of error and more error. In relation to schools, feedback comes in terms of long-range outputs (e.g. graduates of a four-year program) and on a daily basis (e.g. reports from parents). Although negative feedback is important, some systems tend to make their own boundaries less permeable in an attempt to protect the system from what are viewed as threatening forces or information. Consequently, much useful feedback is also shut off and the system cannot easily and rapidly correct internal processes in relation to changing environmental needs for different outputs. The short-range effect is a sense of security in a threatening environment. The long-range effect is a dysfunctional system that has difficulty surviving in a changing environment.

Schools, in particular, are wrought with problems of maintaining optimal boundary permeability. Persons who work within the system may feel the school has a very "thin skin" (Miles, 1967) which makes them subject to demands, criticisms, and controls by "outsiders," from politicians to parents (not to mention psychology consultants). Outsiders may feel the schools have impermeable boundaries and are no longer subject to local control, a traditional American value in relation to public schools. Parents in the inner city may feel particularly hesitant or powerless to enter into the system, literally or figuratively.

Another requirement for optimal systemic performance is subsystem interdependence. Breakdowns in any one of the subsystems will produce reactions in other subsystems, although they may occur at different times and places and with varying intensities. The mutual interdependence of certain subsystems (i.e. pupils, teachers, administrators) within a school is very critical but often unrecognized by the participants. Teachers frequently view themselves as independent agents with some common goals and overlapping classes, a situation quite different from *mutual* interdependence. Other subsystems go unrecognized.

A final feature worth mentioning about schools as open systems is the functioning of boundary spanners, persons within the system whose functions include the spanning of boundaries dividing the internal subsystems and/or the environment. The principal, as manager of the system, will usually serve in this role as will all of the faculty to the extent that they relate to parents or other community agents. Students are also a special class of boundary spanners. Boundary spanners are important carriers of feedback, but their effectiveness within the organization is often compromised by insufficient status or lack of trust by others within the organization who often see them as lacking ultimate loyalty to the organization and its values. Key boundary spanners may be viewed suspiciously as possible breaches of secret information to other systems in the environment. To those familiar with inner-city schools, this situation describes some teachers' perceptions of the principal, not as a helpful protector, but as a person to fear and mistrust. In short, boundary-spanning functions affect boundary permeability and subsequent feedback functions.

Process Consultation

Our consultation model derives from the literature and techniques of change theory and organizational development (Argyris, 1962, 1965; Bennis, Benne, and Chin, 1961, 1969; Lippitt, Watson, and Westley, 1958; Schein and Bennis, 1965). It is best exemplified by Schein's (1969) concept of "process consultation." The most prevalent model of consultation could be called the "purchase model" (Schein, 1969). In this case, a buyer (manager of organization) purchases the expert services or information of a consultant to fill an already identified need of the buyer. The success of the consultation will depend on whether the buyer has correctly identified the need, can correctly communicate this need to the consultant, has correctly assessed the consultant's ability and expertise, and whether he has "thought through the consequences of having the consultant gather information, and/or the consequences of implementing changes which may be recommended by the consultant [Schein, 1967]. These four preconditions are frequently lacking and can be expected to be particularly lacking in schools.

Another feature of the purchase model is that upon completion of the sale and the exit of the consultant, the organization is usually status quo in terms of lacking certain resources that required hiring the consultant in the first place. That is, the consultant applies his particular expertise to the organizational problem but does not necessarily teach the organization how to solve or fulfill a similar need by itself in the future.

Quite another approach resembles the doctor-patient model. A consultant is called in by top management to give a diagnosis of the difficulties in a subsystem and is also expected to prescribe a helpful remedy. The diagnosis is generally done with the target subsystem (i.e. the patient) remaining relatively passive while being examined. This model presents two great difficulties when applied to organizational consultation. First, it usually encounters resistance on the part of the subsystem to yield the information needed for an accurate diagnosis. Second, there is frequently no assurance that the total system will understand the diagnosis or be able to implement the cure.

In contrast to the above models, process consultation involves the organization and the consultant in the *joint assessment* of the problems, with particular focus on the *processes* within the system that need improvement. Unlike the doctor-patient model, process consultation calls for the entire organization to be active, not only in the problem assessment, but also in generating its own remedies. Process consultation, by actively involving the system throughout the problem-solving process, attempts to reduce subsystem resistance and increase the terminal ability of the system to deal with future difficulties.

Finally, it should be noted that the process consultant need not be an expert in solving the problems that are unique to a particular system. Rather, he needs to be an expert at involving people in self-assessment and in teaching general problem-solving skills and strategies. This point is important in relation to schools because it legitimizes, in part, the entry of noneducators into a formal system of education and also offers moral support to psychologically trained consultants when they find themselves in foreign territory, better known as an inner-city school building.

The program described below illustrates to some extent the utility of these two models for consultation within a school system. Not all facets of the total program relate to the two models. In fact, the nature of the final projects carried out by the teachers is more closely related to some traditional principles of psychology. The models are best related to the *processes* by which these projects were developed. The models were most useful in helping the consultants interpret events and direct their behavior in the absence of complete information and experience.

The Consultation Program

In the summer of 1969, the principal of a racially mixed junior high school approached the author requesting graduate students to do counseling for the "emotionally disturbed children" in his school. For many reasons the author rejected this idea but began to explore with him some of the other school problems. This mutual assessment process gradually led both of us to see the necessity for primary prevention strategies, as opposed to the treatment of already existing problems.

Our mutual efforts led to the tentative plan for graduate students to enter the system as consultants to teachers around issues and concerns at the level of the classroom. Only teachers who requested consultation would be seen. *No direct services to individual pupils nor consultation around individual pupils would be provided.* Resisting the invitation to initially enter into direct services or case-centered consultation was difficult, but later proved to be an efficient strategy. The decision was based on practical and theoretical considerations. This important strategy decision, however, warrants more theoretical and empirical attention.

Arrangements were then made through the school board to give volunteering teachers "incremental credits" toward educational advancement and pay raises. While this arrangement provides some status and sanction to the program, it later proved to be less an incentive than did the possibility of improving classroom effectiveness and the opportunity for professional interactions with peers. By and large, it was the new and younger teachers who volunteered (22 of 40 initially volunteered, 16 persisted throughout the program).

The first several weeks were planned as a period of entry

and trust-building. Early in the second week of school, we were invited to the school faculty meeting where we presented our proposal to assist teachers with ideas or projects that were *teacher initiated.* We did not ask for volunteers or commitment at this time. We said we would be around the school each day (two to three consultants were at the school each day) and available for questions or ideas. We stressed our acceptance of their difficulties, the confidentiality of all contacts, and our role as *teacher-oriented consultants,* not as "spies" for the principal or the university nor as providers of direct services to pupils.

Trust came slowly. The fact that we initially crossed the school's boundary at the invitation of the principal did not endear us to those teachers who already felt threatened. The author stresses the gradualness of this process because our acceptance and understanding of their difficulties only became genuine as we gradually immersed ourselves in the day-to-day school operations and did, in fact, begin to see the school environment with the eyes of an "insider."

In moving about the school we remained sensitive to the issues of boundaries and the sanctions needed to cross such boundaries. For example, permission from the teacher was always requested before we entered a classroom for observation. We avoided giving immediate advice for problems that teachers raised, particularly those that focused on individual pupils. At the risk of initially appearing useless, we tried to head off passive requests for direct help by reminding the teachers that after five to six weeks we would work actively with those who indicated a personal interest in some project. This answer was generally accepted. Resistance generally took such passive forms as jokes about headshrinkers or complete avoidance and withdrawal. Because we were not suggesting specific changes, there was not much opportunity for active resistance.

We continued our observations in the school, and during the fifth week we sponsored a one-day workshop on the university's premises for those teachers who were interested in continuing their involvement. The workshop consisted of small group discussions and exercises designed to improve communication and problem-solving skills and develop a sense of group commitment.

The workshop ended with specific teacher-proposed projects and consultant assignments to teacher teams.

The five weeks of field observations and the workshop gave the team of consulants a good idea of the school as a complex organization. The most pressing concerns were for order and personal safety. Control and socialization goals had displaced educational ones. The teachers' interests in revised teaching methods, curriculum reform, and system-wide issues were contingent on classroom order. There was little awareness of teacher-pupil-administration interdependence. In its place was a sense of mistrust, antagonism, or competition among teachers, pupils, and administration. It was difficult in these defensive climates for anyone to engage in self-assessment for the sources of problems or potential remedies. There was also underutilization of valid feedback mechanisms and little use of legitimate environmental support systems. Although morale was low, there was sufficient interest in change for the program to begin.

Our view of the school as a complex open system discouraged us from making early interventions that might eventually lead to problems in other subsystems. We began to see in which ways the various components were interdependent, and part of our process consultation task was to make the persons within the system more aware of such relationships. We hoped to demonstrate, for example, that good teaching at 9:00 A.M. makes it easier for someone else at 10:00 A.M., and that good communication among teachers in the lounge makes a difference in teacher morale, which in turn influences administration, which in turn helps to legitimately support teachers or protect them from unreasonable forces outside of the boundaries, and so forth. In brief, we needed at least six weeks to begin to grasp the systemic complexities and internal norms that governed the system. Our patience paid off when the teachers began to propose their own projects, growing out of their personal interests and specific classroom difficulties. We now had the motivation to change, coupled with responsibility and initiative for directing such change.

Eight teacher-oriented projects emerged during the workshop and were eventually carried out. These projects serve to demonstrate the scope of innovation and change that can develop under such circumstances. Whether or not each individual project has validity for improving education is, at this point, less important than the question of whether or not outside consultants can help persons with a turbulent system undergo self-assessment and self-directed change. Below are listed the eight projects:

1. Development of teacher skills in small-group techniques
2. Behavior modification
3. Videotape recording and playback of teaching styles
4. Motivational development in a special reading class
5. Systems analysis and sociometric patterning in the classroom
6. Use of psychodrama technique for classroom communication
7. Teacher and counselor discussion group for interracial issues
8. Environmental engineering and control of the classroom

During the next six months, the consultants continued to attend my seminar on techniques of planned change, consultation, and group process and were supervised by me. My primary field task was to coordinate the separate projects and to make available the necessary resources through the principal's office or the department of psychology. At some points teachers and consultants in different projects overlapped with one another (e.g. Projects 2, 3, and 8). The author also supported the principal through some anxious decisions and served to interpret the teachers' projects to the principal and other concerned parties.

These first six weeks were the most anxiety provoking for both the consultants and the persons within the school system. Our orientation of process consultation, however, led us to expect anxiety generated by a lack of initial direction.

Program Termination and Evaluation

The projects were carried out over a period of three months, and several continued for another three months. At that time the principal was appointed assistant school superintendent of another area of the city and a new principal replaced him. The new principal was not supportive of the previous principal's policies and began to institute many changes. We were not able to maintain our own sanction and had to withdraw from the system. Several teachers continued to consult with graduate students until the year ended. Teachers reported that staff and student morale had dropped, disruptions were frequent, and racial tensions were evident. It was reported that of forty-five professional employees, twenty-two did not return to the school in September 1970. Another five of the remaining twenty-three left at the end of the first semester (February, 1971). At last report, the school was described as "worse than ever."

Although secondary to the main focus of the article, these data are presented for the sake of historical completeness and to demonstrate the importance of top level commitment in any change program. Leaving aside for the moment the fact that our program eventually collapsed because of a change in principals, what can be said for its outcomes during its existence and how are these outcomes related to our models of schools as open systems and process consultation?

First, the program led to a greater awareness of the interdependence of the pupils, the teachers, the principal, and the school's environment. In particular, the teachers began to see the principal as a source of support and valuable information. His role as a boundary spanner into the community and between subsystems became far less threatening. The teachers in the project became, as expected, more cohesive. Initially, many had expressed resentment about being abandoned in a hopeless situation and cut off from sources of help. Furthermore, they felt that previously most advcie had been given condescendingly and in a critical rather than positive manner, particularly when it came from such sources as supervisory personnel or visiting teachers. Some teachers who had initially planned to terminate their jobs and seek new careers reported that they had decided to give it another try. The teachers reported their own pupils as useful sources of support and asistance (e.g. Projects 1, 5, and 8).

Second, the program helped to open the system to useful inputs from the environment. Not only did the teachers allow greater inputs from the pupils, but they also accepted ideas from our consultant team as well as bringing in new ideas from other sources. The teachers felt the school's skin to be less unbearably thin and felt secure enough to allow feedback to circulate within the system. Some reported more "sense of the community."

Third, the program introduced some specific innovations into the school and, more importantly, began to stimulate a *normative philosophy of planned change, experimentation, and risk-taking.* The willingness to risk change was related, in part, to feelings of less environmental pressures to maintain the status quo which, in turn, was related to new perceptions of the principal and greater openness to complete and accurate environmental feedback asking for change. Teachers also showed a greater trust in their own abilities to initiate and implement innovations. The projects grew out of small-group assessment and planning efforts so that the outcomes of the projects were not seen as the consultants' "expert" solutions for teacher problems.

From a training point of view the program had several beneficial outcomes. It made us more aware of the problems confronting a school principal and teachers, particularly in a racially mixed school dealing with pupils in a critical period of adolescence. It allowed us to try out some models and to test our skills on the firing line. The fact that we left our offices and spent time in the teachers' own territory was a factor helping our acceptance and provided another role model for trainees.

We also learned some useful information about problems in the larger community surrounding the school. Problems of housing, ethnic and racial tensions, unemployment, crime, drugs, and a dozen other issues were expressed in various ways within the school. To this extent the program was one relating to more general community psychology.

Finally, the projects convinced the faculty and students that field research could be combined in a meaningful way with applied consultation. Our major regret is that we did not set up extensive methods to evaluate the overall program. The timing and urgency did not allow for slow and considered research planning.

There were, of course, some failures and shortcomings of the program and the models that we used. We did not reach all the teachers since we rested strongly on motivation and teacher interest. Obviously any program that expects comprehensive results will eventually have to include all of the teachers within the established boundaries. We could have accomplished total commitment given another year in the school. We relied on a very favorable consultant:consultee ratio. A more realistic program would have to develop alternatives requiring less consultant time and energy. We did not persist and follow through when perhaps greater effort could have been expended to assure continual support from the new principal. Graduate student resources, however, were being demanded elsewhere, and the situation deteriorated so rapidly that our own motivation to persist was quickly eroded. To overcome this serious problem, any consultation program should be developed with invitations and sanctions at a level higher than the principal, thereby allowing for better continuity, given a stable source of consultant resources.

Conclusion

It is impossible to describe all of the actions and outcomes connected with this program, but one principle appears highlighted: in gaining entry, in maintaining sanctions ,and in planning change, *do not stray from the primary internal resources of the organization,* the people who make the system operate. The internal operations of any system must ultimately be consistent with the most stable values and needs of the persons within the system. Consultation cannot operate in the long run against these powerful forces. Assuming an open system will make adaptive changes to survive, the consultant can best operate as a mechanism for feedback and a creative source of alternative techniques and strategies from which the system can make its own choices.

Process consultation and open system theory may not be the optimal models to use for school consultation programs. A comparison and evaluation of several models are certainly needed. These two models did, however, provide a starting point and a base of security for some relatively inexperienced graduate students and their equally anxious faculty adviser.

REFERENCES

Argyris, C.: *Interpersonal Competence and Organizational Effectiveness.* Homewood, Irwin, 1962.

Argyris, C.: *Organization and Innovation.* Homewood, Irwin, 1965.

Bennis, W. G.; Benne, K. D., and Chin, R. (Eds.): *The Planning of Change.* (1st ed.) New York, HR&W, 1961.

Bennis, W. G.; Benne, K. D., and Chin R. (Eds.): *The Planning of Change.* (2nd ed.) New York, HR&W, 1969.

Katz, D., and Kahn, R. L.: *The Social Psychology of Organizations.* New York, Wiley, 1966.

Lippitt, R.; Watson, J., and Westley, B.: *The Dynamics of Planned Change.* New York, Harcourt, Brace, & World, 1958.

Miles, M.: Some properties of schools as social systems. In G. Watson (Ed.): *Change in School Systems.* Washington, D.C., National Training Laboratories, 1967.

Miller, J. G.: Toward a general theory for the behavioral sciences. *Am Psychol, 10*:513-553, 1955.

Schein, E. H.: *Process Consultation: Its Role in Organization Development.* Reading, A-W, 1969.

Schein, E. H., and Bennis, W. G.: *Personal and Organizational Change Through Group Methods.* New York, Wiley, 1965.

von Bertalanffy, L.: *General Systems Theory.* New York, Braziller, 1968.

Chapter 24

IMPROVING ORGANIZATIONAL PROBLEM SOLVING IN A SCHOOL FACULTY

(The 1969 Douglas McGregor Memorial Award-Winning Article)

RICHARD A. SCHMUCK, PHILIP J. RUNKEL, AND
DANIEL LANGMEYER

The intervention detailed here was aimed at improving the flexible organizational problem solving of a junior high school faculty. It was pointed toward organizational development, not personal change. Even through the emotional reactions of faculty members were considered in designing the training events, our intervention remained fixed on organizational roles and norms and their interrelationships. We hoped to learn whether improved organizational functioning could be produced in a faculty by integrating group training in communication and problem solving with the normal business of the school. We began our intervention just prior to the academic year and returned intermittently until February.

Data evaluating the effects of the intervention support the claim that a number of salutary outcomes were at least partly due to the intervention. Movement in favorable directions occurred in a number of concrete, observable organizational changes, in verbally expressed attitudes about the principal and staff meetings, in the kinds of innovations reported, and in the changing organizational norms of the faculty. Strengths and weaknesses of the intervention are discussed.

From *Journal of Applied Behavioral Science*, 3:455-482, 1969.

The research detailed here was supported by the Center for the Advanced Study of Educational Administration. CASEA is a national research and development center established under the Cooperative Research Program of the U.S. Office of Education. We wish to thank the faculty of the Highland Park Junior High School, Beaverton, Oregon, for their collaboration. This project will be reported at monographic length by Schmuck and Runkel (in press).

Introduction

L IKE MANY ORGANIZATIONS with traditional modes of operation, schools are suffering stresses to which their customary practices seem ill-adapted. When faced with massive changes in the community, there are at least two strategies a school can adopt. One is for the school to remodel itself into a form maximally adapted to the new demands of the community, e.g. the middle school, the campus school, the unitized school, and the community school. The other strategy is to build new norms and procedures that enable the school constantly to monitor the changing community, to compare the results of its own reactions with what it would accept as movement toward its goals, and to establish new forms whenever the movement toward the goals fall below a criterion. This latter kind of strategy we call *flexible organizational problem solving.* John Gardner (1963) has called it *self-renewal* and Walter Buckley (1967) has referred to it as *morphogenesis.* The purpose of this project was to improve the capability of a school for organizational problem solving.

From the point of view of research, our purpose was to test whether improved organizational problem solving could be produced in a school faculty by training in interpersonal communication skills, where the group processes to be altered and the methods of doing so were consistent with McGregor's (1967) thinking. We assumed, along with McGregor, that functions within organizations are "carried" through interpersonal interactions and that heightening abilities for organizational problem solving must commence with new norms for interpersonal openness and helpfulness. In seeking a lever with which to change group norms, we adopted McGregor's strategy:

> . . . to provide opportunities for members of the organization to obtain intrinsic rewards from contributions to the success of the enterprise. . . . The task is to provide an appropriate environment— one that will permit and encourage employees to seek intrinsic rewards *at work.*

We did this by inviting the faculty to state the frustrations they encountered in the school and to practice a sequence of problem-solving steps to reduce these frustrations. This activity led to reduced frustrations and to the satisfaction of knowing that others valued the contribution one had made to outcomes highly desired by the faculty. It also facilitated changes in organizational norms by requiring staff members to behave in new ways in the actual workgroup where others could observe the new behaviors and see that their colleagues actually accepted the new patterns of behavior in the setting of the school.

In designing this intervention, we made strong use of the laboratory method (Bradford, Gibb, and Benne, 1964). The training often called for conscious observations of the group processes of the faculty; the design required actually practicing new behaviors before using them in daily work. Although the design made use of the school as its own laboratory, we made use of laboratory groups in ways very different from sensitivity training or the T Group. Personal development was not our target. We did not attempt to improve the interpersonal functioning of individuals directly; when this occurred, it was incidental. Our targets were the faculty as a whole and several subgroups within it. We sought to increase the effectiveness of groups as task-oriented entities. We tried to teach subgroups within the school, and the faculty as a whole, to function more effectively as working bodies carrying out specific tasks in that particular job setting. This strategy of training was supported by a recent review of research by Campbell and Dunnette (1968) on the transfer of skills from T Groups to organizations. They found that a T Group, as ordinarily conducted with focus on individual growth in a setting away from the job and without guided application to workaday tasks, has had little effect on organizational development.

In comparison with other efforts at bringing about more effective organizational functioning in schools, our intervention contained a unique combination of three features. First, our training took place with actual groups from the school we sought to affect. Of equal importance, we carried on training with the entire staff of the school, including secretaries, the head cook, and head custodian, as well as all the faculty and its administrators. Finally, during the training, especially in its early parts, we rotated sizes and memberships of subgroups so that every pair of staff members interacted with each other in more than one kind of group.

Training Goals

The major training goals were developed out of a conception of flexible organizational problem solving. It was hoped that the faculty of our experimental school would establish a continuing series of activities for improving its own communication, we held this to be a minimum necessity. Further, we hoped that participation at faculty meetings as well as the initiation of attempts at influence would spread to more and more members of the faculty. We strove to help the faculty increase its discussions about interpersonal or interrole problems and to continue to make conscious use of a sequential problem-solving technique. A related goal was that the teachers would show increased initiative in solving problems they were having with those in higher echelons and that the initiator of an idea would test his idea more frequently than previously with a lower-echelon subgroup before carrying it to the administration. By far the most significant goals had to do with structural and instructional changes in the school. We hoped that the staff would invent some new organizational forms within their school or at least borrow some from our training that would help them to confront problems continuously. Finally, we wanted the teachers to find some uses for the new forms and methods from the training that would have effects on their classroom instruction.

We supplemented these broad goals with more specific ones in designing the initial training events that centered on interpersonal skills and systematic problem solving. We hoped first to build increased openness and ease of interpersonal communication among the faculty by training them in the skills of paraphrasing, describing, behavior describing own feelings, and perception checking. We hoped that through skillful, constructive openness with one another the staff would develop an increased confidence in the worthwhile outcomes deriving from improved communication. We hoped to increase skills of giving information to others about their behaviors and of receiving information about one's own behavior. After increasing communication skills, we hoped to stimulate skill development in using a systematic problem-solving procedure and in helping colleagues to enunciate clearly ideas that might develop into practical plans for solving organizational problems.

The Intervention

We assumed that the faculty members of our experimental school would be likely to attempt new interpersonal procedures if they could first practice them away from the immediate demands of the school day. At the same time, we assumed that transfer of training to the everyday work of the building would be maximized if the faculty expected to continue problem-solving activities on their own after each training event and if the training design called for additional training some weeks and months following the first event. Within this general framework for transfer of organizational training, we made several other assumptions.

We felt that communication could be improved, that feelings of solidarity could be increased, and that power differences could be clarified if virtually every pair of persons on the faculty were brought into face-to-face interaction during the initial training period. Second, we thought that the initial input during training should pose a discrepancy between the ideal and actual performances of the faculty. Out of confrontations with discrepancies would come problem solving. We felt that applications to the work of the school building would be maximized if the faculty dealt with real organizational problems even during the first week of training. Furthermore, we thought that training in a series of overlapping small groups would help individuals to use the skills learned in one group in each of the next training groups, and subsequently, to transfer the accumulated skills to groups in which they work ordinarily. Finally, we assumed that the transfer of the communication and problem-solving skills to the school would be facilitated if the faculty members conceptualized the possible applications of the skills and made plans to try them out in the real school setting.

The training commenced with a six-day laboratory in late August of 1967. Staff members present included almost the entire building staff other than students. There were fifty-four trainees: all the administrators, all the faculty but two, the head cook, head custodian, and head secretary. The first two days were spent in group exercises designed to increase awareness of interpersonal and organizational processes e.g. the NASA trip-to-the-moon exercise, the five-square puzzle, and the hollow-square puzzle. Although these exercises were game-like, they demonstrated the importance of clear and effective communication for accomplishing a task collaboratively. After each exercise, small groups discussed ways in which the experience was similar to or different from what usually happened in their relations with one another in the school. All staff members then came together to pool their experiences and to analyze their relationships as a faculty. Each small group chose its own way to report what it had experienced. Openness and giving and receiving feedback about perceptions of real organizational processes in the school were supported by the trainers. Brief but specific training was given in clear communication, overcoming difficulties in listening, and skills in describing another's behaviors. Selected nonverbal exercises augmented this practice.

The faculty devoted the last four days to a problem-solving sequence, working on real issues that were thwarting the organizational functioning of the school. After a morning of discussion and decisions, which also served as practice in the skills of decision making, three problems emerged as the most significant:

1. *Insufficient role clarity,* especially in the roles of principal, vice principal, counselors, and area (departmental) coordinators.
2. *Failure to draw upon staff resources,* especially between academic areas but also within subject-matter specialities.
3. *Low staff involvement and low participation at meetings* of committees, areas, and the full faculty.

Three groups formed, each to work through a problem-solving sequence directed toward one of these problems. Each group followed a procedure consisting of five steps: (a) identifying the problem through behavioral description, (b) diagnostic force-field analysis, (c) brainstorming to find actions likely to reduce restraining forces, (d) designing a concrete plan of action, and (e) trying out the plan behaviorally through a simulated activity involving the entire staff. Each of the three groups carried through its sequence of steps substantially on its own; the trainers served as facilitators, rarely providing substantive suggestions and never pressing for results.

The group concerned with clarifying roles reasoned that an ambiguous role often served as a defense and that a first step must be to increase trust among the faculty. Accordingly, this group carried out four nonverbal exercises to increase trust among the faculty. The group working on better use of staff resources set up eight subgroups, each of which was to pretend to be a junior high faculty trying to avert a crisis due to lack of texts; each group then developed curricula by drawing upon one another's resources. The group concerned with low staff involvement arranged for three groups to have discussions on role clarification, staff resources, and staff involvement. During the discussions, the more loquacious members were asked one after another to stop participating until there were only two members left. Discussions were then held in each group on feelings about involvement on the staff.

The first week of the training culminated with a discussion to highlight the resources of the staff. Staff members described their own strengths and those of their colleagues. Finally, they discussed what their school could be like if all the strengths of the faculty were used.

During the early fall, we interviewed all faculty members and observed a number of committees and subject-area groups to determine what uses they were making of the first week of training. The data indicated that problems still unresolved were communicative misunderstandings, role overload, and capabilities for group problem solving.

The second intervention for training with the entire staff was held during 1½ days in December. In this session we attempted to increase the effectiveness of the area coordinators as communication links between teachers and administrators, to increase problem-solving skills of the area groups and the Principal's Advisory Committee, to help the faculty explore ways of reducing role overload, and to increase effective communication between service personnel and the rest of the staff. Training activities included communication exercises, problem-solving techniques, decision-making procedures, and skill development in group observations and feedback. On the first day, area (departmental) groups applied problem-solving techniques to their own communication difficulties and received feedback from observing area groups on their methods of work. Problems raised in area groups were brought to a meeting of the Principal's Advisory Committee held the next day in front of the rest of the staff. The staff observed the advisory committee in a fishbowl arrangement, participated in specially designed ways, and later gave feedback on how effectively the committee had worked and how accurately members had represented them.

The third training intervention also lasted 1½ days and took place in February. The main objective was to "take stock of" how the staff had progressed since the workshop in solving the problems of using resources, of role clarity, and of staff participation, and to revivify any lagging skills. A group discussion of each problem area was held. Each teacher was left free to work in the group considering the problem that most interested him. Each group discussed the positive and negative outcomes associated with its problems. For example, in the group discussing staff participation, the question was, "In what ways has staff participation improved and where has it failed to improve?" The group wrote out examples of improvements, no changes, and regression in staff participation. The groups then focused on the negative instances and tried to think of ways to eliminate them by modifying organizational processes in the school. Faculty members continued with this activity in small groups during the spring without our presence.

Organizational Changes

One source of evidence for the effects of the training came in the form of concrete, observable changes in the behaviors of faculty and administration in our experimental school. These data were taken primarily from spontaneous events that were later reported to us and corroborated by the parties involved or by disinterested observers. These actions were not directly a part of our planned training events and, therefore, constituted movements in the direction of increased flexible organizational problem solving.

About three months after the first week of training, a sample of faculty members were interviewed and also were asked to write essays on the effects of the training. From these data we discovered that at least nineteen teachers were applying techniques learned in the organizational training to improve the group processes in their classrooms. Application typically involved such group procedures as "using small groups for projects," "using nonverbal exercises to depict feelings about the subject matter being studied," "using theatre-in-the-round or fishbowl formations for having students observe one another," "using a paraphrasing exercise to point out how poor classroom communications are," "using the problem-solving sequence and techniques in social studies classes to learn more about social problems," and "using small groups for giving and receiving feedback about how the class is going." As far as we know, none of these practices was used by these teachers before the organizational development laboratory.

Previous to our intervention, a group of eight teachers called the Teach Group was granted freedom to alter schedules, classroom groupings, assignment of teachers to classes, and other logistics in attempts to maximize their educational impact on a selected group of students. The group, made up mostly of area coordinators, received many negative reactions from other staff members. They were envied, misunderstood, and often engaged in conflict with others, with the result that their innovative ideas were more often resisted than emulated. However, the organizational training seemed to reduce the distrust, and the end of the year saw the Teach Group's type of collaboration extended to twice as many teachers. At the same time, two other teachers decided to form another team in order to gain some of the advantages of mutual stimulation and the sharing of resources.

The Principal's Advisory Committee, made up of administrators and area coordinators, was raised from advisory status to a more powerful force in the school. It became a representative senate with decision-making prerogatives. During the training event in December, the members of this group delineated and accepted their roles as representatives of their areas and as gatherers of information for the upper-echelon administrators. Later, an actual occurrence lent credence to the power of the advisory committee. Members of the mathematics area decided that they were underrepresented on the committee because their area coordinator held responsibilities in the district as a curriculum consultant. They petitioned the principal through the advisory committee for a new area coordinator and one was chosen. The primary criterion for selecting the person to fill the position seemed to be his recent improvements in interpersonal and group skills. Later in the school year, the advisory committee requested two other training events to help it clarify its role in the decision-making structure of the school.

A number of other events indicated that the quality of relationships on the staff improved because of the intervention. For instance, only two teachers resigned from the staff at the end of the school year, giving the school a turnover rate of only 3 percent. Comparative rates in other junior high schools in the same district ranged from 10 to 16 percent. Several times during the year, faculty meetings were initiated by faculty members other than the principal. Such initiations ran counter to tradition, but nevertheless those meetings ran smoothly, with strong participation from many.

During the spring of 1968, faculty members initiated a meeting to discuss the possibility of having another group-process laboratory before the next school year. Faculty members first discussed the idea in area groups and later asked to meet as a total staff to present recommendations to the advisory committee. The laboratory or workshop was to have two goals: (a) to socialize new faculty members into this group-oriented staff, and (b) to give teachers new skills to use with their classroom groups. The workshop actually took place, without our active participation, in August, 1968.

The principal's interpersonal relationships with staff members were noticeably improved, and he became very much excited about improving further his own leadership skills. He requested funds to attend an NTL Educators Laboratory and was granted them. Later he served as an assistant trainer in a laboratory and performed with great effectiveness. That same summer six members of the faculty planned to go to a laboratory in group process and eventually did go at their own expense.

Perhaps the most dramatic changes after the intervention occurred in the school district. First, a new job was created at our experimental school; namely, vice-principal for curriculum, to act as consultant on interpersonal relationships to task groups within the staff. The role also called for providing liaison between groups, providing logistic support for curricular efforts, transmitting to upper echelons in the district the proposals for curricular development originating at the school, and serving as a liaison with other junior high schools in the district concerning innovations in curriculum. This new vice-principal was asked by the superintendent to maintain a log of his activities and to develop a job description for possible use in other schools. That completed, the school board granted funds for the position in several other junior high schools. The curricular vice-principal, first to hold the role, has been asked to aid the other new vice-principals in learning the role. Still other schools in the district have requested funds for organizational development training for their staffs and the introduction of the facilitator role as a vice-principalship.

Comparisons with Other Schools

The previous section contained descriptions of directly observable outcomes reflecting commitments to action within the school.

This section reports comparisons of data taken from questionnaires administered early and late during the 1967-1968 school year at the experimental school with data from six junior high schools in the New York City area and four junior high schools near the Seattle, Washington, area. None of the New York or Seattle schools was engaged in our kind of organizational training; in their demographic characteristics, too, they met some of the requirements for a control group.

The data for comparing our school with the New York schools came from two questionnaires: one dealing with the faculty's feelings about the principal's behavior, and the other dealing with the faculty's feelings about staff meetings. The data for comparing the experimental school with the Seattle schools came from questions concerning innovations adopted, readiness to communicate about interpersonal relations, and readiness to use and share the resources of other staff members.

The Principal

The questionnaire used to measure the faculty's feelings about the principal contained twenty-four items. Twelve of the items were used by Gross and Herriott (1965) to measure the Executive Professional Leadership (EPL) of elementary school principals; the remaining twelve items were developed by the Cooperative Project on Educational Development (COPED) instrument committee to measure managerial support and social support of the principal for his staff.

The facet of educational leadership studied by EPL deals with the principal's efforts to improve the quality of performance of his staff. Gross and Herriott (1965) found EPL to be related to the morale of the staff, the professional performance of teachers, and learning by students. Hilfier (1969) used the same instrument and found that both EPL scores and social support scores were related to school systems' innovativeness. Because of these findings we felt that the items in this questionnaire were reasonable indicators of the direction the interaction of faculty and principal would take if our training of the faculty approached its goals.

EPL was measured by asking teachers to what extent their principal engaged in activities such as the following:

Makes teachers' meetings a valuable educational activity.
Treats teachers as professional workers.
Has constructive suggestions to offer teachers in dealing with their problems.

A principal's managerial support was measured by items such as the following:

Makes a teacher's life difficult because of his administrative ineptitude.
Runs conferences and meetings in a disorganized fashion.
Has the relevant facts before making important decisions.

A principal's social support was measured by items such as the following:

Rubs people the wrong way.
Makes those who work with him feel inferior to him.
Displays integrity in his behavior.

To compare the teacher's responses to this questionnaire at the experimental school with the responses at the six junior high schools near New York City, we performed a series of chi-square analyses. For each item and every school we let the pretest results be the estimate of expected proportions against which to test the proportions obtained at the posttest, i.e. the proportions of teachers responding in one of six preferred categories. A summary of the analyses appears in Table 24-I where the schools near New York City are labeled A through F.

TABLE 24-I

NUMBERS OF ITEMS SHOWING SIGNIFICANT CHANGES ($p < .10$)
AMONG THOSE IN THE QUESTIONNAIRE ON THE PRINCIPAL

				Schools			
	Exp'l	A	B	C	D	E	F
Positive change	18	1	2	0	0	5	9
No significant change	6	19	17	12	13	19	11
Negative change	0	4	5	12	11	0	4

The results leave little doubt that the faculty of the experimental school changed its perceptions of the principal much more than did any of the other school staffs. At the experimental school, the teachers changed significantly ($p < .10$) on eighteen of the twenty-four items; more importantly, every one of these eighteen changes was in the positive and supportive direction. In contrast, in no other school, except for school F, did the teachers change on more than one-half of the items. Furthermore, in schools A, B, C, and D more of the changes were in a negative direction, indicating that the principal was being viewed less in accord with the EPL ideal at the end of the school year compared with the fall. The staffs of schools E and F changed more positively than negatively, but on far fewer items than at the experimental school.

Specifically, the teachers at our school were reporting that their principal was easier to get along with, made better decisions, helped them more in their own problem solving, improved faculty meetings and conferences, and treated them more as professionals after our training had been completed than before training. Staffs at junior high schools in the New York City area not undergoing organizational training did not report similar changes in their principals' behavior.

Staff Meetings

We were concerned about staff and committee meetings because they are important formal arenas in which communication and group problem solving can occur. Our early conversations with the staff at our experimental school revealed that low participation at staff meetings was viewed as an acute problem. We hoped that improvements in the conduct of meetings would occur as a result of the organizational training. To measure such change, we used a questionnaire to measure educators' responses to the meetings in their schools developed by the COPED instrument committee and reworded in minor ways by us. The questionnaire contains thirty-seven items and has yielded excellent reliability. The total score and subscale scores from this instrument have been found to be related to a school system's innovativeness (Hilfiker, 1969).

The thirty-seven items describe specific behaviors; teachers are asked to rate each in one of six categories of frequency of its occurrence at staff meetings. The following are sample items from the instrument:

When problems come up in the meeting, they are thoroughly explored until everyone understands what the problems are.
People come to the meeting not knowing what is to be presented or discussed.
People bring up extraneous or irrelevant matters.
Either before the meeting or at its beginning, any group members can easily get items onto the agenda.
People do not seem to care about the meeting or want to get involved in it.
People give their real feelings about what is happening during the meeting itself.
When a decision is made, it is clear who should carry it out, and when.

In a manner identical to the questionnaire dealing with the principal, pretest responses for each item and from each school were used as expected frequencies for evaluating shifts in post-test data. Data about staff meetings were available only from three of the six comparison schools, namely, schools *A*, *C*, and *D*. Table 24-II summarizes the chi-square analyses applied to these data. Like the results on the changed perceptions of the principal, the results on staff meetings also show major differences between the changes at the experimental school and the changes at the comparison schools. Among thirty-seven items, our school showed significant positive change in twenty-one, school *A* in three, school *C* in two, and school *D* in six. Changes at our school were almost entirely in the positive direction; among twenty-three significant changes ($p < .10$), only two were negative. In contrast, changes in the comparison schools could hardly have been more evenly balanced between positive and negative. The nature of the items on the questionnaire permits us to conclude that members of the experimental school reported that they could be more open, had improved the conduct of their meetings, dealt with problems more completely, had more commitment to the meetings and observed more solutions emerging from meetings, and felt that meetings were more worthwhile after completing our organizational training.

TABLE 24-II

NUMBERS OF ITEMS SHOWING SIGNIFICANT CHANGES ($p < .10$)
AMONG THOSE IN THE QUESTIONNAIRE ON STAFF MEETINGS

| | Exp'l | Schools | | |
		A	C	D
Positive change	21	3	2	6
No significant change	14	30	32	23
Negative change	2	4	3	8

Innovations

The experimental school and four junior high schools from two cities near Seattle were administered an instrument as part of a larger project. One of the questions in the instrument read:

> How about recent changes that could have useful effects on your school? Have there been any innovations, any new ways of doing things, that began during the last year or two that you think could have helpful effects in the school? If so, please describe each very briefly below. If none, write 'none.'

Teachers' responses to this item were coded into fourteen categories according to the nature of the innovations they mentioned; for this report, we have gathered these categories into the four types shown in Table 24-III. "Packaged" innovations include curricular changes, establishing new jobs or duties, acquiring equipment, and adopting methods of evaluating programs. We describe these as "packaged" because some tanglible set of materials or instructions usually goes along with the innovation such as teaching materials, specifications for a new job, TV equipment, or instructions for a bookkeeping method. Moreover, innovations under this heading can usually be put into effect by training *individuals;* it is not often necessary to establish delicate new role relations or new modes of group problem solving for innovations of this type to be successful. Packaged innovations were mentioned more frequently in three of the schools near

TABLE 24-III

NUMBERS OF TEACHERS MENTIONING FOUR TYPES OF INNOVATIONS

Type of Innovation Mentioned		School				
	Exp'l Dec. 1967 N=46	W N=30	X N=30	Y N=34	Z N=44	Exp'l May 1968 N=39
"Packaged": curriculum, new jobs, equipment, program evaluation	18	25	11	36	22	15
Instrumental in achieving new forms of organization	9	0	3	1	1	16
New methods of problem solving or new organizational structure	21	1	1	0	1	17
Nonspecific improvements and vague answers	6	0	0	0	0	6

Note: Schools W X, Y, and Z answered the questionnaires in January 1968.

Seattle (labeled W through Z in Table 24-III) than in the experimental school.

Another cluster of innovations contained those *instrumental* in achieving new forms of organization and new methods of solving organizational problems. Here we included relations between teachers and students, sharing power among the faculty, and changes in frequency or content of communication, as well as new training of any kind and new attitudes without mention of accompanying actions in organizational arrangements. Although the total number of responses in these categories was generally low by comparison with the first set of packaged innovations, mentions from the experimental school were more frequent than mentions from any of the other four junior high schools.

Innovations of primary importance to our training goals were new *methods of solving problems* or making decisions and *new organizational structure*, such as committees, channels, and conference groups. Table 24-III shows that teachers at the experimental school reported many more innovations in this area than the other junior high schools.

Norms About Interpersonal Communication

We asked the faculty at the experimental school and the faculties at the four junior high schools near Seattle to answer a set of seven questions about their readiness to talk about feelings. Three of the seven questions follow:

Suppose a teacher (let us call him or her Teacher X) disagrees with something B says at a staff meeting. If teachers you know in your school were in Teacher X's place, what would most of them be likely to do? Would most of the teachers you know here seek out B to discuss the disagreement?

    ( ) Yes, I think most would do this.
    ( ) Maybe about half would do this.
    ( ) No; most would *not*.
    ( ) I don't know.

Suppose you are in a committee meeting with Teacher X and the other members begin to describe their personal feelings about what goes on in the school; Teacher X quickly suggests that the committe get back to the topic and keep the discussion objective and impersonal. How would you feel toward X?

    ( ) I would approve strongly.
    ( ) I would approve mildly.
    ( ) I would not care one way or the other.
    ( ) I would disapprove mildly.
    ( ) I would disapprove strongly.

Suppose Teacher X feels hurt and "put down" by something another teacher has said to him. In Teacher X's place, would most of the teachers you know in your school be likely to avoid the other teacher?

    ( ) Yes, I think most would.
    ( ) Maybe about half would.
    ( ) No; most would *not*.
    ( ) I don't know.

Taking those respondents who did not skip the question or

answer "I don't know," we analyzed the responses to these seven items. We found that the faculty at the experimental school reported that more teachers would (1) seek out another person with whom they had a disagreement, (2) tell another teacher when they had been hurt by the other teacher, (3) be less approving of a teacher who tried to cut off talking about feelings in a committee meeting, and (4) be more approving of a teacher who shared his own feelings at a faculty meeting than would teachers from the four schools near Seattle, according to their report. There was no significant difference between the teachers at the experimental school and other teachers in (5) their estimation of the proportion of teachers who would keep a disagreement to themselves (most teachers in all schools felt the majority would do so).

On the other hand, many more teachers in the schools near Seattle than in our school claimed that their fellow teachers would (6) *not avoid* another teacher and would (7) *not* tell their friends the other teacher was hard to get along with if the other teacher had hurt them or "put them down."

On balance, we believe these results indicate that after our intervention the faculty members at the experimental school, to a greater degree than the faculties near Seattle, were more open in their interpersonal communication and were more willing to talk about their feelings.

Norms About Sharing Ideas and Helping Others

Along with items reflecting norms about interpersonal communication, twelve items in the questionnaire concerned the faculty member's readiness to ask for help from other staff members and give help to them. Here are three examples:

> Suppose Teacher X develops a particularly useful and effective method for teaching something. In Teacher X's place, would most of the teachers you know in your school describe it briefly at a faculty meeting and offer to meet with others who wanted to hear more about it?
>
> ( ) Yes, I think most would do this.
> ( ) Maybe about half would do this.

( ) No; most would *not*.
( ) I don't know.

Suppose Teacher X develops a particularly useful and effective method for teaching something. If X were to describe the method briefly at a faculty meeting and offer to meet further with any who wanted to know more, how would you feel about it?

( ) I would approve strongly.
( ) I would approve mildly.
( ) I would not care one way or the other.
( ) I would disapprove mildly.
( ) I would disapprove strongly.

Suppose Teacher X wants to improve his classroom effectiveness. If X asked another teacher to observe his teaching and then have a conference about it afterward, how would you feel toward X?

( ) I would approve strongly.
( ) I would approve mildly.
( ) I would not care one way or the other.
( ) I would disapprove mildly.
( ) I would disapprove strongly.

The faculty at the experimental school reported that they would (1) expect other teachers to report useful and effective teaching methods at faculty meetings, (2) seek administrative support to disseminate these methods, and would (3) approve in a significantly greater degree teachers who engaged in such activities than would faculties of the schools near Seattle. Several items concerned a teacher's attempts to improve his classroom effectiveness. The faculty at our school reported that teachers (4, 5) would ask others, including the principal, to observe their teaching and have a conference afterward, (6) would ask to observe a colleague's teaching to get new ideas, and (7, 8) would approve a teacher who did these things in significantly greater numbers than the faculties of the other schools. The remaining four items showed no significant differences. These results indicate that teachers at the experimental school were willing to share new ideas to a greater extent than in those schools where no organizational training had taken place. Furthermore, teachers at the experimental school were willing to take greater risks to improve their teaching effectiveness.

Lessons for Consultants

In this section we discuss what the consultant can learn from this project that will help him in designing interventions to improve the organizational functioning of school faculties.

Special Nature of This Intervention

The training events in our intervention were aimed at improving the organizational problem solving of a school faculty. The feature that most sharply sets this intervention off from other laboratory training events is that natural workgroups, not individuals, were trained to be more effective. The intervention attempted to influence ways in which the entire faculty or its subgroups carried out their job-related tasks in the context of the school. This was, in other words, a training intervention pointed toward organizational development, not personal development. At the same time, it is an inescapable truism that role-occupants are persons and that the trainees are persons. It is only an abstraction, a way social scientists conceptualize things to say that roles are different from the persons in a particular organization. Persons sometimes invest so much of their personal existence in a role (and this is perhaps particularly true of educators) that strong emotional reactions enter into organizational change of any kind. But even though the emotional reactions of persons always must be considered in designing even *organizational* development, our target remained fixed on roles and norms and their relationships. Organizational training as we conceive it aims at rearranging, strengthening, or in some way refurbishing the relationships among people in various positions in the school.

The Research Evaluation

From the point of view of research, we hoped to learn

whether improved organizational problem solving could be produced by carefully integrating training in communication and problem-solving skills within the context of the living school and by beginning the training just prior to the opening of school and continuing intermittently for some months. We interpret the data to support the claim that a number of desirable outcomes were at least partly due to our intervention. Many teachers began using a greater variety of more effective group techniques in their classrooms. Collaborating subgroups of teachers increased in strength and number. The Principal's Advisory Committee became more potently and specifically representative rather than merely advisory. Faculty turnover decreased well below the rates at the other junior high schools in the district. Additional training in organizational development during the summer following our intervention was initiated by the faculty, and a number of staff members, including the principal, sought training for themselves in communicative skills and group dynamics. The district established a new variety of the vice-principalship, modeled after a role fashioned at the school following our intervention; the definition of the role included skills in group development and problem solving.

These definite changes in organizational practice and structure were accompanied by changes in verbally expressed attitudes about the principal and staff meetings; the nature of reported innovations within the school; and norms concerning interpersonal openness, sharing of influence, and use of staff resources. These changes were found in the school where we conducted our organizational training, but not in other junior high schools not engaged in organizational training.

Strengths of the Summer Workshop

These outcomes indicate that improvements occurred in the school, and we believe that the summer workshop was crucial in getting the project off in a productive direction. Aspects of the design for a training activity like this one can be divided into macro- and microaspects. Macroaspects are the design's overall structure and outline, its sequence of parts, and the general forms through which the individual activities flow.

Microaspects refer to the specific activities played out during any limited period. We feel confident in offering the following features as the most successful macroaspects of the summer workshop.

(1) *Including All Members of the Faculty*: Almost the entire staff was included in the training right from the beginning. This meant that everyone learned about the goals of this training at the same time, that all were in the same circumstances *vis-à-vis* coping with the training activities, and that it was easy to transfer what was learned during the week to the school situation because staff members could remind one another of what happened at the workshop. The importance of everyone's attending was underscored later when the two members of the staff who could not attend posed significant barriers to the staff's further development.

Even a few days' difference can create distance and set up barriers between the trained and the untrained. Perhaps the main reason is that one can feel a threat when others, especially those in roles comparable with one's own or those in roles that are removed only by one hierarchical level, develop skills or procedures that they might "use on you."

The faculty of a not-too-large elementary school or junior high school has no more than three levels of hierarchy: administrators, teachers, and nonprofessional personnel. For many purposes, there are only two layers, with the administrators comprising one layer and the teachers and nonprofessional personnel the other. Such an organization is closer to a primary group than it is to a bureaucracy. In a primary group, where role-takers relate to one another with more emotionality and individuality (in contrast with a more formal bureaucracy), there is no reasonable or legitimate way in which some can be chosen for special training while others are left out.

(2) *Structured Skill Activities*: The macrodesign called for a sequence of training events that started with games and structured skill activities and moved to first steps in solving real organizational problems. This sequence appears to have worked well in two ways. First, we think that faculty members who attend a training event as a duty rather than by self-selection

find their ways into new interpersonal modes more easily via structured skill exercises than through less structured experiences demanding more personal commitment such as the traditional T Group. The skill exercises were chosen because each one, in microcosm, demonstrated organizational issues reminiscent of role relationships in the school. An unstructured T Group probably would have led into considerations of particular interpersonal relationships within the staff; these, we believe, would have set the stage for personal development orientations and would have led away from a focus on organizational problems. Second, the results of the exercise led rather naturally into back-home problem solving and seemed to set the stage for the choices of increasing role clarity, using staff resources, and increasing staff participation at meetings. Unstructured activities probably would have led into work on relationships between certain persons and led away from our goals of working at the organizational level.

(3) *Rotating Subgroup Membership*: The macrodesign called for staff members' rotating through groups of different sizes and compositions during the first few days. This was done to increase the potential network of workable relationships on the staff and to decrease the possibility of an in-group/out-group pattern's emerging. Another goal of such rotating was to increase staff members' identification with the staff as a whole. We felt that some degree of identification with the whole would be necessary for the motivation that would be needed to carry the project through the year, and rotating subgroup memberships appears to have increased the cohesiveness of the faculty.

(4) *Equal Treatment to All Ranks*: The design was consciously contrived to reduce status differences on the staff. No member on the staff was singled out for any special treatment. Rotating the staff through various groups brought teachers and administrators together as well as nonprofessional personnel, teachers, and administrators. The exercise emphasized that persons within groups carry out tasks and that one attempts to do the best he can on a given task regardless of who happens to be in his group. Such an assumption brought staff members

closer together, a prerequisite to achieving more openness and clearer communication.

(5) *Exemplifying New Organizational Forms in the Training*: Group processes, new group forms, and procedures for problem solving were introduced in the design with the assumption that the use of such procedures by staff members would lead to new organizational structures. New structures were expected to arise out of problem solving, and we believe that the macroaspects of the design encouraged that to happen.

Several microaspects of the design for the summer workshop warrant special attention because of their positive effects on the faculty.

(a) The *fishbowl arrangement*, in which a group on the outside of a concentric circle observes a group in the inside working, became especially useful to this faculty. The arrangement used most often called for two or three empty chairs left in the inside group. Members of the outside group were invited to enter the inside when they chose to communicate something to the insiders. During the summer workshop, this pattern was used in the problem-solving phase late in the week. Later, in a follow-up session when the Principal's Advisory Committee met in front of the rest of the staff, the same group formation was used. We learned that the faculty spontaneously employed such a formation several times during the school year to increase communication flow and participation between groups.

(b) In several activities during the training we emphasized the importance of *two-way communication*. The impact on the faculty was great indeed, for it especially affected the shape of the area coordinator's role. Area coordinators were encouraged by their colleagues to serve as communication links between the Principal's Advisory Committee and the area groups. This was an instance when learning about new processes motivated structural change. The new structure was similar to the *link-pin* organizational structure described by Likert (1961). Likert's link-pin structure uses small face-to-face groups as multiple-path communication channels in themselves; work units are organized across hierarchical levels, and members participate in group decisions at levels both above and below their own. In our school, the area coordinators were to represent their area colleagues in the Principal's Advisory Committee and to communicate actions of that advisory committee back to the members of their area.

(c) Working through the *problem-solving process step by step* was another important micro-element. We returned to this problem-solving sequence many times. It became a convenient mnemonic device for staff members. They could easily keep the stages in mind and, in fact, made use of several of them spontaneously during the school year.

Strengths of Training During School Year

Next we wish to describe the things which we believe went especailly well during the remainder of the period of intervention. Five training activities stand out as crucial aspects of the training during the school year. One was the fishbowl technique which we have already mentioned. The other forms were as follows:

(1) *Interviews After Summer Training:* The interviews brought our training staff psychologically closer to the faculty and gave us a number of key ideas for designing training events during the school year. We interviewed staff members during the hour set aside for them to prepare for their teaching. We interviewed some in groups and others individually. Where we seemed to get contradictory comments, we tried to probe for clarity or to go back to a person who had been previously interviewed to ask a few more questions. We tried to keep the interview process open to easy surveillance. All staff members knew that we were at the school on the day of the interviews, the interviews were held in accessible spots in the school such as the teachers lounge, and staff members were invited to sit in or nearby while others were being interviewed.

(2) *Problem Solving in Natural Groups:* During the first follow-up training session, we set up meetings of the area groups and asked them to carry out the problem-solving procedure. This simulation of a real meeting was a significant force in transferring learnings about problem solving to new group procedures in the area groups during the school year.

(3) *Review of Progress Before Departure of Trainers*: A significant contribution to the total design occurred during the February follow-up session when the staff reviewed how far it had progressed toward solving its basic problems of role unclarity, low use of resources, and lack of participation at meetings. The session had three helpful effects: (a) It encouraged continuing discussions and collaborative problem solving that had just begun to emerge. (b) It helped faculty members to recognize that already they had accomplished many positive things. (c) It helped set the stage for a graceful departure of the training staff without also indicating that the project was over.

(4) *Final Unstructured Session*: A significant event in the total design was the unstructured session, in the manner of a T Group, held for a complete day with the Principal's Advisory Committee. Members of the committee originated the session, involvement on the part of most was very high, and the results led to a strengthening of the group.

Weaknesses in the Summer Workshop

Certain features of our design were noticeably weak. We mention below some features we think could be bettered in another application.

(1) *Making Specific Plans*: First, we believe that we should have encouraged the faculty to commit themselves to more specific and concrete action steps at the end of the summer workshop to be used in specific problem-solving processes back home. In essence, the problem solving was learned as a process and used rather well later in the year, but more gains in terms of concrete actions could have come from the problem solving if the faculty had been enabled to use action steps started at the workshop as a springboard.

(2) *Dealing with Absent Persons*: The two staff members who did not attend the summer workshop never were brought into the training psychologically. One attempt was made to bring one of the noninvolved persons in by conducting a discussion about the workshop with that person together with three of her closest associates. At that meeting, events of the workshop were interpreted to the absent person, and feelings within

the group appeared to be supportive and positive. However, little improvement seemed to occur after that meeting. In retrospect, we feel that a session should have been designed in which the problem of informing those who were not present would be dealt with openly and skillfully.

(3) *Information-gathering Techniques*: The problem-solving sequence lacked attention to concrete techniques for diagnosing organizational processes. The training could have included some diagnostic tools in the form of self-report questionnaires, brief but systematic interview schedules, and categories for observation that staff members could have used during the year to diagnose their own organization.

Weaknesses of Training During School Year

Three circumstances may have had adverse effects during the school year.

(1) *Demands on Personal Energy*: Many teachers came to the training sessions after a difficult week of teaching. The training events constituted additional burdens for them to bear. We are now considering ways of arranging training episodes within the context of the school day itself, and we are having some success with meetings during free periods and by using substitutes part of the time. We are also making use of parts of vacations and the weeks immediately before and after the school year.

(2) *Changing Trainers*: Only two members of our training staff remained throughout the project. At times, the faculty was not sure who were our staff and who were not. Some of our own confusions probably sent confusing messages to the faculty.

(3) *Lack of Clarity of Expectations Among Trainers*: Along with our own staffing difficulties, it should also be pointed out that our training plans often were not extensive and at points not sharply enough defined. This led to uneven performances, especially in subgroups within the faculty, when different trainers were involved. We tried to correct for this by rotating trainers continuously.

In conclusion, this project was salutary for a school faculty and contains valuable lessons for consultants or change agents. For us, it serves too as a preface to a series of forthcoming interventions in schools with different structures.

REFERENCES

Campbell, J. P., and Dunnette, M. D.: Effectiveness of t-group experiences in managerial training and development. *Psycho Bull,* 70:73-104, 1968.

Bradford, L. P.; Gibb, J. R., and Benne, K. D. (Eds.): *T-group Theory and Laboratory Method: Innovation in Re-education.* New York, Wiley, 1964.

Buckley, W.: *Sociology and Modern Systems Theory.* Englewood Cliffs, P-H, 1967.

Gardner, J.: *Self-renewal: The Individual and the Innovative Society.* New York, Har-Row, 1963.

Gross, N., and Herriott, R.: *Staff Leadership in Public Schools.* New York, Wiley, 1965.

Hilfiker, L. R.: *The Relationship of School System Innovativeness to Selected Dimensions of Interpersonal Behavior in Eight School Systems.* (Technical Report No. 70.) Madison, Research and Development Center for Cognitive Learning, 1969.

Likert, R.: *New Patterns of Management.* New York, McGraw, 1961.

McGregor, D.: *The Professional Manager.* New York, McGraw, 1967.

Schmuck, R. A., and Runkel, P. J.: Organizational training for a school faculty. Eugene, Ore.: Center for the Advanced Study of Educational Administration, Universtiy of Oregon, in press.

Watson, G. (Ed.): *Change in School Systems.* Washington, D.C., National Training Laboratories, associated with the National Education Association, 1967.

Chapter 25

FROM CONFRONTATION TO COLLABORATION

IRVING N. BERLIN

Of what help can mental health professionals be to teachers and administrators who find themselves directly on the firing line with rebelling students? This paper describes group role playing and discussion sessions with school personnel that eased their tautness and actual fear by giving them a framework for understanding confrontations.

Confrontation of authority, in all avenues of life, is with us today. Youth confront their teachers, school, and college authorities; blacks confront the white community and its agencies. Confrontation and its usual result, counterconfrontation, leads to riots, chaos, disorganization, and to backlash and revengeful calls for law and order. The role of mental health professionals in this process is unclear; but an analysis of some of the problems already examined by sociologists and social psychologists, plus some understanding of the individual dynamics in these situations, provide a dynamic framework within which both individual and group confrontations can be examined and illustrated. Such a framework can help mental health professionals to help others more effectively assess the problems.

It is clear from the writings of Cohn-Bendit (1968), Deutsch (1968), Shoben (1968, 1969), and others that there are some prerequisite conditions for student confrontation and rebellion.

From the *American Journal of Orthopsychiatry*, 40:473-480, 1970.

They appear to have validity for many individual confrontations as well. These conditions are as follows:

1. Legitimate complaints about an institution's failure to meet its students' needs.
2. Arbitrary and authoritarian reactions of administrators and others in power toward the demands.
3. Refusal to listen to and understand the students' anger about existing problems and lack of readiness to negotiate with the students.
4. A moral rather than a task-oriented approach; that is, the right of students to make demands indicates they are ungrateful for the schooling made available versus having a common problem, i.e. "How do we get the best education possible in our institution?"
5. Retaliatory feelings and behavior on the part of challenged administrations and faculty when they feel incompetent either in the work they are doing or in the face of the challenges and when they have no techniques for managing them.
6. Fear of democratic participation in decision-making, especially about potential loss of power and authority.
7. Most institutions have become rigidified and do not change to meet the challenges of technology, population mobility, and the new curricular and teaching alterations required for relevance.

Thus, many administrators and faculty members find a need to defend the status quo because dynamically radical change provokes anxiety and is frightening. Confrontation about these issues, therefore, often results in irrational responses (Gans, 1968; Trimberger, 1968; Widmer, 1969).

Our experiences with individual confrontation were brought to our consultation seminars by mental health workers from ghetto junior and senior highschools. Their experiences confirmed our previous work in another ghetto area. The complaints of teachers and administrators and their pressure on guidance personnel and others to solve the problems did more than reflect the chaos in the schools and the poor learning atmosphere due to defiance by minority students; it also said a great deal about the people involved. Most teachers and administrators involved were anxious about open challenge to their authority, reluctant to examine the relevance of their teaching methods, and in contrast to effective teachers in the same schools, they could not ignore testing behavior, such as keeping coats on and swearing in class, and they attended only to the problem of increasing the learning possible in the classroom (Friedenberg, 1963; Goodman, 1962). In addition, some teachers avoided confrontation by ignoring events that seemed to be leading to a crescendo of definance and breakdown of the learning situation. In desperation they would then finally demand prompt punitive action by administrators to restore order in the clasroom (Rosenberg, 1965; Solnit, et al., 1969).

Authoritative and secure administrators were able, by example, to be helpful to their teachers. They not only could recognize very early signs of trouble among the students and talk about school problems, but they would look with their faculty at the need for bringing about curricular change, etc. Though these efforts were difficult and painful, they did not result in authoritarian, repressive measures which escalate school confrontation and conflict. The school guidance worker, who had, with consultation, been able to work with the faculty, began to share some of our previous experiences. We discussed some possible methods of working with these overwhelmed teachers. We had in mind two tasks: (1) helping these teachers find some alternatives to their almost invariable response to challenge; and (2) heping them reassess their educational tasks as teachers with these children.

The author will illustrate efforts with groups of teachers and with a group of administrators who met with several of our guidance staff around the problems of individual confrontations and challenges posed by what were always described as "irrational and hostile demands" of militant students. We combined two methods, the use of group demonstrations and discussion augmented by frequent individual consultation.

Group Sessions with Teachers

First we did a series of demonstration group workshops, two each week for three to four weeks, in the target schools with twenty teachers at a time. A very forthright social worker who could enact the violent, angry, abusive adolescent confronted another worker as teacher. In this setting we had the worker, as a teacher, do two things. First, his observing ego described his feelings on confrontation, his anxieties, fear, anger, frustration, desperation, and violent desire to hit back. Second, we had the worker demonstrate the way in which one could try to listen to the angry fury of the student and reduce its intensity by concerned interest in the adolescent and by attitudes and words which used a theme and variations of, "Okay, you're mad as hell at me, but I'm not sure I understand what you want of me and how I can be a better teacher for you." The student then replied with specific accusations and examples of the teachers' not caring about the student as a human being, his retaliatory, often racially biased, behavior, his lousy and indifferent teaching, the poor and often inappropriate curriculum planning, etc. The concerned teacher responded with, "Okay, maybe some of these complaints are justified but where do we start to change them?"

The first reactions from the groups were always shock at the accuracy of the hostile, vituperative nature of the portrayal of the minority adolescent. There was usually clear agreement about the accuracy of the description of the teachers' feelings while under attack. However, usually there were very mixed reactions about the methods demonstrated in dealing with the confrontation. We then asked some fairly secure teachers to play the adolescent, which they did with scathing effectiveness. On subsequent occasions we asked the less secure teacher to play that role as a more secure teacher tried to deal with the confrontation. We stopped the role play at critical moments to evoke comments and suggestions for behavior on both sides. The discussion was always lively and heated. Finally, we involved the least secure teachers in the role of the confronted teacher.

During this period of three to four weeks, two sessions per week, the workers talked individually with the teachers most in trouble to inquire about how the group sessions could be more useful. During consultation we got the teachers involved in discussing their own reactions to difficult students. The consultants' understanding comments about how threatening these confrontations were would occasionally help some teacher to consider with the worker how he might try to consistently use one of the attitudes suggested in the group meeting when dealing with a very difficult youngster. Subsequent consultations were used for discussion of what did or did not work and what modifications seemed in order. This on-the-spot followup and encouragement seemed to work very well. More teachers were able to be more flexible with their students, more open and less repressive. Often consultation continued much beyond the period of demonstration.

One of the outcomes of the group sessions was the learning of alternative methods of handling confrontation. Some desensitization took place as teachers identified with the actors and later were able to participate. A beginning consideration of the previously unalterable and unsuitable curriculum and a hard look at some of their teaching methods also resulted as the teachers tried to meet these youngsters' needs. Sometimes the worker acted as a catalyst to get administrators to join the group in discussing how the curriculum could be altered to be more interesting and useful. In this setting the more flexible and creative teachers had their long-awaited hearing as they described those techniques in their subject that seemed to work and interest their students.

Again, individual consultation was helpful to some very rigid teachers. Persistent encouragement in their efforts to change their teaching style and to find new curriculum aids was enhanced as the consultant clearly acknowledged how difficult such change was and how much guts it took to make such efforts. After a time, some of the teachers discovered that they could teach differently without loss of classroom control. Several teachers voiced satisfaction about beginning to again feel competent and effective as teachers as their efforts began to pay off.

One of the most dramatic moments in the demonstrations usually occurred when we tried to illustrate that attacks and confrontations were not just aimed against teachers as individuals. The worker who demonstrated the teacher role asked in bewilderment, "Why me? I'm trying to be understanding and helpful. What's so terrible about me?" The worker playing the student replied that he hated any smug, sweet, superior, aloof authority. He wanted some sign of individual concern and understanding of his needs and problems. No matter how "nice" the teacher was, he felt usually rejected and actually experienced some retaliation because of racial and cultural differences, expressed attitudinally, which unless explicitly pointed out with examples were not in the awareness of educators.

Group Sessions with Administrators

We did a similar series with administrators where the author played teacher, since it was evident that the administrators would enjoy having someone with greater status on the hot spot. The prompt follow-up with individual consultation was equally important and sometimes helpful with rigid, retaliatory administrators who were in real trouble.

We moved from discussions of individual confrontations to discussions with administrators of their problems around group confrontations, especially their dealing with the angry and sometimes irrational demands *en masse.* We used case histories of successful and unsuccessful meetings and confrontations to demonstrate what seemed to work and to analyze the data together. For example, one rather mild, elderly high school principal's office was invaded at 4:30 P.M. by fifteen minority activists who demanded that three fourths of the teachers be fired, a new curriculum be instituted, and that they be given authority to interview and hire all new teachers and approve all the curriculum. They threatened to burn down the school that night if their demands were not met. The principal, alone with a custodian and a few scattered teachers in the school, felt helpless and very frightened. Under the circumstances, however, he asked the group into the conference room to discuss the problems with them. During an hour of discussion, the principal agreed with the students' criticism of the curriculum and the unhelpful attitudes of some of the teachers. He asked the students to name a committee of students and teachers to meet with him to plan a more relevant curriculum. At the end of an hour the principal asked the students if they wanted to wait and present their problems to the superintendent that same day so they could together secure his support of the needed changes. The students agreed that the next day would be fine.

In another instance a very secure and flexible administrator in a similar confrontation became rather angry with the irrational aspects of the demands and made a counterdemand of the students after he had listened carefully for a time. It was *their* education and he wanted *them* to come up with some ideas and plans for implementation of their valid demands. He understood the problems but felt helpless about obtaining the needed official support to institute change. In the furious debate he maintained his concerned interest, and no matter what the provocation he demanded the students' thoughtful participation in solving the problems raised. He asked them to get some parents, teachers, and community representatives involved. One of the minority student leaders said later, "I didn't know the old man really cared. He seemed kind of out of it before. We really dug his demands, especially because he believed we had ideas about what and how we could be taught better and who could do the job." This is an excellent example of the authoritative versus the authoritarian approach.

We were also able to use an example known to all that was disastrous. A junior high school principal, a former physical education teacher who ruled by brawn and threat, called the police in the face of a mass confrontation. This led to a riot and the closing of the school. Since some of us had worked with this administrator, we were able to describe where we had failed. First, in case discussions around individual confrontations, he could not be helped to consider the distinction between confrontation as a challenge to his authority, which was in part always there, and confrontation as a statement about the problems and the troubles of the ghetto youngster. He could not recognize a confrontation as a student's comments regarding his hopeless world and the school's failure to help him find any way out. No matter how much data about the family problems, previous schooling, or neighborhood history, etc. that we presented, this principal still saw any angry, threatening kid as a personal affront. It meant not being liked or respected, a very personal threat that could only be met with force. Thus, we could not help him to talk to students about how change could be brought about to meet their needs. His way had to be the only way, and his decisions were final. In contrast was our success in demonstrating to this administrator how to interview paranoid, angry parents. He could understand the parents' pathology and did not feel as personally involved. Thus, he learned to listen and to be helpful and flexible in working things out with them. It was clear to all the administrators, some who were not unlike the principal under discussion, that the sense of insecurity and urgent need to use force to maintain order posed a very severe problem. As we examined case studies together in terms of the impact of counterforce and retaliation on the learning process and the school atmosphere, they could agree that it only increased the need for violent rebellion, reinforced the conviction that administrators were the enemy, and that under these conditions no learning could take place.

After four months of weekly meetings and many individual consultations, one of the administrators in our group, the junior college dean of men, helped us to recognize that we had not correctly understood several aspects of the problem underlying mass student confrontation. He described in detail the events of the previous week which had been a failure in handling a confrontation. Police were called to handle the riot, and massive destruction of the school property had occurred. He described how for some weeks minority students and student activists had made repeated efforts to meet with the administration. Some faculty had also supported the students' position; yet after several meetings with administrators, the massive confrontation nevertheless occurred with bitter results. He first described his own sense of bewilderment and helplessness that reason, efforts at conciliation, and dialogue had not been enough. Only as the details unfolded did we gain some understanding of what had been missing.

The several minority groups of students and other activists had presented the administration with demands for a greater say in the curriculum and greater involvement in its teaching. They protested that as a vocational college it ill-prepared them for jobs; its equipment was ancient and in no way similar to that they would use on a job. The black, Mexican-American, and Indian students demanded that their history and literature be properly presented in the curriculum. Most of all they resented that their instructors and the administrators felt they were still children who did not know what was good for them and should have no voice in what was taught, how it was taught, and who taught it. They demanded change *now*. They had waited long enough in their ghettos for others to recognize and respond to their needs. They intended to force change *now*. The urgency, anger, and impatience with endless dialogue and administrative delays were not correctly assessed, nor was there clear student involvement in problem-solving. The administration's repeated pleas for patience and their use of a chart to illustrate the chain of command they had to go through only gave the students a sense of the impotence of the faculty and administration to effect change. They were, therefore, determined to force it in any way possible (Fanton, 1963; Fever, 1968; Malcolm X, 1965; Rosenberg, 1965). One of our consultants, a black social worker who had been consulting with that particular administrative staff, sharply pointed out that his warnings and predictions had been ignored.

We began to see how unprepared a school or college system was for rapid response and integrative action. There was little evidence of creative anticipation of problems and almost no community involvement of school people. The estrangement between the school and the community made responsiveness, communication and mutual engagement in problem solving impossible. Several of the administrators voiced their troubled beliefs that one could not find integrative solutions to such situations.

It was almost as if they were hoping that if one lived through one or two of these difficult experiences that the troubles would then go away. The dean of men spelled out the realities, the schools were not out of the woods and he at least wanted some help with planning for the troubled future. Again we turned to our black social worker consultant who restated his perceptions and offered some tentative solutions that had emerged from previous meetings.

We had data now from several schools whose continued involvement of concerned school personnel with the community kept the schools in tune with the community needs. School people learned especially how the schools might become more responsive in their curriculum and their teaching methods and how school mental health workers might be more responsive to the particular needs of some students and parents.

We used this data from school-community efforts to discuss with administrators how they might help some of their teachers become more alert to the possible meanings of difficult student behaviors, as well as to the educational needs of their students. More flexible and more imaginative teaching was a must. The administrators then began to talk about their own difficulty in shifting from set curriculum standards which are prescribed by the system to a curriculum that would educate more of their students. Some of them were espeically concerned with their own tendency to take the easy way out and expel difficult students rather than to learn what it takes to help the students learn more and stay in school. Adapting more rapidly to changing student needs, involving students more in the assessment of these needs, and evaluating the effectiveness of the schools' efforts, raised the spectre of loss of authority and status. These issues were repeatedly considered and examined most effectively in the context of the schools' role to educate students to become responsible participants in their society.

Summary and Conclusions

After these discussions and the crises that had occurred, it became evident that schools needed to use their mental health personnel to work with teachers and administrators to keep the students in school rather than to get rid of them. This also required new roles of mental health workers, and only a few of them had learned to work in this way.

The threat of crises and violence forced the most adaptable of the administrators to begin to plan ahead to avoid trouble by inviting student and community involvement in planning for a more meaningful education. Other administrators, although they could see the effectiveness of these methods, were unable to participate in such involvement or to use consultation to improve their capacity to deal with confrontation more flexibly and to reexamine their function in the schools. Under the great and repeated stress, many of them left these schools.

We were able through demonstrations and discussion followed by individual consultation to give some administrators and teachers a framework within which to understand confrontations. As they could acknowledge the legitimate complaints, distinguish between authoritative and authoritarian responses, and recognize from our role playing and discussions how one could understand anger and respond to it positively, they seemed more at ease in their schools. The efforts to help educators distinguish between moralistic attitudes which turned kids off and task-oriented ones which involved them in mutual problem solving was more difficult to get across. In our role playing we were able to indicate the universality of retaliatory feelings on being confronted and to demonstrate techniques of becoming aware of such feelings and not acting on them. The need for participation of students and community members in planning and evolving better education was both threatening to some and appealing to others because it meant getting community help to mount needed programs. Many educators expressed greater willingness to try new methods and approaches after these sessions.

For mental health personnel it required some role changes as well. They often had to be the ones who could interpret both student and community needs as well as be able to help educators find a more flexible and integrative way to meet these needs. Some school guidance personnel found themselves unable to function in these roles. Others found these roles compatible with their understanding of interpersonal and organizational dynamics and their capacity to function flexibly in a variety of new roles with students, educators, and the community.

In conclusion, our experiences in this school system very greatly paralleled the necessary and requisite factors for confrontation described by some of the authors quoted. It was our experience that our efforts, successful and unsuccessful, could be understood as part of a dynamic process.

REFERENCES

Cohn-Benit, D., et al.: The student rebellion. *This Magazine Is About Schools*, Summer, 1st section, 1968.

Deutsch, M.: Conflicts: productive and constructive. In *Kurt Lewin Memorial Address*. Am Psychol Assn, Washington, 1968.

Fanon, F.: *The Wretched of the Earth*. New York, Grove, 1963.

Feuer, L.: *The Conflict of Generations*. New York, Basic, 1968.

Friedenberg, E.: *Coming of Age in America*. New York, Random, 1963.

Gans, H.: Toward the "equality revolution." *New York Times Magazine*, Nov., 1968.

Goodman, P.: *Compulsory Mis-Education*. New York, Vintage Books, 1962.

Malcolm X: *Autobiography*. New York, Grove, 1965.

Rosenberg, M.: *Society and the Adolescent Self-Image*. Princeton, Princeton U Pr, 1965.

Shoben, E.: Means, ends, and the liberties of education. *J Higher Educ*, Feb.:61-68, 1968.

Shoben, E.: The new student: implications for personnel work. *CAPS Capsule*, Spring:1-7, 1969.

Solnit, A., et al.: Youth unrest: A symposium. *Am J Psychiat*, March:39-53, 1969.

Trimberger, E.: Why a rebellion at Columbia was inevitable. *Transaction*, Sept.:28-38, 1968.

Widmer, K.: Why the colleges blew up. *Nation*, Feb.:237-240, 1969.

> Chapter 26
>
> # PREVENTIVE COUNSELING FOR TEACHERS AND STUDENTS
>
> Matthew Snapp and J. Neville Sikes

$\mathbf{M}$ANY PUBLIC SCHOOLS today, especially those in big cities, seem to be in a state of perpetual crisis. Again and again administrators find themselves trying to patch up and having little time left to plan ahead in an attempt to prevent problems.

Yet in the face of these problems, the delivery of counseling services has largely been limited to remedial individual treatment of the more seriously disturbed children. Relatively little has been done to teach "healthy" children how to cope with the pressing tensions of their environment.

While mental health workers may be swamped with referrals of disturbed youngsters, it is becoming increasingly important for these workers to take the time needed to set up preventive mental health programs; programs aimed at dealing with problems before they require remediation. One such program, instituted on a trial basis this year in Austin, Texas, is the focus of this paper.

The Goals of the Program

The major goal of the program was to prepare youngsters to deal constructively with racial-ethnic tensions and discrimination. It was not expected that prejudice and misunderstanding would end, but that students would learn to cope with their fears and

From *The Guidance Clinic*, 4, 5-8, 1972.

distrust without fighting, insulting, and name-calling.

It was hoped that communication skills could be improved so that if conflict arose, it could be resolved in a manner in which both parties would feel, at least, that they had been heard. Individual students still might not like each other, but they would have learned to see beyond the stereotypes to the individuality of other persons.

While developing these communication skills, it was hoped that enough contact between ethnic groups would occur to maintain healthy tri-ethnic relationships. And finally, there was the desire to build trust between teachers and students.

Program Preparations

The program in Austin was initiated at the suggestion of a committee appointed by the principal of a junior high school to consider ways to improve teacher-student relations. This committee, which consisted of one counselor and a small group of teachers, felt that discussion groups of students led by teachers would be a partial answer. The district school psychologist was invited to consult with the principal and the counselors on ways to develop a group counseling program which would serve large numbers of students and teachers.

Initial Encounters: The consultation resulted in a plan which began with an encounter group for teachers, counselors, and the principal, co-led by a school psychologist and one counselor. Another psychologist, in addition, co-led two encounter groups with each of the participating counselors. The members of the latter two groups were students who would later serve as co-leaders with teachers of broader student groups.

Group Structure: Small tri-ethnically balanced discussion groups (five boys and five girls) were to be led by one student and one teacher. These groups were to meet for one hour a week during school time for a period of six weeks.

These groups were not conceived of as therapy groups, or even encounter groups, but rather as rap sessions which would give students an opportunity to talk about whatever they wanted within a minimal structure. The leaders were to be members, but members who, because of their greater experience, could help to model constructive communication patterns.

Leadership Training: The selection and training of teacher and student leaders were very important. It was decided that all teachers and counselors would be invited to participate, but that required training would take 1½ hours a week *after* school time. While it was hoped that enough faculty members would participate to enable the program to reach a large number of students, only teachers who were willing to commit their own time and their emotional energy to learning more direct means of communicating would sign up.

Adult Participation: The principal, the two counselors, and nine teachers made the commitment. For eight afternoons and two Saturday morning sessions they participated in a group led by the psychologist. Role barriers were quickly broken down. The members practiced open communication, with the opportunity for feedback as to how they were affecting others and an opportunity to experience increased self-awareness.

Student Training: The student co-leaders were chosen by the counselors from a list of students nominated by individual teachers. One group of ten seventh graders and two groups of ten eighth graders were selected for training. Each group was composed of one-half girls and one-half boys, four Anglos (83% of the school population), four blacks (15% of the school population), and two Mexican-Americans (2% of the school population).

Each group of student leaders was co-led by a psychologist and one of the counselors and met during the school day for one hour a week for eight weeks. Every student who was asked to participate eagerly agreed, even though he would be responsible for making up work missed in his classes. Of these thirty students, thirteen were selected by the counselors as co-leaders for the first round of groups. Many of the others co-led later groups.

Group Formation: Toward the end of the eight-week training period, students in the school were notified that they could sign up for groups which would be meeting for one hour a week for six weeks. Of the 250 who signed up, 130 were chosen for thirteen groups; the others were told that they would be assigned to a group during the following six-week period.

In the two weeks before the general student groups started, key leadership issues were discussed with the participating teachers, issues such as how to avoid relating to students as authorities or as therapists. The teachers then got together with their student co-leaders to discuss how they would work to share their joint leadership responsibilities.

Implementing the Program—Problems and Solutions

Scheduling: In order to get broad student involvement, it was felt that group meetings needed to be scheduled during school hours. This would have posed no problem had there been study halls. Because there were no study halls, the meeting time was changed each week for each group, so that no student had to miss a given class more than once during the six-week period.

Teachers were freed for their groups by having other teachers in the program fill in for them during their free hours. It was thought that asking nonparticipating teachers to take extra classes so that teacher-leaders could be freed for the program might cause resentment, but some teachers welcomed the opportunity to help out in this way.

An added incentive for taking a colleague's class was that the teacher was encouraged to teach anything about which he was personally excited. An example of this interdisciplinary exchange was an art teacher who talked to a history class about the place of art in the study of history.

The Danger of Polarization: Once the training program for teachers was under way, there developed a strong support base for the program among those directly involved. The teachers who participated were very excited about the program's potential value. While this support is necessary for the success of the program, inherent in it are pitfalls that need to be avoided.

In situations such as this, strong feelings can develop of an "in group" and an "out group." Special alliances between the principal, the counselors, and the participating teachers can be seen as posing a threat to those who are "outside." When special relationships with students are added to these alliances, where communication is presumably freerer, the nonparticipant may perceive the group as having awesome power.

Encouraging Cooperation: Two ground rules were found to be important in assuring the goodwill and cooperation of other teachers:

1. Participating teachers were not to discuss the groups in the lounge or elsewhere in the presence of nonparticipating teachers, so that teachers in the training groups would not appear to be closing ranks and excluding the outsiders;
2. If teachers were discussed in the student groups, the leaders were to try to ensure that names were not used.

In fact, a strong attempt was made to keep the discussion focused on the present, with the members of the group, rather than on persons who were not present. If an uninvolved teacher heard that he had been "discussed," resentment and hostility might result.

Other techniques used to involve the nonparticipating teachers were to solicit recommendations from them for student leaders and discussion topics, and to offer a program at a faculty meeting in which a discussion was conducted to illustrate what occurred in the groups.

The Fear of Change: One of the major problems this program encountered was the apparent fear of the faculty related to change. As was mentioned in the introductory paragraphs, education is in a state of flux today, particularly in newly-integrated schools. This school was attempting to meet these changes with innovative programs, several of which demanded new types of teacher behavior. Some teachers resisted any change, saying that it was "impossible to teach these kinds of kids," and that, "if the principal would support teachers more and paddle the acting-out students, we could reestablish discipline."

The mental health program became a target for the teachers' distress over the changing school environment. The program was highly visible, since students left the teachers' classes for group meetings. Often asked was, "Why should a student miss a class, even if it is only *once* during the year, in order to participate in something 'nonacademic?' What are the priorities to be?"

In order to reduce some of these fears, the counselors tried to understand the monumental problems facing these teachers and to empathize with their frustrations. They worked to find areas in which their goals coincided and helped to find ways in which counselors and teachers could work together.

Expanding Participation: A greater number of capable teachers could have been involved in leading discussion groups had there been more avenues open for training than just the teacher group which met after school. Three teachers who wanted to participate but were unable to attend the after-school sessions were trained individually by the school counselors. They became co-leaders in the January session of the program.

Another means of giving teachers experience in group leadership would have been a six-hour communications laboratory for interested teachers conducted on a workshop day or on a weekend. This might have been held in addition to, or in lieu of, the eight after-school meetings.

Next year, this school is going to have a communications lab for the entire faculty on the first day that the teachers report to school. Its purpose will be to help people to get acquainted and to encourage discussion of anticipated problem areas. Special emphasis will be placed on tri-ethnic communication.

Evaluating the Effects of the Program

Confrontation: Observations in other schools in the system had suggested that as integration proceeded, the number of fights increased. Therefore, there had been an increase anticipated in the number of physical confrontations between members of different ethnic groups. What occurred, however, was a dramatic increase in the number of *verbal* confrontations and a concomitant decrease in the number of fights, compared with the previous year.

Crisis Groups: The principal and the conuselors believe that the real "pay off" of the program was in these verbal confrontations. When the pressure built within a group of students, they were encouraged to come to the counselors' office to "hassle their problems out" together.

These gatherings were called "crisis groups" and were sometimes led by a counselor and at other times, met without a leader. The students would remain in the group room (a small, empty, carpeted room adjacent to the counselors' office) for from one-half hour to four hours, until an understanding was reached.

Often one or two students would come to the office saying that they were having trouble with four or five others. A request would then be made of the counselor to send for the others so that they could "get it together." Sometimes a group would be about to fight and would be stopped by the counselors or administrators and told to sit down and talk out their disagreements.

By the middle of the school year, there were one or two crisis groups meeting each day. The principal, counselors, and consultants were very impressed with how well the students who had participated in the program could work things out with each other in a crisis group. Instead of name-calling and ascribing blame, they told each other how they felt, what had made them feel this way, and what would make them feel better.

Most of the problems were found to be the result of misunderstandings due to gossip and rumors, and could readily be cleared up with direct, nondefensive communication.

Intergroup Relations: Another apparent effect of the program was that students sat down and talked with someone of another ethnic group, in many cases for the first time. Beginning this new understanding was often difficult, but students indicated that they learned that many of their stereotypes were wrong. They also learned that there are some very real differences between people of different ethnic background.

Teachers co-leading the groups said that they learned to be much more "human" and "open" with their students, as their students were more open with them. And several students who had never before spoken up in class, were able to participate freely after having been in a group.

As in any new mental health program, it is very difficult to say what caused what effect. The results of the program could be due to factors not considered here. However, the participants in the program, particularly the adults, were very enthusiastic. At least it seemed to begin the difficult process of building bridges between persons.

Chapter 27
SYSTEM INTERVENTION IN A
SCHOOL-COMMUNITY CONFLICT
GILBERT LEVIN AND DAVID D. STEIN

IN THE FALL OF 1968, New York City was hit by a long and bitter school strike. During those harrowing two months, when schools opened periodically only to be closed down again after a day or so, parents' concern over their children's education began to affect and to be affected by the issues that had first caused the controversy, decentralization of the school board, community control, and teachers' job security. As the resultant community feeling of helplessness grew, the pressure increased on various community agencies to do something, *anything*, either to help to end the school strike or to aid the children (and their parents) in the interim.

One agency affected by these pressures was the Sound View-Throgs Neck Community Mental Health Center (CMHC) in the Bronx; and, as the community cries for action became more insistent, center staff members responded by helping to plan and execute a forum in school-community relations. The intention of the forum was to channel existing conflicts in the direction of the community's long-term benefit. The result was not only an apparently successful program but also an increased closeness and understanding between the CMHC and the community it serves.

From the *Journal of Applied Behavioral Science,* 6:337-351, 1970.

Background

CMHC is a comprehensive mental health program staffed by more than 200 professional and nonprofessional workers which serves a population of about 180,000 residents of New York City. Its central purposes are to provide a continuum of psychiatric and rehabilitative services to the chronically mentally ill and to increase the problem-solving ability of the community by providing technical assistance to indigenous organizations and agencies. The population it serves is ethnically and economically heterogeneous. It is in the process of transition from a predominantly blue-collar white population to a black and Puerto Rican population of relatively lower socioeconomic level.

Planning for the forum began within CMHC. In the school year preceding the strike, CMHC had built a number of significant consultative relationships with schools in its catchment area. When, in the fall of 1968, the school opening was delayed and the schools were later closed by the strike, the center felt various conflicting pressures, from teachers, from principals, and from parents, to act in ways that each group construed to be in its behalf. Because of the highly mixed character of the population, there was significant conflict within role groups as well as between and among them.

Local Group, a local grass-roots group of parents whose children were enrolled in schools throughout the center's catchment area, which CMHC had helped to organize for more than a year, was seriously split within itself on the numerous questions that divided the school and the community. A significant portion of the membership favored keeping the schools open in defiance of the United Federation of Teachers (UFT); others favored keeping the schools closed. Some members of both factions supported and contributed toward the setting up of temporary classrooms outside school buildings; others in Local Group opposed this action. While this subgrouping was, in a degree, along racial and ethnic lines, it was not exclusively so. Indeed, CMHC was aware of several incidents of conflict and alienation between neighbors who had maintained amicable, even friendly, relationships over a period of years.

Within CMHC itself there was considerable tension during the initial weeks of the dispute, as conflicting pressures were placed upon CMHC staff to provide services and/or take sides. For example, at least three principals approached CMIIC staff known to and trusted by them with requests for services in their schools, this during a period when picket lines composed partly of other CMHC clients were up and attendance at schools was low. Simultaneously, other teachers and parents from these same schools requested space in the CMH Center to hold informal classes. At first, the center tried to ride out the storm. The "typical" staff member's response, if indeed there was any during those chaotic days, was to favor acting on the needs of his individual clients but to refrain from doing so out of an awareness that the collective organizational clients of CMHC might not be served in that way. Each staff member, of course, was in actual or potential conflict with one or more other CMHC staff members whose personal clientele advocated a contradictory behavior from the group. As time passed, staff members became increasingly aware that relationships they had labored to build were in jeopardy due to inaction. In addition, CMHC observed that its passive attitude was shared by virtually every other organized group with a mandate to act. It was these pressures building up from both within and without the center which eventually forced CMHC to design an intervention.

Steps Toward a Forum

After some preliminary planning was completed, CMHC approached Local Group leaders and invited them to collaborate in sponsoring and implementing an open meeting aimed at managing the conflict. At the suggestion of its president, a planning committee of Local Group was formed consisting of members who took different positions on the strike, thus giving most parties in the conflict a voice in planning. While CMHC and Local Group agreed that a full resolution of the various conflicts was dependent on city-wide forces and negotiations at that level, they also felt that it would be possible to design and implement a program aimed at limited but nevertheless significant objectives, which were clearly explicated in the joint planning sessions.

In the defused atmosphere of a forum format:

1. People with strong feelings and definite opinions would be able to examine them in a more rational light.
2. Angry persons on each side of an issue would have an opportunity to "hear" (understanding) the opposing point of view.
3. People with legitimate differences of opinion would be able to come to mutually agreed-upon accommodations.
4. Stereotypes would be reduced, and members of particular groups, either racial or ethnic; whether teachers, parent, or student, and so on, would be able to discover advantages in working together.
5. Various groups might be able to use a variant of the design to resolve continuing and new conflicts arising in their environments.

These objectives were spelled out after several sessions in which members of the planning committee confronted one another with some stereotyped notions. Some parents, for instance, assumed that all teachers were in favor of the strike, an assumption obviously untrue, although few teachers who opposed the strike could afford to make public declarations of their position. Charges of anti-Semitism and black militantism were leveled when persons disagreed and did not want to confront the substantive issues underlying their differences. Such stereotypes were actually more pervasive in the day-to-day contacts among community members than in the joint planning sessions, where they played a minor role, probably because the committee members seemed quite anxious by that time to do something constructive.

The Forum

Design—Intergroup Exercise

As a result of the planning sessions, the Local Group and CMHC decided to invite a large number of persons from both the schools and the community to participate. The capacity of the available auditorium necessitated scheduling two consecutive weekday evenings, with 125 persons invited each night. The invitation list for each evening included forty-eight parents (from the 16 public schools in an area defined by the Local Group as its community), thirty-two teachers, eight school principals, twenty-five students (grades 9-12), one to three clergymen, three to four businessmen, one to three district school superintendents, one to two local school board members, and one policeman from the local precinct. Personal contacts were made to ensure the attendance of parents and teachers representing different points of view on the issues.

The forum was held at the CMH Center. The schedule of events, modeled after a typical residential laboratory intergroup exercise, was as follows:

7:30–8:00 P.M.	*Warm-up*
8:00–8:15	*Welcome and orientation*
8:15	*Sheets containing "Suggested Issues for Discussion" passed out*
8:15–9:05	*Platform and Nomination*
9:05–9:30	*Speeches (5 minutes each)*
9:30–9:35	*Election (ballots passed out at 9:30)*
9:30–10:15	*Discussion of process and results*
10:15–10:30	*Follow-up steps*

From 7:30 to 8:00 P.M., each person was greeted and registered. At the moment of his arrival, each person became involved in the business of the evening. Folding chairs were set up to create five separate groups. Those attending were assigned to groups by a procedure that ensured a relative balance of role membership (i.e. teacher, parent, student, principal, and so on). Those who came in pairs or cliques were deliberately split up in order to facilitate contacts with other persons and points of view.

In each group circle was a small table on which were placed pencils, pads, and envelopes. Each envelope contained the answer to one of the the ten multiple-choice questions the guests received upon entering the auditorium. The questions were concerned with demographic and educational matters related to the schools in the area. Each person was allowed to open only one envelope containing an answer. In this way, all persons were guaranteed of being included in the discussion, people came to know one another, and they also learned something about the schools in their area. A CMHC staff member was present in each group as a facilitator only during the warm-up period.

The boredom and alienation of clique formation, which often builds up at community meetings as those who arrive early wait for those who arrive late, was avoided. Group cohesiveness developed during the warm-up period, thus enabling people to handle the major tasks of the evening requiring a cooperative problem-solving set. Since each person could make a specific contribution to his group when he arrived by opening an envelope and giving the group an answer to a question, his sense of inclusion was enhanced.

The Task—Platform of Concerns

The second phase of the program started around 8:15 P.M., when a member of Local Group and a member of CMHC made brief welcoming remarks. The participants, situated in five groups, were then given instructions concerning their task for the next hour. Each group was requested to develop a platform on a series of education-related issues and, at the same time, to nominate one of its members as a candidate for "mayor" in a mock election. The issues suggested were construction and physical improvement of schools, curriculum, parental participation in planning and decision making, conflict and polarization within and between various groups, the disruptive child, and decentralization.

The groups went to work promptly. Participation was complete except for one member of the local school board who declined, explaining to members of the CMHC in the hall that she felt her access to private information about school matters would inhibit her participation in the forum. This failure of communication is testimony to the gap between the school board and its constituency both in this and many other communities.

By about 9:15 P.M., each group had nominated its candidate for mayor and the "campaign" began.

The ten nominees (selected from the two evening sessions) included parents, teachers, principals, and students, suggesting no particular role bias in the groups' choices of representatives.

Common to most of the campaign speeches was a stress upon the value of having persons with different views get together to talk productively about issues. Students wanted more opportunity to get to know their teachers and to eliminate the drudgery of schoolwork in favor of exciting educational experiences. The specific suggestions are summarized below:

1. Neighborhood facilities used as classrooms to alleviate over-crowding
2. Housing construction curtailed unless new school facilities included in plans
3. Community residents employed in paraprofessional and tutorial roles
4. Minority group teachers hired in greater proportion
5. Textbooks geared toward minority group experiences and curricula including such neglected areas as "heritage" studies and history of labor unions
6. Computer instruction
7. School programs for children two- and three-years-old.
8. Vocational training programs placing noncollege-bound students in skilled and respected positions
9. Student influence in school program and policy
10. An accountability system, more specific yet fair, for teachers and school administrators
11. Public election of local school boards
12. School facilities used during free hours for community recreation and social services, such as family and legal counseling.

It should be noted that the forum was not designed to include action assignments but merely to generate major educational concerns.

Findings

Group Process in Platform Preparations

Following the campaign speeches, an election was held by individual written ballot. While the votes were being tallied, the CMHC chairman suggested that someone from each group share his particular group's experience in working together with the total group.

Most groups felt overwhelmed by the difficulty of the task and, therefore, selected those issues which held the greatest meaning for their members. The spokesmen reported an open, but not always heated, exchange of views of the various "camps" represented. They mentioned their pleasant surprise at being able to see proponents of differing views as people rather than as ogres. While some persons tended to dominate the discussion in the beginning, no group felt that this continued for very long.

Candidates were nominated mainly on the basis of their verbal skills as demonstrated in the group discussions, the spokesmen explained. On a few occasions, students were nominated to represent the group because "this was about their education."

When the total assembly was asked whether there were any reasons for it to meet again, the main reaction was that this type of forum should continue, but should be organized in individual schools, not at the CMHC.

Group Cohesiveness in Election Results

The tabulation of the ballots permits an assessment of in-group identification, or group cohesiveness. Since participants in each group had worked together for a measurable period of time, one would expect a greater proporton of votes for a group's own candidate than for others. The level of commitment of each group to its candidate appeared to be high, as comments were made about "our man" or "our girl." Group solidarity had developed quite strongly in most groups, and participants found it preferable to maintain allegiance to their own group's candidate than to cast a vote for someone else whose presentation might have merited equal endorsement. "Pulling together" to accomplish a clearly designated task no doubt facilitated the development of solidarity; group forces operated toward achieving a consensus on issues, and divergent views had either to be ignored or assimilated into the platform. A rough measure of this variable is presented in Table 27-I.

TABLE 27-I

BALLOT COUNT PROVES GROUP COHESIVENESS

FIRST NIGHT

Group	N	Total Votes Received	Votes From Own Group	Proportion of Actual Own Group Votes to Total Possible Own Group Votes (%)	Chance Expectation of Own Group Votes (%)
1	14	10	9	.64	.20
2	16	17	9	.56	.20
3	15	29	10	.67	.20
4	16	16	11	.69	.20
5	14	3	2	.14	.20
SECOND NIGHT					
1	11	13	11	1.0	.20
2	11	3	3	.27	.20
3	11	17	11	1.0	.20
4	12	13	9	.75	.20
5	11	10	7	.64	.20

Of note here is that in eight of ten groups, candidates received appreciably above random endorsement from their own group. The two contradictory cases (Group 5 on the first night and Group 2 on the second) can probably be accounted for by the relatively desultory campaign speeches of those candidates. Of importance is the field "validation" of the behavioral science principle of in-group choice. There have been numerous examples in laboratory settings demonstrating this phenomenon after the completion of certain group tasks. But in this situation, despite the fact that people with different ideological and attitudinal viewpoints, exacerbated by the school strike, were asked to work together cooperatively on a task, these predisposing factors did not obliterate the effect of in-group identification. This result tends to support the authors' guarded optimism about working with community groups in conflict.

Aftermath—Local Initiative Facilitated

The evaluation of the forum by the CMHC and the Local Group was positive. They were delighted that people with opposing points of view could work together productively and were especially pleased with the attitudes and enthusiasms expressed by the many students who attended. Most participants left the meeting with increased feelings of respect for one another. Since the forum, the authors have heard several accounts of persons', formerly isolated by their opposing positions on sensitive issues, becoming willing to meet to discuss their differences.

Some reservations about the success of the forum were voiced by members of the joint CMHC-Local Group planning committee. For some the process was not so easy or smooth as it seemed. These people could not fully warm up to the point of expressing openly and honestly some of their very strong feelings on the issues related to the strike.

In general, however, the hopes and expectations for the forum cited above were met. Some of those who attended immediately began planning future meetings aimed at coping with these major problems. CMHC intends to assist in the development of such programs.

As the process of decentralization proceeds in New York City, it is imperative for this community to take steps to avoid the kind of chaotic circumstances which surrounded the Ocean Hill-Brownsville experiment. The school strike mobilized many people to take an active concern in the functioning of the schools, and the authors view this as a time of opportunity to assist people in realizing their desire to improve the situation. As decentralization takes shape, a number of issues will need to be confronted, among them the election of local school boards, the determination of what kind of teaching and other activities are to go on in the schools, the role of nonprofessionals, and a greater decision-making and advisory role for students, among others.

As a result of the forum, a number of parent associations have requested consultation from the CMHC to help set up similar kinds of workshops directed toward establishing clearer goals and priorities. Local Group, on its own initiative, planned another community-wide forum to convert the positive feelings engendered by the earlier meeting into positive action. With CMHC assistance, Local Group worked out its own design for a community-wide meeting aimed at setting priorities for local educational improvement and creating task forces to begin implementation.

At the meeting in March 1969 three task forces composed jointly of school personnel and community residents were established. They were concerned with narcotics problems of youth, more effective teaching, and improvement of school-community relations.

The narcotics task force has begun to work on a monitoring system whereby volunteers patrol designated areas in the community and report any drug activity to a central telephone service. Speakers have also been invited to talk on the nature of drugs and on the various drug programs in operation locally and nationally. This task force was also influential in getting CMHC to hire a community organizer to work with community groups on the narcotics problem.

The more effective teaching task force has sponsored a course for teachers and parents entitled "A Community's Concept of Human Relations." The parents are planning and designing the course and will lead most of the discussion sessions. Participants will take a tour of the community and will meet with local shopkeepers, librarians, and others. Teachers enrolled will receive course credit from the board of education.

The school-community relations task force has determined which schools have the most severe problems in school-community relations and is developing a plan for consulting with these schools. In addition, the task force has started a "courtesy campaign" focused on how parents should be treated in the schools. This task force is also working on plans to enable students to assume certain decision-making powers in their schools.

The success of the forum has legitimized the instrumented laboratory within this community and paved the way for organizational development activity on a community-wide scale. The authors see this as a logical extension of current OD theory and practice. As human service organizations become increasingly aware of the need to operate in a community context, new models and plans must be developed to come to grips with this singularly inelegant system. Similarly, those who act as consultants to business organizations might well begin to consider the "community of consumers" as part of their OD work.

Significance of Intervention

Certain generalizations formed from this experience are warranted and may be useful to others.

Entry During Conflict

The risks of entering a community conflict situation are great; they seem even greater when the consulting organization invites itself in. Any unsolicited action could easily antagonize a whole client population, thus destroying whatever effectiveness it might have had in the first place. For whatever the interorganizational dynamics may be in fact, it is clear that a norm within this local community, and one that seems pervasive in our society, is to stay out of a fight unless you are a principal to it or until you are invited in. One has only to recall the paradigm of the battling husband and wife who join forces to oppose the policeman summoned by the sounds of their violence. In advance of the forum CMHC staff experienced anxiety on several counts. They feared that no one would attend the forum; that CMHC staff would "blow" the implementation; and even that one or another of the parties to the conflict would picket the forum or otherwise create an organized disruption. That none of these catastrophes occurred is due in part to careful planning and to the design of the forum itself, and in part to the fact that staff apprehensions stemmed more from pervasive norms shared by them as consultants with parties to the conflict than from the realities of group dynamics.

Statutory Relationships

Unlike the private consulting firm which operates in a relatively free market, accepting contracts that satisfy its needs and rejecting those that do not, a community mental health center, supported as it is by tax funds, is obliged to limit its clientele to agencies and organizations within its designated catchment area. The statutory nature of the relationship differentiates the activity of a CMHC from the in-house consulting/ training unit as well. The actual relationship between a center and its clientele may be thought of as midway between those two extremes, more akin to the marriage relationship than the love affair. The parties to it are in a no-exit situation. Some of the implications of this sort of relationship are a reduction in glamour, an increment in mutual dependency, and, because of the dependency, a multiplication of the risks of termination. In this context, the relationship established between the CMHC and the local education system during the previous year had some of the characteristics of courtship. Therefore, the fact that many school system members gave only token support to the forum (a community-directed action) and at the district level behaved as if the collaboration between the CMHC and the Local Group was a flirtation becomes comprehensible. During the two evenings of the forum, for example, only three out of a possible twelve district-level representatives attended, one of the three refused to participate, and another departed early, the only person present to do so.

There is no way of predicting the long-term consequences of the CMHC-school system relationship. The alternatives open in either the in-house or free market situation (firing, termination of contract, and so on) are clearly not available here. The two parties must continue together. In the immediate post-forum period, the form of the relationship was primarily one of mutual avoidance. One of the three local boards is still at odds with CMHC in spite of efforts to ameliorate the difficulties. These strains will continue to exist until the school system and its clients are able to shift attention from territorial prerogatives to educational accomplishment. The popular election of local board members to take place during this school year may be a step in this direction.

Reporting These Results

Preparation of this case study in itself raises some issues of professional ethics and determinants of professional effectiveness. The forum was successful largely because a trusting relationship between CMHC and many members of Local Group was developed over a substantial period of time. One of the conditions of that relationship is that the scientific and career-building interests of CMHC are subordinate to community service. For this reason the authors refrained from suggesting systematic data collection for research purposes. Although CMHC is working toward evaluation of its programs, with community groups taking a major role in designing and implementing studies, the authors felt that under these particular circumstances it was best to avoid risking a loss of trust which might have resulted from any kind of data collection. The hope is that when members of the Local Group (who must necessarily remain anonymous) read this article, they will not feel that this condition has been violated.

High Turnout

The size of the turnout for the forum was strikingly large. Approximately 150 of the 250 persons specifically invited attended. This was due partly to systematic telephone and personal contact and partly to the urgency of the situation. In a significant sense, however, the result was the product of hundreds of hours of personal contact between CMHC's community organization staff and residents of the community over a period of one year. The level of cooperation between Local Group and CMHC was high; Local Group did the bulk of the telephoning to community members; CMHC aided in bringing out teachers and administrators. Had the forum been sponsored solely by CMHC, it would have been impossible to tap the informal social network of community residents that produced the high turnout.

The Design

The most unique features of the forum design were (a) the warm-up period, permitting significant group-building interaction to occur for each person upon arrival and thus short-circuiting clique formation and other distancing maneuvers that often interfere with the success of public meetings; and (b) the translation of a laboratory intergroup excrcise into a format that works in a community conflict situation. It is probable that the translation was successful because the content of the exercise had high face validity (i.e. it permitted discussion of the very educational issues that brought people to the meeting) and because the warm-up period helped the groups develop to the minimum level of solidarity necessary to carry out the exercise.